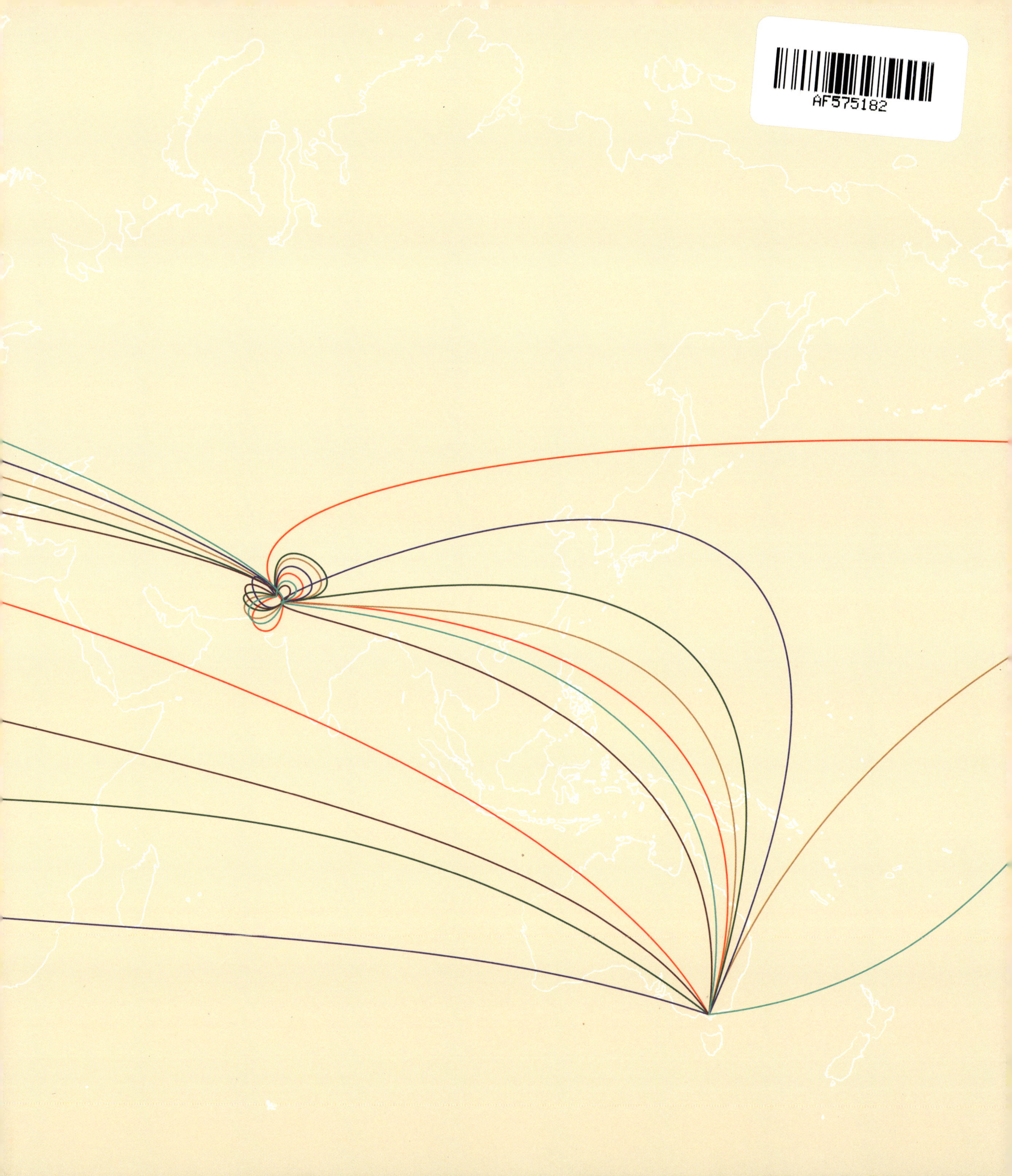

Karkhana

The Aldrich Contemporary Art Museum

green cardamom

karkhana: Urdu (n.) a factory; a workshop; a laboratory
Medieval Persian (n.) a manufactory of public works; an imperial atelier

Karkhana

A Contemporary Collaboration

M. Imran Qureshi
Saira Wasim
Hasnat Mehmood
Nusra Latif Qureshi
Aisha Khalid
Talha Rathore

Hammad Nasar

Qamar Adamjee
B.N. Goswamy
Salima Hashmi
Jessica Hough
Sandhya Jain
John Seyller
Anna Sloan
Virginia Whiles

The Aldrich Contemporary Art Museum
green cardamom

Published in conjunction with the exhibition

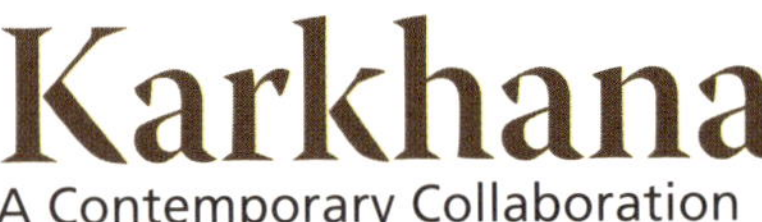

A Contemporary Collaboration

Originally conceived by Muhammad Imran Qureshi
Curated by Jessica Hough, Hammad Nasar, and Anna Sloan
Organized as a traveling exhibition by The Aldrich Contemporary Art Museum

Exhibition tour

The Aldrich Contemporary Art Museum

The Aldrich Contemporary Art Museum, Ridgefield
August 21, 2005 – March 21, 2006

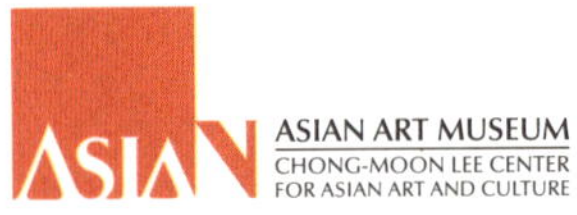

Asian Art Museum, San Francisco
August 4, 2006 – November 5, 2006

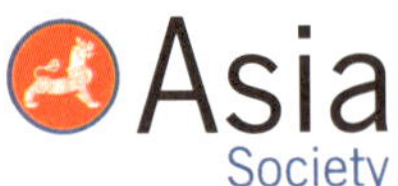

Asia Society and Museum, New York
Spring 2007

Museum funding provided by: Alex G. Nason Foundation, Altria Group, Inc., Connecticut Commission on Culture & Tourism, Danbury Porsche Audi, Edelman Leather, Ironwood Gallery, Purkiss Capital Advisors LLC, Anne S. Richardson Fund, Ridgefield Bank, UST, and U. S. Trust.

Education funding provided by: The Barnes Foundation, Inc., Boehringer Ingelheim Cares Foundation, Inc., The Estate of Ruth I. Krauss, Fairfield County Community Foundation, Institute of Museum and Library Services, The Goldstone Family Foundation, National Endowment for the Arts, Newman's Own, and The Smart Family Foundation.

Exhibition funding provided by: The Andy Warhol Foundation for the Visual Arts, The British Council, Danish Arts Agency, Elizabeth Firestone Graham Foundation, Hersam Acorn Newspapers, Islamic World Arts Initiative, a program of Arts International generously supported by the Doris Duke Foundation for Islamic Art, and The LEF Foundation.

Media sponsorship is provided by: Connecticut Cottages & Gardens, Fairfield County Weekly, and Ridgefield Magazine.

Library of Congress Control Number: 2005928683
ISBN: 1-888332-26-3

Cover
From left to right: details from *Karkhana 1, 5, 9, 7, 7* and *10*

Produced by
Green Cardamom, London
www.greencardamom.net

Edited by
Hammad Nasar
with Anita Dawood-Nasar

Designed by
Vipul Sangoi, Raindesign, London
www.raindesign.info

Printed by
Die Keure, Bruges, Belgium

Published by
The Aldrich Contemporary Art Museum
258 Main Street
Ridgefield, CT 06877, USA
www.aldrichart.org
and
Green Cardamom

This publication has been made possible
by generous support from:
Fayeeza and Arif Naqvi
Huma and Asif Alam
Association of Pakistani Professionals
Natasha Kazmi and Qaisar Hasan
Pervaiz Lodhie and Ledtronics Inc.
Munir and Zeelaf Mashooqullah
Shezi and Emily Nackvi
Waqas Wajahat LLC, New York
And other donors who wish to remain
anonymous

Contents

7 Foreword

8 Introduction

12 Painting Workshops in Mughal India
John Seyller

18 In the Spirit of Improvisation
Jessica Hough

26 Karkhana: Revival or Re-invention?
Virginia Whiles

34 Postcards to Empire:
The Politics of Resistance in the Karkhana Project
Hammad Nasar and Anna Sloan

42 Journey's End: The Making of Karkhana
Salima Hashmi

48 Innovations to a Timeless Practice:
Materials and Techniques of the Karkhana Artists
Qamar Adamjee and Sandhya Jain

54 The Karkhana Project

104 Artists' Biographies

108 Works in the Exhibition

111 Contributors

112 Acknowledgments

Foreword

Miniatures as we know them, or knew them till yesterday, have been likened to couplets from an Urdu *ghazal*:[1] terse, precious and filled with resonances. This makes it appropriate to recall, in the context of the *Karkhana* project, some old practices from the world of poetry. There was, for instance, the much loved but challenging maneuver of *girih lagana*: to take a given *misra* or hemistich and "knot" it with your own to complete a verse or *sher*; or *dakhl* poetry, where you "entered" into someone else's verse in your own manner and turned it on its head, or nudged it in an altogether different direction. There was a delight in these exercises, and the excitement of anticipation, but also a sense of venturing into the unknown.

One can be certain that the six young talents involved in this *Karkhana* project must have had the sensation of venturing into the unknown, at least when they began; for, the idea of collaboration and of parceling out different elements of work notwithstanding, the karkhanas of old functioned very differently. Here, there is no stern Mughal *ustad* masterminding the project, conceiving a design, allocating tasks; empowered to amend, approve or reject the finished product. There is not even the intimacy of atmosphere, or informality, that one imagines belonged to a family workshop, as in the Rajasthani or Pahari traditions. Here, each artist was on his or her own: free, conscious of what the others were capable of doing, but unaware of what it was going to be; putting first thoughts down on paper and then leaving the work to develop slowly in other hands, like a Polaroid image evolving over time and space.

Astonishingly, however, and to one's delight, what one sees in the finished versions of the works are not some images hung upon the fading walls of memory, but works that look fresh and provocative. It all comes together in these works: Hasnat's stamped impressions, Imran's layering, Talha's piercing botanics, Saira's wit, Aisha's veiled references, and Nusra's wispy outlines seeking new contexts. As things unfold or evolve, textures are added, outlines start filling up, margins expand, colors fade in and out. But also, mallets materialize, holy men grow satyrs' feet, and lions roam the earth. There are no chance encounters; one gets the feeling of minds peering within themselves, and then out. Like the couplets of old, these works are terse and precious and filled with resonances. But also brave.

It is difficult to predict where all this is headed but easy to see that there are sets of issues here, some consciously raised, and others that simply arise. In the context of the tradition of painting on the sub-continent, all these issues need to be faced before a whole generation grows weary of that tradition, and a pall begins to descend upon the act of viewing. This karkhana, with the excitement that its concept and its works afford, sends some of these questions hurtling along their courses, a momentum one can only celebrate.

B.N. Goswamy

Note

1 The *ghazal* form of poetry originated in Iran and arrived in India by the twelfth century. *Ghazal* means a conversation with the beloved—mortal or divine. It consists of a series of *shers* (couplets) that need not be related, and are considered to be poems in their own rights.

Introduction

"Everyone instinctively understood that they were taking turns at having complete ownership of each piece—I am sure no one would have blinked if someone had washed a painting and started afresh." [1]
Muhammad Imran Qureshi

"Because collaboration defines art as a problem of cultural form—its use-values—it brings the category of art face to face with its most cherished expectations and ideals—individual authorship and autonomy—and thus addresses the very basis of art's relationship to democracy." [2]
John Roberts and Stephen Wright

Karkhana: A Contemporary Collaboration presents twelve paintings by six artists. Each work is composed of imagery laid down by the artists in discrete succession without any pre-established "plan" for its content or visual structure. Together they record a seriated performance—an improvisational act involving creative destruction, semiotic play and dynamic adaptation. Like other contemporary collaborations, the project wove many visual threads into a single artistic vision; this one however, was inspired in part by the cooperative nature of miniature painting in South Asia's pre-modern courts. Its name, "Karkhana," is borrowed from the Urdu term for the painting workshops patronized by the Mughal emperors, who ruled the territories of present-day India and Pakistan between the sixteenth and mid-nineteenth centuries.

Though aspects of the project are embedded in history, this new karkhana represents a break with the traditional institution and reflects a distinctly contemporary moment. The project's multiple and diffuse authorship, spread among six equal partners, questions the limits of the individual artistic ego and explores the possibilities of collective expression. In another break with historical precedent, the *Karkhana* paintings were fashioned over intervals of time and across geographic space. They embody the correspondence and spirit of collaboration between artists located on three continents. Muhammad Imran Qureshi, who initiated and guided the project, brought together a group of six, bound by a coherent artistic ethos.

The artists—Aisha Khalid, Nusra Latif Qureshi, Hasnat Mehmood, Talha Rathore, Saira Wasim, and Qureshi himself—are linked by the extensive training they received in miniature painting at Lahore's National College of Arts. There, they developed a set of subversive tactics characterized by improvisation, wit, and irony, and exemplified by Mehmood's trompe l'oeil postage stamps. Pictorial strategies such as mimicry, pastiche, punning and iconoclasm provided a common language for the group, as they passed paintings from one artist to the next during the project, in what amounted to a visual dialogue. Individual works by Khalid, Latif, Qureshi, Mehmood, Rathore, and Wasim reveal distinct personal experiences and political visions. And yet, the *Karkhana* project affirms a set of shared perspectives grounded in their homeland's history of colonization, Partition, and nationhood, and in an acute sense of political marginalization.

After the American military response to the events of September 11, 2001, the significance of the past gained a new expedience for members of the group, catalyzing the project's realization. Suddenly, Pakistan's colonial history acquired a new context in this fresh wave of imperialist aggression in the Middle East and South Asia—a theme that provided a coherent focus for *Karkhana*. In light of the artists' shared history and focus, such a project became not only plausible, but imperative.

By default and design alike, the *Karkhana* paintings reflect the multi-nodal geography of the artists' lives. Inscribing (and thereby also validating) a pattern that defies Empire's centrifugal model of artistic production, Qureshi devised a process that involved transferring the paintings by mail and international courier service between the artists, who live in Lahore, Melbourne, Jhelum, New York, and Chicago. Three of the six artists live outside the country of their birth, and the sense of dislocation inherent to diaspora, provides a coherent thread throughout the series of paintings. The imagery gathered within them honors multiple sites of subjective experience.

In the course of the project, as artists applied their own individual techniques and motifs to the paintings, each layer of marks interacted with those already on the picture surface and, in turn, personal expressions acquired a deeper, multi-faceted resonance. These layers of imagery and symbols interact directly in a dialogic manner, and in some instances they present what appear to be several dimensions of reality at once. In this manner, the viewer is confronted with elements from the present, past, and future concurrently: a useful device for viewing a world where the space age and the medieval co-exist.

The exhibition, *Karkhana: A Contemporary Collaboration*, brings together this unique series of experimental paintings with individual works by each of the artists. The project's significance extends beyond the surfaces of these paintings to the collaborative processes by which they were produced. To expose these underlying processes, both the exhibition and this catalogue are accompanied by visual resources representing the paintings' multiple layers. It is hoped this will help viewers engage with the works by unraveling some of the densely packed ideas embedded within them.

The twelve *Karkhana* works were first exhibited in Rochdale, UK, in 2003-4.[3] In organizing the current exhibition, we sought to fulfill two objectives: firstly, to bring the exhibition to its unspoken but obvious audience—America; and secondly, to more fully explore the challenges presented by the rich layers of coded signs contained in each work. The layered quality of the paintings has provided an organizing principle for both the exhibition and its accompanying catalogue. Within the exhibition, comparative works by the six participating artists highlight their individual motifs and techniques. Viewed in conjunction with the *Karkhana* series, the comparative works reveal the roles played by personal idioms in the collective project. This exposure to each artist's visual vocabulary will help viewers recognize the building blocks of the collaborative series. A digital program displaying images of the works-in-progress reveals the six stages that ultimately produced each painting, providing a virtual re-enactment of their physical construction. At the same time, by presenting and documenting the twelve paintings in series, the exhibition and catalogue respect the coherence of the final project. The metaphorical edifice thus erected does not seek to fix absolute meaning; the works are rich enough to hold on to their ambiguities, offering universal appeal with personal meaning.

The nature of the *Karkhana* project is vast and multi-faceted. It explores the possibilities of collaborative practice and political resistance, the reinvention of a "tradition," and the expression of diasporic identity. It also raises broader questions about globalization and political marginalization. This catalogue has been structured to mirror the multifaceted nature of the project: six essays approach the exhibition from contiguous and, at times, overlapping perspectives. The result is a quilt-work of critique covering historical origin (Seyller), comparative practice (Hough), context (Whiles), political engagement (Nasar and Sloan), representation (Hashmi), and technique and materials (Adamjee and Jain). Each of these essays suggests modes of viewing, which, it is hoped, will prove useful in engaging with the paintings.

John Seyller's essay lays out the historical context against which we might consider the output of the contemporary karkhana. As evident in his piece, Seyller's scholarship has begun to elucidate the inner workings of the Mughal atelier, where supervisors dictated the subject matter and composition of most paintings. The "seemingly constrained operation" of the Mughal atelier afforded artists little of the spontaneity that characterizes the new *Karkhana* paintings. If, as Seyller indicates, individual painting styles had "little significance in the collective undertaking" at the Mughal workshop, its contemporary counterpart leads us to pick out and marvel at the work of individual hands.

With a simultaneous recognition of individual and collective identities, *Karkhana* represents a distinctly contemporary phenomenon. The self-consciousness with which six artists have modulated these identities in the project occurs in the wake of the modernist experiments described by Jessica Hough in her essay. If collective consciousness runs counter to the modernist ideal of the individual artistic ego, the "psychologically fraught" condition of the collaborator is mediated by the solidarity gained in the collective process. For the *Karkhana* artists, separated spatially by three continents, and psychologically by the dislocations of the post-colonial condition, the collective process offers a return of sorts. Or, as David Humphrey of the artists' collective Team SHaG suggests, collaboration offers a "shared orientation towards psychologically rich subjects" from which the *Karkhana* artists have clearly benefitted in their project. While the contributions of each particular artist remain discrete in the *Karkhana* paintings, their signature motifs and eclectic marks contribute, nonetheless, to a coherent whole.

At the root of the artists' shared vision is the defining experience of their training at the National College of Arts in Lahore. Virginia Whiles's essay examines the education they received at Pakistan's oldest art school—the only one in the world with a department dedicated to miniature painting. The institution not only exemplifies the persistence of the colonial legacy but also the inevitable dislocation of post-colonial identity. The two predominant pedagogical styles at the school presented the artists with a dialectic choice between an allegiance to "tradition" and the imperative to innovate. The *Karkhana* artists have each shunned the obligation to seek "authenticity" through a rigid return to the Mughal precedent. Mehmood's modernist grids, Qureshi's Dadaist marks, and Latif's bold silhouettes all present new approaches to the miniature, which incorporate ideas from myriad sources available in the contemporary world.

Even prior to *Karkhana*, there was an obvious political charge to much of the artists' work, a facet that has been enriched by the collaborative process. For instance, where Qureshi's abstract "mapping points" and geographic symbols intersect with Khalid's burqa-clad women, they evoke the global media's exploitation of Afghan women in the aftermath of the attacks on the World Trade Center. In another work, Qureshi's target symbols appear adjacent to Rathore's subway grids and cypress trees, provoking the viewer to think about who is targeted. The marks culled together in the *Karkhana* project reflect post-September 11 realities for many citizens and visitors who are asked repeatedly by immigration officers and police "but where are you really from?"[4]—a question that disregards the complexities of contemporary identity. Hammad Nasar and Anna Sloan explore this and other political perspectives behind the project's post-colonial "postcards to Empire."

Salima Hashmi describes the *Karkhana* paintings as a coded language that requires active viewing and, in many cases, a formidable background of historical knowledge and local experience. The problem of interpretation, she suggests, is among the themes consciously invoked by the series. Admittedly, some of the imagery in the *Karkhana* paintings is more familiar to American audiences than others—a fact that Latif has often addressed in her work. By adding Urdu words comprehensible only to those with proficiency in the language, Latif points to the inevitable difference between local Pakistani interpretations of imagery and foreigners' interpretations. Her use of the strategy in the *Karkhana* project satirizes foreigners' long-standing misinterpretations of her homeland and explores the implications of these. The effect, magnified by the presence of six artistic voices, presents viewers with a high-speed visual banter.

Key to the paintings' visceral power are the materials chosen by the artists and the techniques by which they were applied. Qamar Adamjee and Sandhya Jain interrogate these through a forensic examination of the works and a series of detailed interviews with the artists. Their resulting contribution is a lucid account of the paths traversed by the *Karkhana* artists in bringing the miniature tradition into the twenty-first century.

In her discussion of the *Karkhana* project, Virginia Whiles notes the power inherent in performance. Cultural anthropologists have long noted that performative modes of action can harness local sources of resistance and prompt social change. Victor Turner, Stanley Tambiah, and Maurice Bloch, for instance, have described ritual performance as a space of social negotiation, in which the status quo is either reiterated and secured or, alternatively, disturbed and destabilized. In their analyses of ritual, it is the components of performative action—collective experience, symbolic repetition, and movement through space and time—that allow normative patterns to incur significant deviations.[5] These "disturbances" enable traditional symbolic forms to take on new meanings, and as a result, they bear the potential for creative acts of dissidence. This particular facet of the performative process was the driving force behind the artistic maneuvers executed by Khalid, Latif, Mehmood, Qureshi, Rathore and Wasim in the course of their collaboration. With the *Karkhana* project, the six artists have infused Pakistan's most acclaimed traditional art practice with new political significance, transforming the space of the "workshop" into a stage for social and political resistance.

Jessica Hough, Hammad Nasar, and Anna Sloan

Notes

1 Interview with Hammad Nasar, March 2004.

2 John Roberts and Stephen Wright, "Art and Collaboration—Introduction," in *Third Text*, Vol.18, Issue 6 (2004), pp.531-32.

3 The exhibition, *Karkhana: Contemporary Pakistani Miniatures*, took place at Touchstones Art Gallery in Rochdale, UK, from November 15, 2003 to January 4, 2004.

4 Anonymous quote in Hammad Nasar, "Sidestepping Stereotypes," in *Herald*, Karachi, August 2004.

5 Victor Turner, *The Ritual Process: Structure and Anti-Structure* (Ithaca, NY: Cornell University Press, 1969); Stanley Tambiah, *Culture, Thought, and Social Action: A Performative Approach to Ritual* (Cambridge, Mass: Harvard University Press, 1985); Maurice Bloch, *Ritual, History, and Power: Selected Papers in Anthropology* (London: Athlone Press, 1989).

Painting Workshops in Mughal India

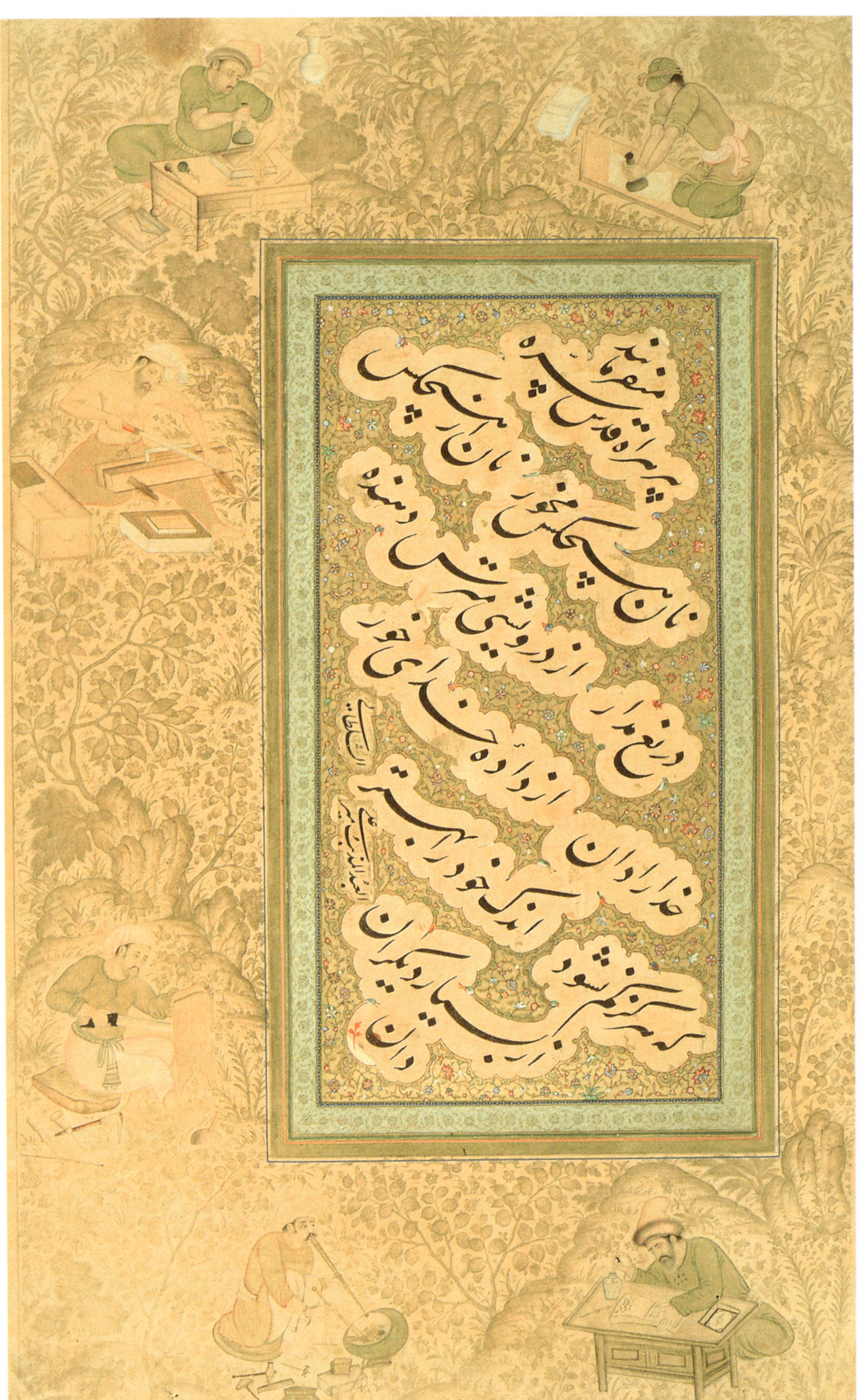

John Seyller

The painting workshop at the imperial Mughal court in the sixteenth century was more complex in organization than any atelier India had ever seen. Most earlier Muslim courts in India had enlisted the services of one or two Persian émigrés and a few locals who struggled to imitate the style of their masters. Most indigenous Indian courts, both before and after the heyday of the Mughal empire, had their painting needs satisfied by a family or two of local artists. The resources of the Mughal Empire allowed its painting workshop to draw upon a much larger pool of talent, including Persian artists in search of new patrons, and Indian artists from the many regions that had recently come under Mughal control. The Mughal workshop started out large and grew rapidly, so that a heterogeneous group of about 50 artists in 1565 had reached the unheard of scale of about 130 painters by 1600. As might be expected in a land where hereditary occupations are prevalent, family ties figured prominently in this recruitment, with sons following their fathers into imperial service. The sheer number of artists enlisted, and the complexity of coordinating their tasks, was beyond the capacity of traditional familial hierarchies, and so the Mughal workshop quickly developed a bureaucracy to ensure that this accumulation of talent could be harnessed to work together in a fruitful and efficient manner.

Once a text was selected, suitable paper made, sized, and burnished, and the written surface marked with discreet guidelines and preliminary rulings, a calligrapher was summoned to write out the text. The nature and sequence of these activities can be discerned from a close physical examination of particular manuscripts. Several processes are depicted in the margins of a well-known page from the Jahangir Album attributed here to Madhava (Fig.1). Since many favorite texts were copied repeatedly, the calligrapher could often refer to an existing manuscript of that text in his patron's library. This measure of dependence on the library is one reason why those involved in the making and illustrating of books usually operated in or near the library, where they would also occasionally be called upon to refurbish damaged or incomplete holdings.

Calligraphers, who trained for years as apprentices under the masters of their day, approached their tasks with tremendous care. Relatively few manuscripts bear signs of correction, of accidentally omitted or repeated phrases, or of inadvertent lapses in the even spacing of words within a given line of text. This level of perfection was achieved at a painstaking pace, with one of the most highly esteemed calligraphers completing no more than seventeen lines of the text of Nizami's *Khamsa* in a single day.[1]

Contemporary literary references and the valuations of manuscripts make it clear that calligraphers enjoyed the greatest prestige within the Mughal *kitabkhana* (literally, "book-house" in Persian—a specialized term for the imperial workshop where books were prepared and collected). Nonetheless, in manuscripts intended to be decorated with illustrations, they often tailored their work to painters' concerns. Before many illustrations were started, for example, the calligrapher was compelled to write out several lines—sometimes as much as an entire page—of text in oblique configurations. This decorative device stretched out the text so the painting would have an attractive and sufficiently large physical presence on the page, and simultaneously appear immediately below the relevant passage of text. It is very unlikely that the number and subjects of illustrations were the prerogative of the calligrapher; rather, these overarching decisions, which affect the putative visual program and ultimate quality of the book, were probably made by a project supervisor, perhaps in consultation with the patron, well before the calligrapher took up his pen.

Despite the careful coordination of text passage and intended image, it appears that painters rarely took their cue from the wording of the actual text. Instead, the subjects of their illustrations were dictated by supervisors in the form of oral instructions or written ones, inscribed either at the bottom of the folio or within the area to be painted. The content of these prescriptive notes ranges from a few words, such as the notes scrawled at the bottom of a double-page composition in the 1596-97 Beatty *Akbarnama* (Fig.2): "A picture of the victory over the fort of Chitor," and "Two pages are to be done,"[2] to the relatively complete description of the scene of Iskandar meeting Dara at Mosul (Fig.3): "From two directions the armies array, wait anxiously, and make a compact."[3]

Such a succinct synopsis of the text simplified the artist's task of knowing what to paint. This was handy for painters who might not be able to pick out the relevant narrative details from the subtleties of the full Persian text, especially in poetry, or who might even be unable to read the Persian language at all. Mughal artists then decided how to give pictorial expression to these subjects, most often resorting to compositional formulas that they or their peers had developed for similar subjects in other manuscripts. When the painter Ahmad needed to show Akbar at the siege of the fortress of Chitor (Fig.2), he could draw upon earlier depictions of the siege of any fort, whether of Chitor itself or of nearby Ranthambor. In this case, he actually combined the two, retaining the tent compound in the lower corner and the breached walls from the former, and Akbar's active role on the ramparts from the latter.

For most kinds of sixteenth-century Mughal manuscripts, the task of producing these miniatures was given over to various teams of painters, with one painter, usually a senior artist, being charged with the design, and another, usually less experienced or talented, asked to finish up the image by coloring in the forms. Assorted unfinished paintings help us to understand the distinction between

Fig.1 (left)
Attributed to Madhava
Folio from the Jahangir Album with border scenes depicting six artisans of the library making books, Mughal, ca.1610
Ink, opaque watercolors, gold on paper
42.2 x 26.5 cm (16 1/2 x 10 3/8 inches)
Freer Gallery of Art, Smithsonian Institution, Washington D.C.: Purchase F1954.116 recto

Fig.2 (below)
Ascribed to Ahmad
Akbar shoots Jaimal during the siege of Chitor; Mughal, 1597
Ink, opaque watercolors, gold on paper
Painting 24.3 x 13.2 cm (9 5/8 x 5 1/8 inches)
Akbarnama, Chester Beatty Library Ms.3, f.133b
© The Trustees of the Chester Beatty Library, Dublin

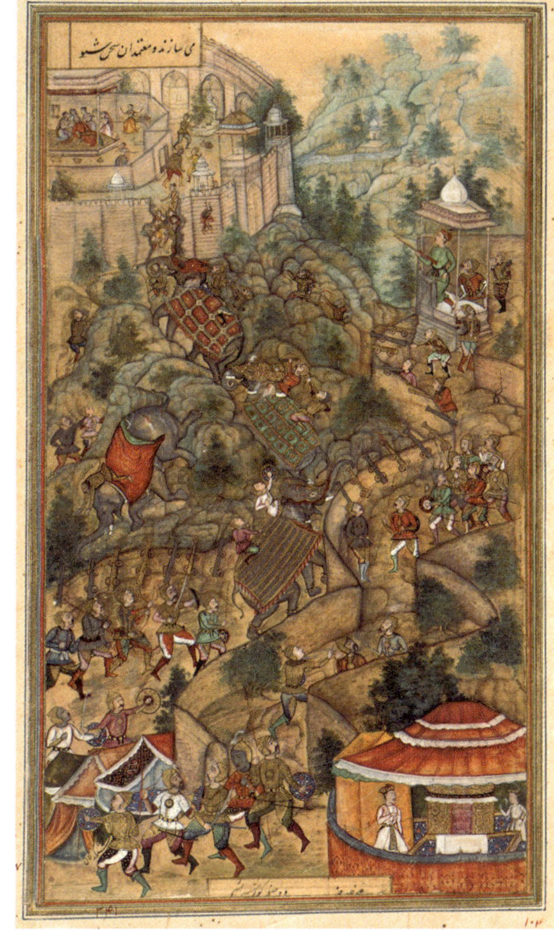

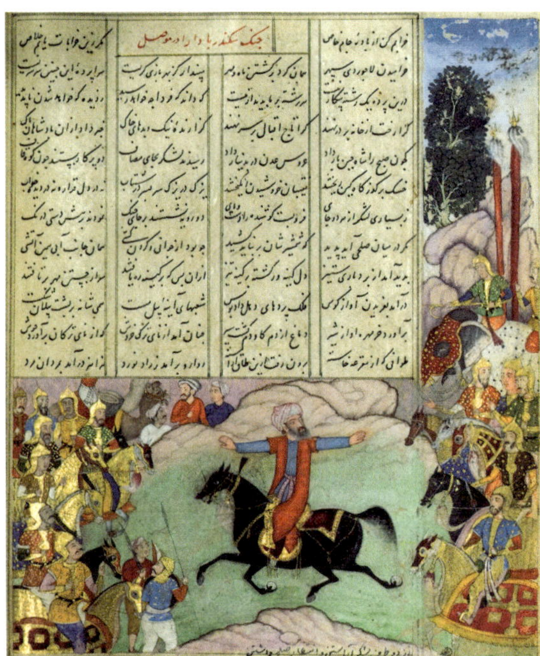

Fig. 3
Ascribed to Makara
Iskandar meets Dara at Mosul, Mughal, ca.1598
Ink, opaque watercolors, gold on paper
Painting 17.9 x 15 cm (7 x 6 inches)
Sharafnama, School of Oriental and African Studies
Ms.24952, f.27b
Courtesy School of Oriental and African Studies, London

the two phases of painting. In one representative example, depicting Akbar receiving Prince Salim, the composition is fully worked out and the faces of all of the figures have been sketched in—a detail so essential that one face has been covered over with white paint and replaced with an improved likeness (Fig.4). A second artist working downward from the top of the painting has only begun to lay in the colors for the largest areas in the background, such as the pavilion, canopy, and distant landscape. From this point, he would proceed to render individual figures, first doing their clothing and finally their faces and surface ornaments, with little or no guidance from his senior partner. Often the elder artist would step in towards the end to paint the faces of a few of the major figures, in this case certainly those of the emperor and his son. In very rare instances the role of providing special portraits was given to yet a third artist. This bi- or tripartite division of labor is documented sporadically in informal and formal ascriptions written below the manuscript illustration, and can often be detected in works in which there is an obvious shift in style. This inscriptional and visual evidence runs counter to some scholars' claims that artists might specialize in details as limited as landscape elements or decorative patterns, and that as many as four or five individuals might routinely participate in a single work. While a few artists did come to be associated with a given genre, such as Husayn Naqqash with illuminations or Mansur with animal painting, most artists shifted readily from one kind of work to another, so that at one time or another landscapes, architectural passages, figures, and floral and geometric border decorations all fell within their purview.

Surprisingly, Mughal painters labored under considerable time constraints. Some supervisors' notes specify the number of days that artists should spend on an individual miniature, and others indicate the date by which the painting should be completed. These directives had a profound impact on an artist's imagination and workmanship. Figure 5, for example, belongs to a fable book illustrated about 1595, one of the most cursory manuscripts produced in the imperial Mughal atelier. A note in the lower left of the painting field orders the artist Jagana (also known as Jagannatha) to have the painting ready in "five or five and a half days by the 14th of the month of Azar." So even before Jagana took up his brush, he knew that he had to work quickly and efficiently. Accordingly, he limited the scene to a pair of washermen too busy to take heed of the fox about to lure their donkey to his death. The figures and animals are drawn simply, and the landscape is nothing more than a series of lightly colored washes. Now compare an illustration done by this same artist, Jagannatha, for a poetical text, the 1595 *Khamsa* of Nizami, now at the British Library, one of the most luxurious manuscripts ever produced by the Mughals (Fig.6). Here we see what Jagannatha was capable of doing when he had ample time and money. Most obvious is the dramatic increase in the number of figures in the composition. The inclusion of the many servants buzzing around the princess and the guards conversing before a series of gates, is a stylistic choice, not a requirement of the story, which needs only to show a princess painting her self-portrait. The setting too, is far more elaborate, from the frieze of warriors adorning the outermost wall, and the numerous buildings sprouting up around the courtyard, to the magnificent carpet on which the princess is seated. But even individual forms are treated differently. The facial features are finer, the patterns of clothing more intricately detailed, the colors far richer. Most remarkable of all is the fact that this same elevated level of pictorial complexity and technical finish runs throughout this copy of the *Khamsa*, transcending the work of any particular artist. That this pattern of homogenization recurs at some level—high, ordinary, or even low—in virtually every manuscript of the period is an unmistakable sign that the imperial Mughal workshop had developed supervisory mechanisms to ensure that a given project would present a consistent look or quality in every one of its constituent parts. To understand Jagana as an artist, we must consider both kinds of his work, simple and lavish alike, as well as something of the general conditions under which the paintings were made.

Hence, in the Mughal workshop of the late sixteenth century an artist was regularly told the subject he was to depict, the collaborator with whom he was to work, and the amount of time in which he was to bring his creation to completion. In this seemingly constrained operation, what room was there for the individual artist to develop his own visual ideas or habits?

Although the thousands of manuscript illustrations made by the scores of painters active during this period do show some formal variety, the stylistic differences among them are far more subtle than one might expect from a group so large and potentially diverse in background. Indeed, the calculated and overriding stylistic coherence of the Mughal workshop is easily contrasted with the stylistic heterogeneity of their modern counterparts, the artists tapped to contribute to the *Karkhana* project, whose artistic training is, if anything, more uniform in nature. Yet within the confines of a common formal vocabulary, most Mughal artists did develop a set of distinctive idiosyncrasies that they applied throughout their work. These distinguishing traits rarely rise above the level of such minor details as a penchant for certain types of faces, a preference for particular colors and degrees of tonal contrast, or a predisposition for formal devices drawn from European art.

Scholars often learn to associate these subtle distinguishing details with individual artists and subsequently venture attributions for many a painting. Although this kind of connoisseurship can be enticing, especially when it holds out the prospect of affording the modern viewer a personal—and thus more readily satisfying— account of the creative process in another time, it can all too easily obscure a larger issue, that is, whether the attribution of individual credit was a matter of any real significance in these historical collective undertakings. The regular presence of official ascriptions naming the two or three individual contributors to a given Mughal manuscript illustration suggests that the identity of the individuals did matter. But to whom and to what end?

One possibility is that these ascriptions were a kind of work record for purposes of compensation, which, as Mughal court annals indicate, was issued in the form of monthly salaries with the occasional bonus. Yet this function is belied by the very prominence of these ascriptions, which are ordinarily written in a fine hand beneath the painting, sometimes alongside the formal description of the subject; if this information were no more than a mundane account of employment, it probably would have been recorded in a less conspicuous place, such as on a flyleaf at the back of the manuscript or in a separate logbook. A more likely possibility is that this unprecedented record of artistic contributions is both an expression of a Mughal inclination toward systems, and part of an increasingly widespread pattern of acknowledgment of the work of individual painters in Muslim courts, throughout South and West Asia from the late sixteenth century onwards.

Despite the apparent increase in the prestige of painters, there is no evidence that what modern critics would call a painter's personal artistic vision ever factored in the commissioning or evaluation of a Mughal work of art at the end of the sixteenth century. Ascriptions naming an artist are found rarely on independent paintings, that is, those intended to stand apart from the context of a manuscript. Similarly, inspection notes written nearly contemporaneously on the reverse of these paintings inevitably mention the subject of the painting but never the name of the artist. Finally, extant examples of contemporaneous numeral evaluations of paintings have been shown to be tied to workmanship and visual complexity rather than to the reputation of one artist or another.[4] Although seventeen individual painters are singled out by name in Akbar's court annals, they are lauded repetitively and almost exclusively for the marvelous fastidiousness of their work, which is never extolled as an expression of their own distinctive creative temperaments.[5] Thus, while individual painting styles and talents were probably recognized within the community of artists employed in the workshop, they had little significance in the collective undertaking, and would not have been picked out from the final product. What mattered instead was the imagery and finesse of the final product, for only if an object was perceived to be free of the imprint of another

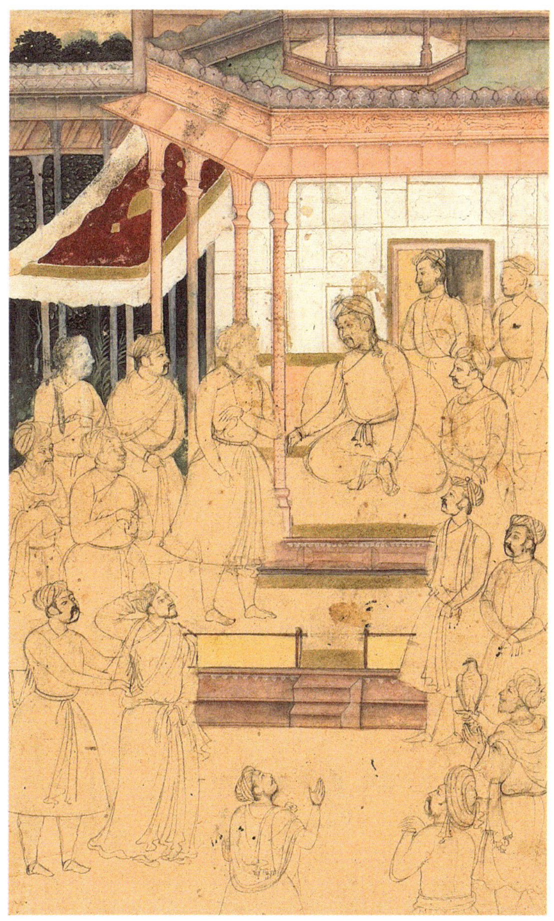

Fig.4
Unknown
Akbar receives Prince Salim, Mughal, ca.1595-1600
Ink, opaque watercolors on paper
20 x 12.6 cm (7 7/8 x 5 inches)
Musée Guimet MA 1026
Courtesy Musée Guimet – musée national des Arts asiatiques, Paris

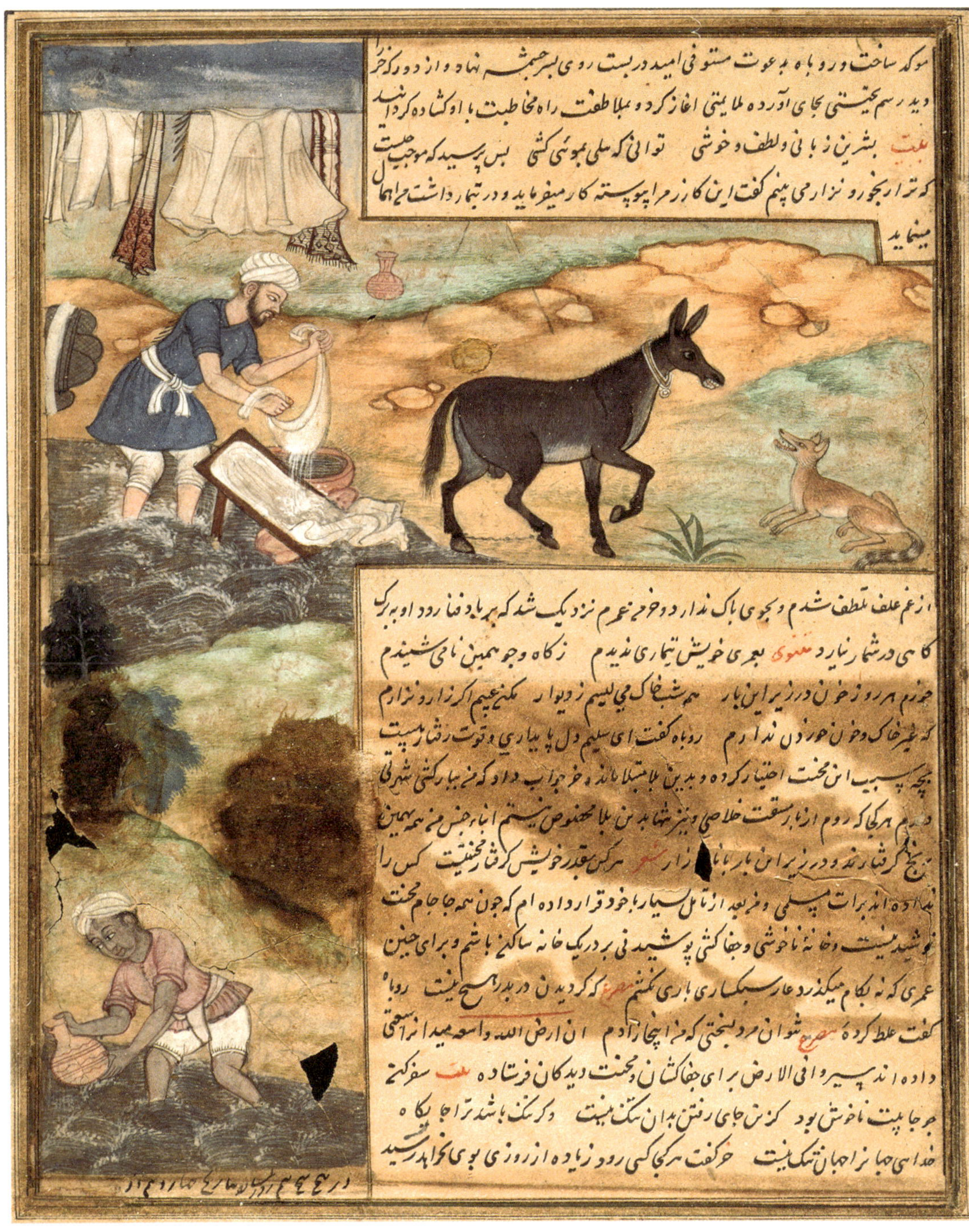

Fig.5
Ascribed to Jagana
As washermen tend to clothes, their donkey listens to a fox, Mughal ca.1595
Ink, opaque watercolors, gold on paper
Painting 13.3 x 9.6 cm. (5 1/4 x 3 3/4 inches)
Folio from a dispersed *'Iyar-i Danish*. Chester Beatty Library, Ms.4, no.52

individual's spirit could it reflect the patron to his best advantage.

While the exceptionally deep documentation of the imperial Mughal atelier at the end of Akbar's reign makes it a comprehensive model of workshop processes, other Mughal workshops followed that model in only the broadest outline. The painting workshop maintained contemporaneously by Prince Salim at Allahabad, for example, commanded a roster of artists only a fifth as large as that of its imperial counterpart. Only rarely is there evidence of the collaboration of two or more artists on a single work, and never is there a trace of a supervisor's directive or deadline. Ascriptions appear less frequently below the illustrations of the manuscripts produced there—a trend possibly exaggerated by accident of preservation—but are supplanted by some artists' signatures on the paintings themselves.

This pared-down structure took hold of the royal atelier too, when Salim ascended to the Mughal throne and adopted the regnal name of Jahangir (r. 1605-27). The corps of imperial painters was reduced drastically, apparently to no more than a couple of dozen artists. Illustrated manuscripts lost their primacy, ceding that favored position to albums filled with exquisite specimens of calligraphy and independent paintings, usually ascribed to individual masters. Together with Jahangir's boastful claims of his own connoisseurship of painting, purportedly honed to the level that he could discern the work of different artists in various parts of a single painted face, this tendency underscores a general shift away from collectively produced paintings and toward individualized efforts.

Meanwhile, other Mughal painting workshops continued to operate along traditional lines. Akbar's mother, Hamida Banu Begum (d. 1604), kept both a small library and painting studio of her own. The evidence for these has come to light only recently, but the two illustrated manuscripts that can thus far be associated reliably with her attest to a workshop limited to about six painters, only one of whom is documented by name in the manuscripts.[6] In many illustrations a key figure or two is rendered in a conspicuously more refined manner, a phenomenon that points to a master artist both overseeing and intervening in the work of his colleagues.

A contemporary biography of 'Abd al-Rahim (1556-1626), the highest ranking noble at the courts of Akbar and Jahangir, sheds light on another well-established Mughal library and workshop.[7] The financial and personnel matters of this library, which had some ninety-five employees, were overseen by a supervisor (*nazim*), who rose to this position by virtue of his manifold skills in poetry, calligraphy, painting, and other arts of the book. Below this rank was a deputy librarian (*darogha*), who managed the staff of calligraphers, painters, and bookbinders. Despite their subordinate place in this hierarchy, a few artists became the personal confidants of their patron, a status that the biographer cites to extol 'Abd al-Rahim's uplifting effect on his retainers but which, he also admits, led to some jealousy within workshop ranks. Ascriptions and signatures on the illustrated manuscripts and independent paintings produced by this atelier yield the names of twenty-one painters, all of whom worked single-handedly. If this lack of collaboration is one sign of a loose workshop structure, another is the unexpected duration of some projects—at least seven years for a wholly original manuscript and fourteen for the refurbishment of one collected piecemeal. Such occasionally extended production times almost certainly included some hiatuses, which, given the relatively stable roster of artists in this atelier, probably reflected the distraction of a patron buffeted by sudden changes in political fortune.

As these examples demonstrate, the most elaborately developed painting workshops in Mughal India were essentially hothouse creations. They thrived when personal inclination and social circumstance combined to motivate a patron with ample resources to call together and sustain a group of talented painters, and collapsed when that sponsor died or lost interest for some reason.[8] The striking exception to this trend is the imperial Mughal workshop, an institution whose sheer size and official status enabled it to weather Akbar's death and to adapt to the new aesthetic values being advanced by Jahangir. In most other cases, however, a painting workshop simply dissolved upon the demise of its patron. Its members scattered across India in search of employment, almost never finding new situations as ambitious or cohesive. Some artists were absorbed into short-lived commercial workshops that turned out mostly humdrum imitations of styles that had long since passed from fashion at the Mughal court. Others made their way to the new ateliers being set up at regional courts in Rajasthan or the Punjab Hills, where they served as catalysts for new chapters in the history of Indian painting.

Notes

1 John Seyller, "Scribal Notes on Mughal Manuscript Illustrations," *Artibus Asiae* 48, nos.3/4 (1987), p.258, n.55.

2 The Persian inscriptions read: "*taswir-i fath-i qil'a-i-chitor* and *do safha guzashta ast.*" Both halves of the double-page composition are discussed but not illustrated in L. Leach, *Mughal and Other Indian Paintings from the Chester Beatty Library*, vol. 1 (London: Scorpion Cavendish, 1995), nos.2.119-120.

3 The Persian inscription reads: "*az do taraf lashkar arastan wa intizar sulh dashtan.*"

4 J. Seyller, "A Mughal Code of Connoisseurship," *Muqarnas* 17 (2000), pp.178-203. Basavana, for example, has works rated both 1 and 2 on a scale of 1 to 3, and some paintings even have individual figures rated above or below the number assigned to the work as a whole.

5 For an explication of this often-cited passage from the *A'in-i Akbari*, see J. Seyller, *Pearls of the Parrot of India: The Walters Art Museum Khamsa of Amir Khusraw of Delhi* (Baltimore: Walters Art Museum, 2001), pp.30-31.

6 These manuscripts, a dispersed *Ramayana* dated 1594 and a *Dvadasa Bhava* of about the same date, are presented respectively in C. Black and N. Saidi, *Islamic Manuscripts* (London: Sam Fogg, 2000), no.44; and G. Fantoni, *Indian Paintings and Manuscripts* (London: Sam Fogg, 1999), no.19. L. Leach, "Pages from an *Akbarnama*," in R. Crill, S. Stronge, and A. Topsfield, eds., *The Arts of Mughal India* (London and Ahmedabad: Mapin, 2004), pp.42-55, has associated the dispersed *Akbarnama*, which has recently appeared on the London art market, with Hamida Banu. This association, based almost exclusively on the hypothetical prominence of women in its surviving illustrations and the unsupported assumption that a female patron would automatically be exceptionally interested in such scenes, is rejected here.

7 For a more complete account of 'Abd al-Rahim and his library establishment, see J. Seyller, *Workshop and Patron in Mughal India: The Freer* Ramayana *and Other Illustrated Manuscripts of 'Abd al-Rahim* (Zurich: Artibus Asiae, 1999), pp.45-63.

8 M. S. Simpson, "The Makings of Manuscripts and the Workings of the *Kitab-khana* in Safavid Iran," in P. Lukehart, ed., *The Artist's Workshop* (Washington, D.C: National Gallery of Art, 1993), pp.104-121, arrives at similar conclusions in her discussion of painting workshops in sixteenth-century Iran.

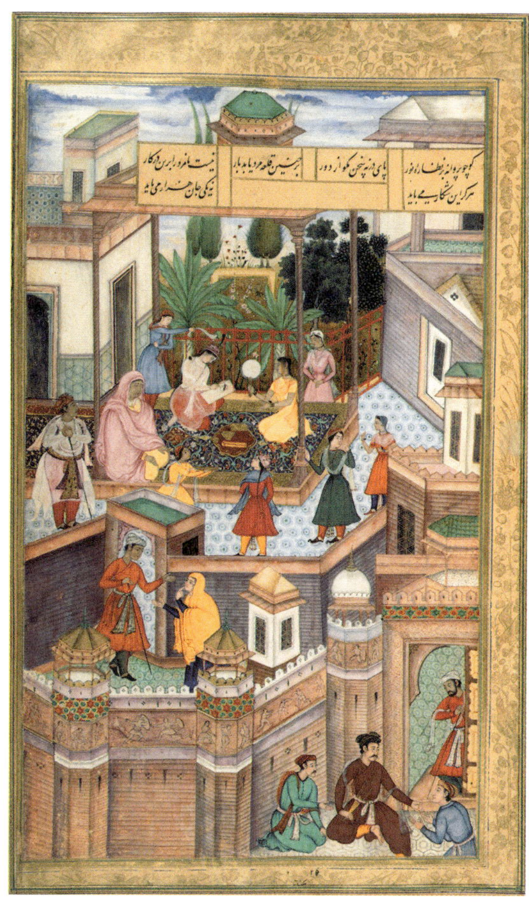

Fig.6
Ascribed to Jagannatha
The princess paints a self-portrait, Mughal, 1595
Ink, opaque watercolors, gold on paper
Painting 23.8 x 14.6 cm (9 3/8 x 5 3/4 inches)
Khamsa of Nizami, British Library Or.12208, f.206a.
By permission of the British Library, London

In the Spirit of Improvisation

Jessica Hough

"...I love that I can have a perceived idea of what a work is going to turn out like, yet someone else takes that idea and runs with it, but in an entirely different direction, but not far enough so that I won't still love it. That's where the element of surprise comes into play, and trusting someone else enough with your own drawing to allow them to add their own sensibility. There is no room for ego."[1]
Marcel Dzama, The Royal Art Lodge

Artists have always enjoyed the company and stimulation of other artists, and for many these relationships are essential. The history of art is dotted with references to communities of artists, sometimes informal groups of like-minded colleagues working together, or, more often in the twentieth and twenty-first century, "official" groups working under a group name or philosophy. Some of these relationships resulted in fascinating examples of jointly-produced works of art, which stand out for their unique contribution to an artist's body of work. Of particular interest are collaborations in which artists work in turn on a single object reacting to each other's additions. In most of these cases, the artists' individual contributions are evident and their distinct identities retained. The contributions can be surprising and revealing; offering examples of improvisation, problem solving, spontaneity, and insights into the artists' solo practice. Artists are more likely to take risks in jointly-made works, and these experiments outside their studio parameters can often help feed new ideas into their solo work.

The nature of collaborative work varies considerably depending on the arrangement between artists. In some situations, artists come together to form a group with a single identity, producing work in such a way that the product does not outwardly appear to have been made by more than one person. One such collaborative ChanSchatz (Eric Chan and Heather Schatz) is formed as a unified artist-partnership. Their output is a result of negotiations and experiments, with one unified voice that ultimately comes through. Interestingly, their work also involves collaboration with their audiences, further complicating its authorship. Work made by collectives such as their's raises questions about identity, process, authorship, and inspiration, and is a form of collaboration quite distinct from the process of working in turn.

There are many reasons why artists enter into an art-making relationship. Artist David Humphrey described a game that he and his wife, also an artist, regularly play. He challenges her to draw something arbitrary, a nurse mowing a lawn for instance. She might then ask him to add Gore Vidal having a cup of tea, and so on; each artist must make the next addition work within the context of what has already been drawn on the paper.[2] The game loosens up the couple's creativity, provides amusement, and forces them to be bold and brave in the face of art-making. In some cases, artists might venture into collaboration because they believe it will help them access ideas and imagery they could not give shape to on their own.

The Dadaists and the surrealists, well known for their collaborations, were searching for a similar creative spontaneity through collective work. The Dadaists, in particular George Grosz and John Heartfield, are credited with having invented photomontage, a process by which fragments of photographs are combined to make a composition. According to Grosz, the first photomontage and subsequent ones were made together, and some of them signed "Grosz-Heartfield Combine."[3] We might imagine the artists seated side by side in Grosz's Berlin studio in 1916, cutting up found printed material and pasting down scraps onto a piece of cardboard. Each would work in turn, necessarily reacting to what had just been placed down. Photomontage and collage became a popular way of working among the Dadaists. The format naturally lends itself to multiple inputs, and works were often created in collaboration. The clippings often included text so that the final collage was not only a visual composition but also contained poetry. Members of the international Dada movement sought creative spontaneity and chance occurrences in their visual art, music, and poetry as a way of working against what they perceived as a war-supporting European culture. Having more than one creative mind work on a single piece must have seemed like a way to break free from the influences and parameters of society, so easily ingrained in human behavior.

The surrealists invented the game of *The Exquisite Corpse* (*Cadavre Exquis)* to stimulate, entertain, and mine the subconscious of its players. Andre Breton, founding father of surrealism, describes *The Exquisite Corpse* as a game of folded paper, in which several people compose a phrase or drawing collectively, without knowledge of the preceding contribution or contributions. The now famous example, which gave its name to the game, is the first phrase obtained in this manner: "The exquisite corpse shall drink the young wine."[4]

The Exquisite Corpse resulted in works that were clearly collaborative, in which each artist's hand is easily distinguishable. If the game was played according to the rules that Breton outlined, the collaboration was "blind." In this way, the artists were not reacting to what came before, but rather playing a game of chance in which disjuncture was a valued outcome. The surrealists also ventured to make their contributions immediate and instinctive, so as to access true thought as opposed to thought mediated by reason. In one example of *The Exquisite Corpse* (Fig.1), it is easy to see the process by which Joan Miró, Man Ray, Yves Tanguy, and Max Morise (from bottom to top) each added to the composite. This is a very different process than working with full knowledge of what came before. With *The Exquisite Corpse*, the clash between both individual artists' styles and content created a finished work of heightened disjunction. The exercise suited the surrealists' desire to be non-conformist and access a freedom unconstrained by the analytical mind. Non sequitur, disjunctive and contrasting imagery were hallmarks of surrealist work, which strove to avoid reason.[5] The resulting drawings and collages were pregnant with metaphorical meaning which could then be the nucleus of creative inspiration.

In the example shown here, it is interesting to note that the contributions by each artist are not necessarily made in their signature style or medium. The artists may have experienced a freedom to take risks outside of their studio practice.

The Exquisite Corpse has been played among artists since the early twentieth century, with extant examples by artists from recent art history, including Joseph Beuys, Gerhard Richter, and Wifredo Lam. In 1993 independent curator Ingrid Schaffner, working with artists Kim Jones and Leonard Titzer, revived the surrealist game on a large scale for an exhibition titled *The Return of the Cadavre Exquis* that opened at The Drawing Center in New York and traveled to four additional venues. The organizers were so overwhelmed by the requests to participate that they had to postpone the exhibition twice. When the show was finally hung it included 600 drawings, by more than a thousand artists.[6] Around the same time, two comic artists, Art Spiegelman and R. Sikoryak, embarked on a similarly ambitious project, in which they invited graphic artists to contribute to what they called *the narrative corpse*, the

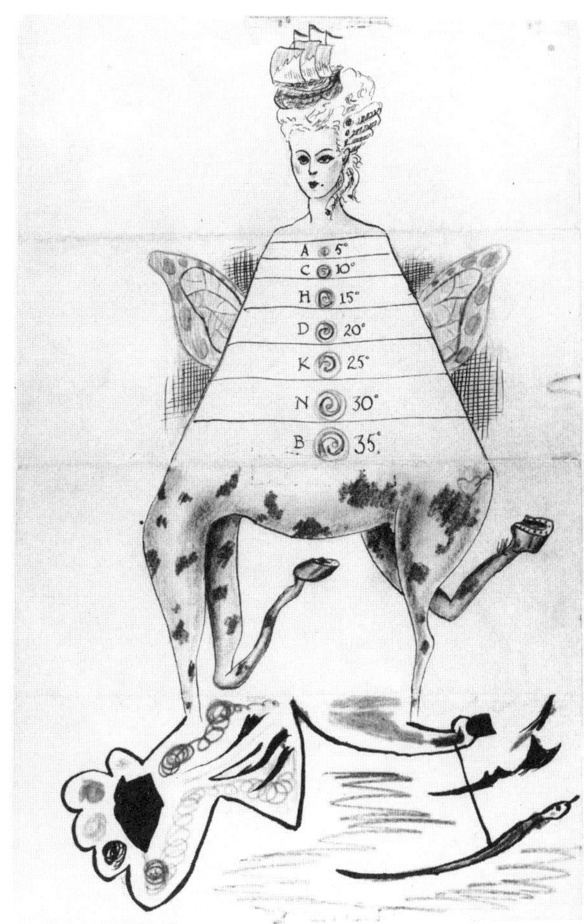

Figure 1
Joan Miró, Man Ray, Yves Tanguy and Max Morise
Exquisite Cadaver, 1927
Game of paper folded in four, each artist working on their section without seeing the other sections and knowing only the title
Private collection
Photo credit: Snark /Art Resource, New York

comic variant of the game. Sixty-nine artists participated by writing and drawing three consecutive panels in response to three made by an artist sequenced before them. None of the artists ever saw more of the story than those three panels of the narrative.[7] The final product, published in book form in 1998, is criticized for its lack of narrative cohesiveness but lauded for its experimental quality.

Some of the best-known collaborative paintings of the twentieth century were made by Jean-Michel Basquiat, Francesco Clemente, and Andy Warhol. According to one account, these artists were brought together by friend and dealer Bruno Bischofberger. Bischofberger had been fascinated by works made collaboratively by other artists whom he collected. He also witnessed several informal collaborations between artists and his daughter Cora, who at the time of her collaboration with Basquiat was only four years old. Cora made drawings with both Clemente and Basquiat on different occasions when the artists were visiting the Bischofberger home. These experiences led him to initiate a discussion about arranging a collaboration between artists he admired, at first with Basquiat, who was very open to the idea of working in collaboration, and then with Warhol and Clemente. Bischofberger has described the arrangement: "To get the most spontaneous work into the collaborations I suggested to

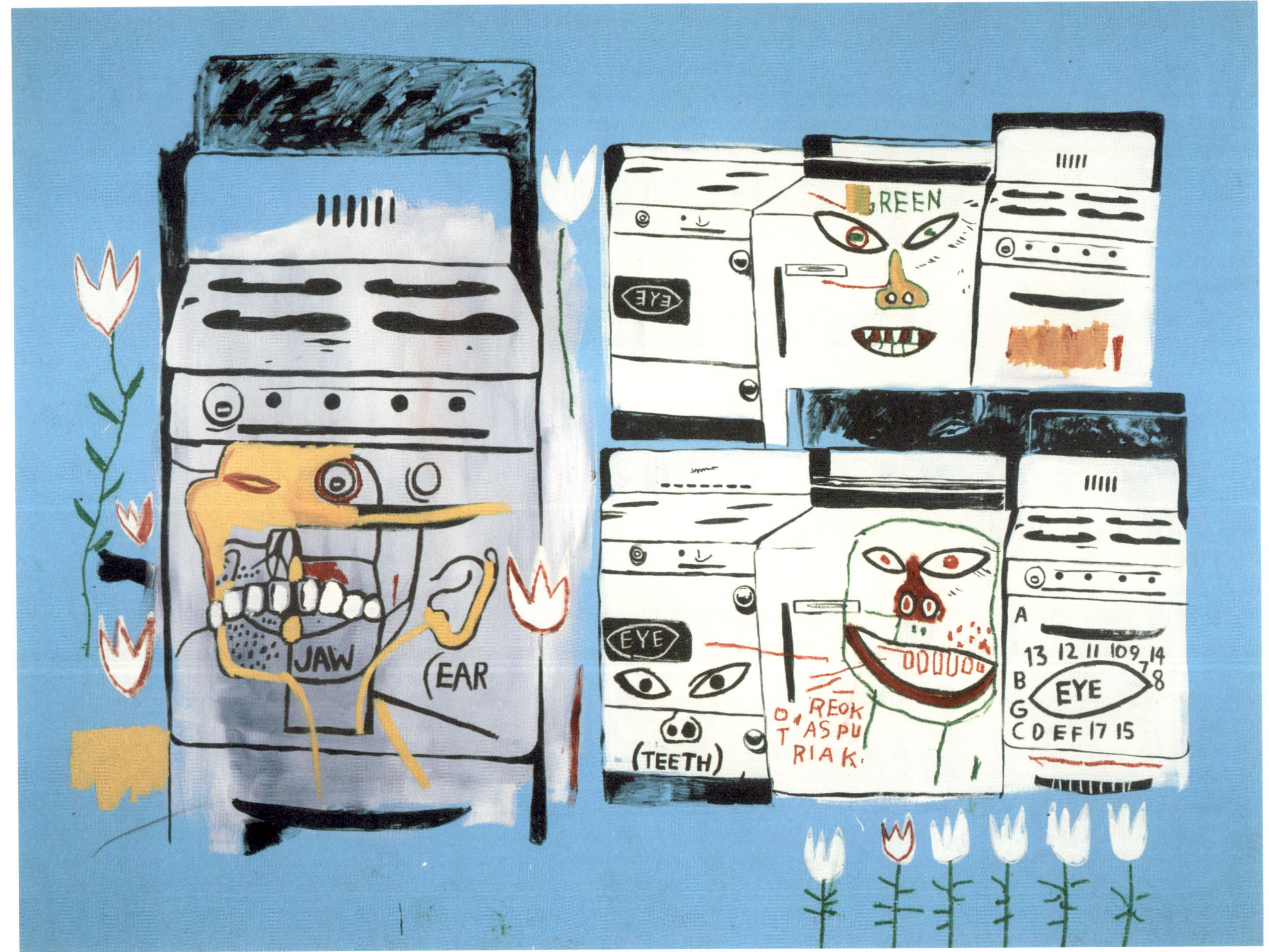

Figure 2
Jean-Michel Basquiat, Andy Warhol
Stoves, 1985
Acrylic, oil crayon on canvas
80 x 107 3/4 inches (203 x 274 cm)
Private collection
Courtesy Galerie Bruno Bischofberger, Zurich

Basquiat that every artist should, without conferring with the others about iconography, style, size, technique, etc., independently start the paintings, of course in the knowledge that two further artists would be working on the same canvas, and that enough mental and physical space should be left to accommodate them. I further suggested to him that each artist send one half of the started collaborations to each of the other artists and the works then be passed on to the remaining artist whose work was still missing. Basquiat liked my proposal and agreed."[8] Fifteen works were completed at that time and they were shown as a group at Bischofberger's Zurich gallery in 1984.

Although it was Bischofberger who did the match making (not the most romantic way to enter a relationship), it seems that the artists were curious enough about it to agree to the engagement. Interestingly, this initial collaboration led to a further series between Warhol and Basquiat alone (Fig.2), which took place in Warhol's studio. Artist Keith Haring, a friend of both Basquiat and Warhol, wrote a short essay describing their working relationship, which he witnessed numerous times: "Painting with Jean-Michel was not easy. You had to forget any preconceived ideas of ownership, and be prepared to have anything you'd done completely painted over within seconds. It was a kind of total abandon, which required total trust and respect. Andy loved the energy with which Jean would totally eradicate one image and enhance another...They worked on many at the same time, each idea inspiring the next. Layers and layers of ideas would build towards a concise climax."[9] According to legend, Jean-Michel's compliments, and their painting sessions together, re-directed Warhol back to painting with a brush, an early technique that he had since nearly abandoned to silk-screening.

David Humphrey, artist member of Team SHaG, describes a similar atmosphere of both trepidation and trust when working in this manner with other artists. He and co-members Elliot Green and Amy Sillman have been painting together since 1996, and each has a somewhat different role within the group. David sees himself as an adapter but describes his partners differently: "Elliot is more of an illustrator and less happy to see his work obliterated. Amy is a 'schmearmeister'. A little addition turns into a total repaint... The Amy-factor unnerves him [Elliot]. He can't bear it because it all may be destroyed right then." Team SHaG was originally conceived among three friends who loved each other's work. It started with idle chat at a party and turned into a body of work, as they began painting on a group of prepared canvases that Green had available at the time. A dozen canvases were split among them, each started several paintings, and then passed them on to the other members. When each had had an opportunity to amend the paintings, the group gathered together to finish the works. This process is generally "psychologically fraught," says Humphrey, as they work towards getting each painting to a point that they all can agree is finished.

Humphrey points to the shared orientation towards psychologically rich subjects, which made their collaboration appealing to him and also, perhaps, possible at all. To some extent they were all dealing with the same subject in their work, interiority and the imagination, and using a cartoon-like figuration (Fig.3). Similarly, Warhol and Basquiat shared certain issues; such as their interest in emblems or totems, and appropriated cultural material. Although the painting styles of Warhol and Basquiat are quite distinct, their jointly-produced paintings, like those of Team SHaG, do have a visual cohesiveness. They both paint in shallow space, for example, and share an interest in imperfect finishes; these qualities hold the paintings together.

It is not a surprise that Warhol and Basquiat agreed to collaborate; in many ways their individual practices were suited for it. Both, in different ways, allowed external creative energy to enter their work. Warhol depended on a team of people working in the "factory" to produce paintings, films, photographs etc. While these individuals may not have been collaborators in the sense we are discussing here, they would have had an unavoidable and lasting impact on his work. Basquiat started as a graffiti artist working on the facades of buildings, subway cars, and other urban surfaces. Much of his work was a visual response to what was already present.

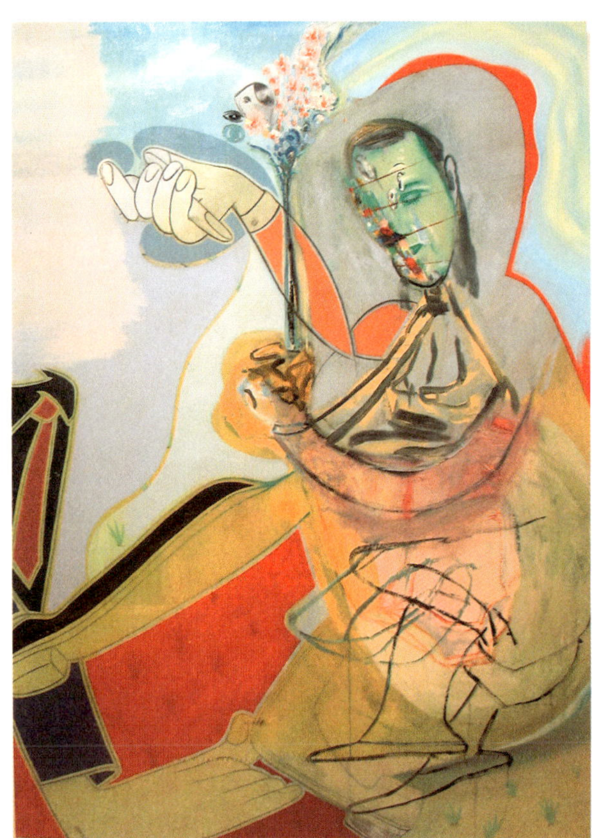

Figure 3
Team SHaG (Amy Sillman, David Humphrey, and Eliott Green)
Girl With Flowers, 2001
Oil on canvas
64 x 44 inches (162.5 x 112 cm)
Courtesy of the artists

He would respond to the language of a sign or previous graffiti tag, or the texture of a distressed surface. In this way, he rarely began with a blank canvas but rather by making sense of, and responding to, what was already there. In a sense, he was prepared for the experience of collaborating.

Basquiat was not prepared, however, for the public reception of his collaborative works. When the new works were finally exhibited at Tony Shafrazi Gallery in SoHo in 1985, they were poorly received with a *New York Times* review that was especially biting. This negative criticism was a blow to Basquiat and the stimulating painting relationship did not continue.

Collaborative works made by artists such as Warhol and Basquiat generally sell for far less at auction than their individual works, even in this example of two artists of legendary status. According to Amy Cappellazzo, international co-head of post-war and contemporary art at Christie's, the market is influenced by the perception that collaborations never produce the best of an artist's work and that the compromises made on both sides do not serve the final artwork.[10] Similarly, team SHaG's paintings have not reached the market value of the artists' individual works. Team member Humphrey feels that collectors may be concerned that the collaboration may be short-lived—only a novelty.[11]

One novel "collaboration" that has become a legend is Robert Rauschenberg's *Erased de Kooning Drawing* of 1953. The young Rauschenberg approached the established master artist, Willem de Kooning, and asked for a drawing. He returned to his studio and proceeded to erase nearly all evidence of the image, destroying one work of art in the creation of a new conceptual work. It was essential to the success of the piece, in Rauschenberg's mind, that the erased drawing was by an established and successful artist. This way no one could dispute that it was "art" that had been erased. The radical gesture of obliterating a work of art was, for Rauschenberg, not a rejection of de Kooning's work but "a celebration."[12] With the *Erased de Kooning Drawing* an experiment took place across generations, as Rauschenberg both acknowledged a debt to the older generation, and moved the history of art forward. De Kooning's willing participation (although he told Rauschenberg that he didn't like the idea) was an affirmation of the younger artist and his ideas.

Keith Haring, who himself engaged in collaborations, articulates his thoughts on the relationship between working artists: "For an artist, the most important and most delicate relationship he can have with another artist is one in which he is constantly challenged and intimidated. This is probably the only productive quality of jealousy. The greatest pleasure is to be provoked to the point of inspiration... This provocation, coupled with a little self-confidence, can create an intense working atmosphere." Both ego and camaraderie have played an important part in collaborative art and often the tussle between them, has been the creative force.

Recently, art audiences have been very curious about the compelling work of a group that calls itself The Royal Art Lodge. The group of eight Canadian artists from Winnipeg, who started working together in 1996, has made a name for itself as a successful collaborative. Much like the surrealists, who gathered often and relied on the salon atmosphere for many of their collaborations, these artists work in the same studio and often discuss the drawings as they are being made. Drawing is their primary medium of collaboration, and also the main interest of most of the artists in the group, although they also produce paintings, video, performances, and even puppets.[13] The Royal Art Lodge members (Michael Dumontier, Hollie Dzama, Marcel Dzama, Neil Farber, Drew Langlois, Myles Langlois, Jonathan Palypchuk, and Adrian Williams) all engage in a slightly bleak and off-color view of contemporary life—sharing a sensibility in their solo work, which like the other successful collaborations of Team SHaG and Warhol/Basquiat, seems to be helpful in these efforts.

Their name provokes images of a secret society or a turn-of-the-century private club. In reality, the Art Lodge isn't so much a place as an intimate group. Member Adrian Williams says, "It eventually and increasingly seemed to serve as a mysterious-yet-socially-okayed therapy group for mildly dysfunctional (myself included), highly imaginative people who liked to draw."[14] Intimacy and camaraderie seem essential to this group, whose work sometimes makes obvious the hands of multiple artists and other times looks completely cohesive (Fig.4). Artist-member Neil Farber has described his involvement in the group: "For me the point of collaborating with other artists has always been for the social aspects of working together. When we started the Art Lodge we began making drawings together and we made them very quickly, which was kind of an exaggeration of the way some of us were working at the time. This way of working is very automatic and improvisational, for me it's always been a fun way to spend an evening. We didn't intend to do much with our drawings originally so there wasn't much pressure to make them especially good or presentable. Because of this most of the work focused on entertaining or impressing each other."[15] Farber's description of a relaxed atmosphere of improvisational play makes it clear how for a group of curious artists this could be the source of new visual material and continual ideas.

This social group, who gathered for the fun and stimulation of improvising on paper, soon generated an enormous body of work. Gaining recognition as a collective, they began to pay more attention to the quality of the drawings they were creating, and developed an editing process. Editing jointly-made works is something even the surrealists, who were committed to chance and spontaneity, admitted to doing.[16] The editing method developed by The Royal Art Lodge for their collectively-made works has been described by Neil Farber: "Often, after a meeting, we will sort the drawings into one of five suitcases. The worst drawings go into the To Be Destroyed suitcase; these are usually terrible jokes, disturbingly ugly, or really boring. This was the first suitcase we started using to separate drawings, and it was to prevent these drawings from escaping to the outside world. We have plans to eventually destroy the drawings or maybe bury them somewhere. The Sad Cloud suitcase holds drawings on the lower end of the middle class of drawings. These drawings are usually boring but may also be kind of ugly. Occasionally, drawings I like quite a bit—if they are disturbing or ugly, but also funny—will end up in the suitcase; I will lose the vote to bump them up to the Pink Heart-Faced suitcase. The Pink Heart-Faced suitcase holds the higher end of the middle-class drawings. These are usually nice enough to look at, or smart enough, but are missing that special quality that shows up in the best drawings. The Sun-Faced suitcase contains the best drawings we make; these are the ones we generally use to show people or put in exhibitions."[17] The intimacy and sense of humor shared by the group extends to their process of deciding which works are ready for the outside world.

Collaborations have also been driven by more philosophical concerns. Cobra, a group of artists who took their name from the cities they worked in—Copenhagen, Brussels, and Amsterdam—founded their group in 1948 with a view to reject mainstream society and access real emotion. This they believed only existed apart from dominant culture, through a primitive expressionism.[18] They saw all people, including artists, as constrained by the culture of the individual, which they believed was propounded by the West. In their view, society's hierarchy of classes only supported artists who served the upper class and so unavoidably reflected its constraints. While these artists were influenced by surrealism, they believed that it too had been a product of a class culture and therefore failed to impact society. Artist member Constant Nieuwenhuys explained the group's perspective on art in a written statement: "A new freedom is coming into being which will enable human beings to express themselves in accordance with their instincts. This change will deprive the artist of his special position and meet with stubborn resistance. For as his individually won freedom becomes the possession of all, the artist's entire individual and social status will be undermined."[19]

The idea that art is the purview of the masses and that the artist should not be thought of as a distinguished individual naturally led group members to experiment with collaborative works. Despite the pithiness of Nieuwenhuys's words, the artists still signed their individual and group-generated works with their names, retaining to this extent their own sense of individuality.

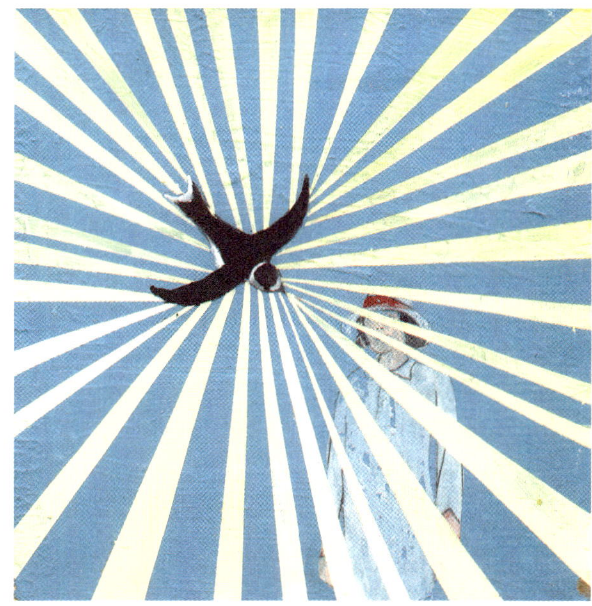

Figure 4
The Royal Art Lodge
Untitled, 2004
Mixed media
6 x 6 inches (15 x 15 cm)
Courtesy of the artists

It was during the years immediately following World War II that the artists first started working together—the historical moment probably contributing to their interest in collective work. The artists worked in a style influenced by the art of so-called primitive cultures, folk art, and the art of children and the mentally handicapped, whom they believed were uninhibited by the constraints of formal society. In at least one instance the seven-year-old son of artist-member Klaus Jorn painted alongside his father and other artists on an unusual and ambitious project. Group members worked together on cladding the interior of a house of an architect friend with floor-to-ceiling murals, in some cases painting the ceiling as well. More than a dozen members participated, spending one month living and painting together. However, the artists seemed to divide the space into discrete areas—for example, the fireplace of the sitting room was painted by Stephen Gilbert, the space around it by Klaus Jorn, the right-hand wall by Carl-Henning Pedersen, and the door by Jorn's son. While the artists had distinguishable styles, their work shared enough characteristics that the murals held together in a somewhat cohesive way.

Working together on drawings and wall paintings must have been a fruitful way for the artists of Cobra to access spontaneity and draw attention to the art-making process, which was also very important to their goal of genuine (and not culturally repressed) expression. In a jointly produced work titled *Some of These Days*, six Cobra artists worked on one lithograph measuring only fifteen by fifteen inches. It appears that each artist in turn drew a creature on the lithography stone, and then went back multiple times to add to the child-like drawing. It is a composition that is clearly unplanned; there is no clear orientation to the work and it feels most akin to a page torn from a sketchbook.

The sketchbook is an interesting comparison to work made in collaboration. Generally, the sketchbook is a place for an artist's most intimate expressions—a private place. A collaborative team, Beattie & Davidson (Drew Beattie and Daniel Davidson) who painted together through the nineties, kept jointly-made sketchbooks. In them, one can see how the artists developed imagery and ideas through the doodling, collaging and sketching typical of a single artist. They have described the source of the imagery in their paintings as either coming directly out of their heads or, as Beattie says, "the quotations are mainly of ourselves from previous paintings or sketchbook energy."[20] This idea of "sketchbook energy" might be a good way of describing the spirit of collaborative works. Many have an immediacy and rawness that makes a viewer sense the artists' presence more directly. But while Beattie & Davidson's paintings tend to be fragmented and absurd, they are not irrational or spontaneous (Fig.5). Curator Larry Rinder writes about their work: "However random their imagery may appear, it is always selected and refined to convey a particular emotional tone: psychological states are the glue that holds their worlds together."[21] In the same interview Davidson goes on to explain, "We're big doubters of the business of the artwork being the representative of the singular soul, the absolute, singularized, centralized self."[20]

This sentiment may be at the core of much of the work discussed here. Despite the assorted motivations for entering into a collaborative arrangement, each artist may maintain some doubt about the validity or even the honesty of the individual expression. And perhaps collaboration is a way to test themselves and their own work, to look at what might arise from joint expression.

The stereotype of the solitary artist working away in private has dominated the recent history of Western art, but in the end we are social beings. The truth is that artists feed off their relationships with other creative people. These few examples of successful and productive collaborations give concrete form to the important exchanges we so rarely get to witness as viewers outside the art-making process. We might look to these improvisations as opportunities to see other dimensions of the artists whose work we think we know. In these instances, they are less confined by a single style, more playful, and in the end, perhaps, more dimensional and human to us.

Thanks to Amy Cappellazzo, Jim Hett, David Humphrey, Mariya Rivera, Ingrid Shaffner, and Jessica Zucker for their help with research on this essay.

Figure 5 (right)
Beattie & Davidson
Blue Monkeys, 1997
Acrylic, mixed media on canvas
90 x 58¼ inches (229 x 148 cm)
Collection of Deborah Oropallo, Berkeley, CA
Courtesy of the artists

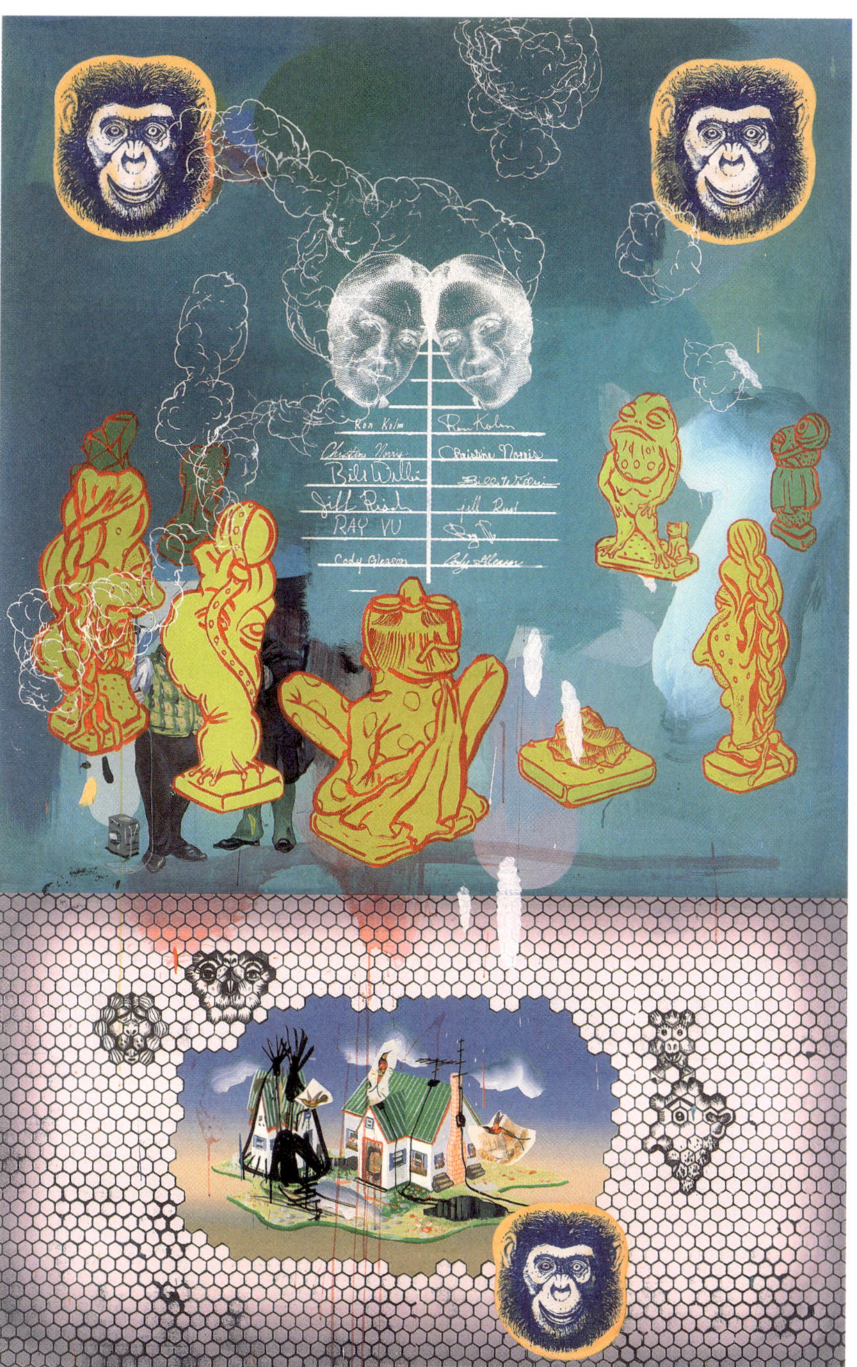

Notes

1 Wayne Baerwaldt and Joseph R. Wolin, "An Interview with The Royal Art Lodge," in *The Royal Art Lodge: Ask the Dust Dictionary of Received Ideas* (New York: The Drawing Center, The Power Plant, De Vleeshal, Plug In ICA, 2003), p.25.

2 A real example provided by the artist, phone conversation with the author, February 1, 2005.

3 Cynthia Jaffee McCabe, "Artistic Collaboration in the Twentieth Century: The Period Between Two Wars," in *Artistic Collaboration in the Twentieth Century* (Washington DC: Smithsonian Institution Press, 1984), p.20.

4 André Breton, "The Exquisite Corpse, Its Exaltation," *Dictionnaire Abrege du Surrealisme* (1938); reprinted in *The Return of the Cadavre Exquis* (New York: The Drawing Center, 1993), p.13.

5 "Surrealism, n. Psychic automatism in its pure state, by which one proposes to express—verbally, by means of the written word, on in any other manner—the actual functioning of thought. Dictated by thought, in the absence of any control exercised by reason, exempt from any aesthetic or moral concern." Andre Breton, *Manifestoes of Surrealism*, trans., Richard Seaver and Helen R. Lane (Ann Arbor: University of Michigan Press, 1972). Originally published as *Manifestes du Surrealisme* (Paris: J.J Pauvert, 1962).

6 Ann Philbin, Foreword, *The Return of the Cadavre Exquis.*

7 Art Spiegelman and R. Sikoryak, eds., *The Narrative Corpse: A Chain-Story by 69 Artists* (Richmond, VA: Raw Books and Gates of Heck Inc, 1998), p.1.

8 Bruno Bischofberger, "Collaborations: Reflections on and Experiences with Basquiat, Clemente and Warhol," reprinted in *Basquiat* (Milan: Edizioni Charta, 1999), p.150.

9 Keith Haring, "Painting the Third Mind," reprinted in *Basquiat*, p.XLVII.

10 E-mail correspondence with the author, August 24, 2004.

11 E-mail correspondence with the author, February 15, 2005.

12 Interview with Robert Rauschenberg (video), from San Francisco Museum of Modern Art, *Making Sense of Modern Art,* http://www.sfmoma.org/msoma/artworks/93.html (accessed March 14, 2005).

13 Interview by Wayne Baerwaldt and Joseph R. Wolin from *The Royal Art Lodge*, p.7 & p.23.

14 Ibid., p.11.

15 E-mail correspondence with the author, July 28, 2004.

16 Mary Ann Caws, "Exquisite Essentials," *The Return of the Cadavre Exquis*, p.34.

17 Neil Farber in an e-mail correspondence, printed in *The Royal Art Lodge*, pp.14-16.

18 William Stokvis, *Cobra: An International Movement in Art after the Second World War* (New York: Rizzoli International Publications Inc., 1988), p.8.

19 Ibid., p.30.

20 "Weedy Snowball: David Humphrey Talks with Beattie & Davidson," *Beattie & Davidson* (Santa Monica, CA: Smart Art Press, 1998), p.58.

21 "Cars without Shadows: Recent Paintings by Beattie & Davidson," *Beattie & Davidson*, p.12.

22 "Weedy Snowball: David Humphrey Talks with Beattie & Davidson," *Beattie & Davidson*, p.59.

Karkhana: Revival or Re-Invention?

Virginia Whiles

We are tackling something that has been in hibernation and then commandeered by people who are trying to retain it in a 'pure' state for the sake of tradition. As artists have started to experiment, there is a freshness emerging, making the form as well as the tradition grow.[1]
Aisha Khalid

Cultural anthropologist Johannes Fabian's view of performance as a dialectical relationship, *"...making, fashioning, creating what I call a sociality...a social praxis,"*[2] suggests that performance allows people to empower themselves at a local level by acting out their anxieties. The *Karkhana* project is a collaborative performance at a distance. It is also the outcome of an extraordinary mutual trust and respect between six artists. Their set of twelve paintings stands as a testimony to their comradeship, critical wit, and curiosity about the miniature tradition. The artists of the *Karkhana* project form the core of a group who believe in an experimental play with the practice of miniature painting. This experimentation has been inspired largely by the artist Zahoor-ul-Akhlaq, a former head of the fine arts department at their old art school: The National College of Arts (NCA) in Lahore. The curiosity and innovative approach of the *Karkhana* artists is not the norm in contemporary practice, and the current head of miniature painting at the NCA, Ustad Bashir Ahmad, sustains a more conservative line, steering the department along the orthodox patriarchal path of the traditional workshop. This is the path chosen for their practice by most students, who see experimental work as risky. The tension between the orthodox and experimental factions that has unfolded within the department—the only one of its kind in the world—over the past years, lies at the heart of this practice. While one faction magnifies the myth that miniature painting is an endangered species, the other explodes all such preservationist paradigms.

Tradition and Patriarchy

The Department of Miniature Painting at the NCA maintains the teachings of a meticulous technique through the rigorous copying of existing works from various schools of painting, mainly those of the Mughal courts. This revivalist path illustrates the familiar nationalist strategy of "inventing tradition" by constructing a "continuity with a suitable past,"[3] but the appropriation from the Mughal school by the practitioners in this exhibition is in a radically different spirit. These artists have rejected the purist myth, and reclaimed the original eclecticism of the Mughal style—one that owed its rich hybridity to the collaborative nature of miniature practice. It is the intercultural dialogue encouraged by the Mughal emperor Akbar that suggests an appropriate precedent for these artists. Their revision is less in the spirit of nationalist discourse, and more a celebration of the freedom to experiment in an arena of many cultural influences. Curiosity about what would be gained through collective practice led to the *Karkhana* project on show here.

The traditional Mughal karkhana was a collective workshop with a complex hierarchy of artists, and collaborative practice was the norm. The version of the workshop reproduced at the NCA attempts to preserve the role of the *ustad*, or master, and conceives of his role as not only the senior teacher, but also a dominant father-figure for students. The strong linear dependency created by such a hierarchy and the notion of mastery at its core extinguishes any spirit of dialogue, collaboration, or indeed experimentation. The lack of studies that critically analyze the historical evolution of miniature practice, ironically justified by the orthodox argument that training has always been oral, has also not been conducive to open discourse. Even the form of collaborative practice found in the Mughal karkhanas has been neglected in the NCA's orthodox training program. This is strongly related to the tension, mounting in Pakistan as elsewhere today, between traditional patriarchal attitudes and more avant-garde forces. The current revival of the orthodox tradition is so intent on maintaining its hierarchy that it cannot risk potential disruption from rebels—often female.

The structure of miniature painting workshops has always been patriarchal, and specialized knowledge has been transmitted from fathers to sons. Since the techniques of miniature painting were protected by the workshop system, trade secrets were kept within the male side of the family, and it was often felt that they should "...not be passed onto daughters in case they gave or made them available to other painters' families into which they married."[4] Excluding daughters from trade secrets was the "social response" of male painters to the threat of lost status. Historical accounts mention only four females as practitioners of painting within Mughal courts: the Empress Nur Jahan, Nini, Raqiya Banu, and Nadira Bano, known as Anarkali, the legendary concubine of Jahangir. The only mention of other women is as assistants responsible for grinding the pigments.[5]

The most remarkable shift in the traditional practice of miniature painting today is the important role that women are playing in its reinvention. The majority of the painters in the radical movement of contemporary miniature painting in Pakistan are female: four of the six participants in the *Karkhana* project are women. Gender issues are tackled by both male and female artists in this group, but are either ignored or disregarded by the orthodox discourse, which continues to deny historical change.

The differences between the *Karkhana* artists and the mainstream view at the NCA department is evident from two separate comments, the first from a student happy to play by the patriarchal and hierarchical rules: "We are lucky to be taught the traditional way, he [Ustad Bashir] trains us all the time. We never feel insecure, we are never disrupted, all thanks to him. He clarifies our minds as to whether a miniature is real or not."[6]

The second comment is from Nusra Latif Qureshi, one of the *Karkhana* artists: "I believe the language of tradition to be a living, potent and valid system of expression, not accepting, necessarily, the ritual. Many of us think of tradition as something of the past, [that] should be treated like a relic and ritualized. I do not attach nostalgia to tradition. The systems that are lost have been lost forever, there is no point in pining for an *'ustad-shagird'* (master-disciple) system... although there are still living examples of both this Eastern 'hallmark' and its Western parallel: the 'master'."[7]

Closely related to the current orthodox discourse is the colonial practice of the manipulation of knowledge, inherited by the present system. The imperialist policy of "civilizing the natives"[8] made for a reactionary attitude towards experimental work. By the mid-nineteenth century, miniature painting in court ateliers had been thoroughly undermined by a double-edged blow: the loss of Mughal patronage and the political deconstruction of indigenous art-making by an imperialist cultural policy. The annexation of Punjab in 1857 brought the dissolution of the last workshops in Lahore. Albums were dispersed as booty or sold into different collections, many of which now reside in Western museums. Miniature painters took to the Punjab Hills or to Rajasthan to look for support in the smaller courts of Rajput dynasties. In Alwar, Patiala, the major Sikh kingdom of the Punjab, a prominent family of Muslim miniaturists became forefathers to the first link in the chain between workshop practice and Westernized education: a scion of this family, Ustad Haji Mohammed Sharif was to become the first official teacher of miniature painting at the Mayo School of Art (later renamed the NCA) in 1945.

The NCA was originally established as an Arts and Crafts inspired school by the British, in 1878. Named the Mayo School of Art after the Governor of Punjab, its first "superintendent" was John Lockwood Kipling, father of the writer Rudyard Kipling, who was also curator at the Lahore Museum from 1875-1893. Like the other principals of colonial art schools in India, such as E.B. Havell and George Birdwood, Kipling leaned towards progressive policies to encourage indigenous craft industries. Miniature painters were by then officially classed as craftsmen "empowered" to decorate walls, furniture, and diverse objects, and it was curious that miniature painting was excluded from the curriculum at this stage. The hierarchic division between art and craft was "a device for maintaining power and stratification in colonial systems,"[9] and miniature painting has been the subject of taxonomic shifts since the colonial period, bearing the status of artifacts or fine art according to its presentation.

This confusion in classification is an outcome of the ambivalent discourse of imperialist art administration and teaching. In the nineteenth century, the indigenous learning process by oral transmission was replaced with design lessons based on "a scientific outlook and the use of reason."[10] The academic program at art schools swung back and forth between the economic push for Indian decorative arts and the romantic pull of imagination and spirituality in the living traditions of Indian fine art and aesthetics. The united call for an "authentic" Indian art on the part of both Western orientalists and Indian members of the *swadeshi* art movement eventually led Havell, then director of the Calcutta Government School of Art, to throw out the school's Greek plaster casts and promote miniature painting as an ideal indigenous model for students in fine art.[11]

The staff at the Mayo School of Art in the 1920s included artists from the Bengal School who were keen to supplant the Western academic system with alternative structures of pedagogy and patronage. This group's commitment to nationalist forms led to a search for indigenous content and, inspired by both Havell and Tagore amongst other orientalists, this quest led them to revive miniature painting. Thus it was that in the 1920s, miniature painting was listed among the techniques to be studied by fine art students at the Mayo School. With the growing confusion between the orientalist influence and the academic call for a modernist syllabus, naturalist drawing vied with the hieratic formalized style. Also, as miniature painting could not be preserved along the master-disciple system within an academic program, a compromise was reached and it was introduced as a minor option.

In 1958, the Mayo School of Art was upgraded to become the National College of Arts and it embarked on a pedagogy influenced by Bauhaus ideas of integrating fine art and design, wholly inspired by the Arts and Crafts ideology. Shakir Ali, considered the founder of the modern movement in Pakistan, and Haji Mohammed Sharif, of the Patiala miniaturist family, were both on the faculty of the Fine Arts department. Yet, in spite of their mutual respect for each other's contrasting views, modernism dominated at the school. When Sheikh Shujaullah, also from a lineage of traditional miniature painters, took over the post from Sharif in 1968, it was still as *ustad* of a "minor" art.[12]

During the 1950s and 1960s, art in Pakistan moved across a wide range, from post-impressionist landscape to cubist and expressionist figuration. Abstraction was slow to dawn and harshly received by the critics. Many artists spent time studying and traveling in the West and became subject to critique from the nationalist lobby. For instance, the critic Jalal Uddin Ahmad argued at this time that "modern Western styles and techniques have been sympathetically studied and pursued, often too vigorously at times, a little too imitatively. Shakir's early works almost seemed to carry the invisible tag: 'Imported from Europe'."[13] Interestingly, his critique reveals a discourse identical to that used today in Pakistan by certain critics with reactionary views about the new miniaturists' "Westernized" tendencies.

Throughout, the quasi-socialist government of Zulfikar Ali Bhutto and the social upheavals in the 1970s, there appeared new configurations of "populist" views on art and identity. Folk art, music, and literature were officially patronized. Miniature painting was officially promoted as the ideal gift to foreign visitors, employing a rhetoric that emphasized its courtly origins and recycled its former role in diplomatic exchange between the Mughals and the Jesuits. Under the subsequent military dictatorship of General Zia-ul-Haq, the orthodox style of miniature painting figured high on the list of officially-sanctioned state art, alongside calligraphy and, paradoxically, Westernized landscape painting. Meanwhile a wave of popular "vulgarization" recycled familiar Mughal miniature themes onto calendars, post cards, cushion covers, and adverts, saturating the tourist market.

At the NCA, up until the 1970s, miniature painting appeared to be caught in the trap of reproduction. Under the *ustads* Shujaullah and Sharif, the Mughal style served as a basis for copying and reproducing miniatures. As witnessed by a contemporary critic, "the creative edge was all but blunted and in the hands of copyists and uninitiated craftsmen, the art of the miniature painter degenerated into the soulless insipid prototypes of which any number can be seen even today in many family collections all over East and West Pakistan."[14] While appreciation of the work of Ustad Sharif concentrated on the craft perspective, "an echo of Mughal and Kangra miniature paintings...outstanding as a master craftsman,"[15] the praise for fine artists who appropriated miniature work, such as Chughtai, acclaimed as the first "National Artist" of Pakistan, had a different resonance: "Chughtai's whole outlook is romantic...a logical evolution of Mughal miniature painting from the illustrational and documentary to the lyrical and the decorative."[16]

The current orthodox appreciation of miniatures with historical themes maintains a similarly romantic myth. Based on the assumption that lyricism preserves the original mood of miniatures, it reflects a mulish rose-tinted interpretation of tradition, especially given the fact that in Mughal painting blood and gore often outweigh romance. One reason for the development of this benign vision could be the replacement of the "documentary" by the "decorative" as a strategy that has suited dictatorships by its denial of content. It is precisely for this reason that the work of experimental artists, such as those of the *Karkhana* project, is so powerful. They have retrieved the essentially content-based nature of the medium rather than approaching it as purely an aesthetic exercise. These artists have questioned the ambivalence of a postcolonial art education. They ask why it should encourage pride in a cultural tradition while mystifying the past through a nationalist propaganda that lacks critical history. They see the reinvention of the miniature that began with Akhlaq as an example of a more positively critical art-form—one that offers a critique through its content as well as its form.

Akhlaq took over as head of the fine arts department of the NCA in the mid 1980s. His experimental work with the miniature coincided with the extraordinary resistance of the women's movement to oppression under General Zia's "Islamization" drive. This was the beginning of a paradigm shift in gender relations in Pakistan. It was against the backdrop of women's activism, which included a significant number of women artists, that the reinvention of the miniature began to take place.

This in turn led to yet another social narrative on *wasli* (layered hand-made paper, p.48), as the medium came to be envisaged by miniature artists as a vehicle for "the personal as political." The alternative movements that evolved from the diverse world events of 1968 also form part of this story: activists for racial and sexual rights within the black power and women's liberation groups all had an influence on the art world. The swing was clearly away from pure formalism and back towards an art linked, in various forms, to its social context.

The Reinvention of the Miniature

Akhlaq's reinvention of the miniature was essentially anarchic in its refusal to toe the nationalist line. Ironically, the process of "vulgarization" and the commodification of the miniature during the Zia years may well have contributed towards Akhlaq's realization of the potential play offered by the miniature medium. Akhlaq had studied printmaking at the Hornsey College of Art in London which, like all art schools in the late 1960s, was seen as a hotbed of rebellion and rock music. The mode for mixed media at the time reflected a motley range of practices, in performance, minimal painting, earthworks, and conceptual semantics. This informality set the stage for Akhlaq to explore a different approach to miniature painting, and inspiration came when he studied the superb miniatures at London's Victoria and Albert Museum as a post-graduate student at the city's Royal College of Arts. He discovered a force of invention in the miniatures, which he simply had not realized before. To juxtapose such material from his own cultural history with contemporary innovations proposed a fresh vocabulary for his painting.

On returning to Lahore in the 1970s, Akhlaq's aim was to encourage students to realize the potential of miniatures for their own work. The painter and critic Quddus Mirza, who was a student of Akhlaq's, remembers how he would point out precise factors of contemporary interest such as "the incomplete areas, the looseness of paint application, the use of collage and the play with margins."[17] This examination of old miniatures could only come about by looking at them critically and in the flesh, not from weary reproductions. Unfortunately, the collection in the Lahore Museum was, and remains, in such a sparse and fragile state that the students are obliged to use poor reprints for the crucial stages of copying. Lahore's heritage of original miniatures was seriously depleted through the double loss of patronage after colonization, and the disappearance of collections in the course of Partition. Major parts of the Lahore Museum's former acquisitions are either missing or else in very poor condition. The students, therefore, scarcely use the Museum. This would have Kipling turning in his grave, since his vision was that students would move between the school and the Museum—the twin towers of Punjabi visual culture—an ideal reflected in Akhlaq's wish that the students examine miniatures directly for their intricate sources of formal inspiration.

Akhlaq's own practice informed his teaching and fired an enthusiasm in his students by way of a "communitas" pedagogy—he believed in seeing students outside the classroom and interacting with them socially as part of his work, rather than being limited by an orthodox classroom environment.[18] While the traditional method, which informed the developing curio market, functioned on "faith in the copy" which was as near as possible to the original, Akhlaq's method advocated the use of photocopies with the intent of disturbing the sense of preciousness attached to the miniature. Inspired by Dada and Pop art, the painting department at the NCA entered an experimental phase. There was no militancy in the deconstructive tactics, but simply a parody of academic principles, both Eastern and Western. As one critic has commented, "his post-modern aesthetic investigated the form and structure of the two-dimensionality in miniature painting through his own work...he believed in the possibility of allowing a viewer to read a painting in many ways and at many levels. But the underlying concern with miniature painting was at the core of his image making."[19] Akhlaq's idea was to make miniature painting alive through absorption into painting of the present day, not to preserve it in any pastoral sense. His post-modern methods were defended by the avant-garde and attacked by the reactionary critics for "being brainwashed" by the decadent West.[20]

Akhlaq's influence resonated to the next generation of miniature artists, such as those of the *Karkhana* project and Shahzia Sikander, who recounts: "Zahoor played a critical role in a conceptual dialogue with the miniature tradition and my interest grew through watching him do the opposite of what I was pursuing—he was deconstructing miniatures in relation to larger size painting."[21] Akhlaq's intention was to provoke a re-invention in the practice through a dialogue between traditional and experimental teaching. He encouraged Bashir Ahmad, his most passionate student of miniature painting, to start up a specialized department for it at the NCA, and proposed that miniature painting and printmaking be offered as major areas of specialization, along with painting and sculpture. He personally supervised the development of courses of study in which he encouraged maximum interaction between the painting and miniature painting departments, complementing the experimental mode with the rigor of traditional practice. The complexity involved in putting theory into practice, both at the intellectual and practical levels, was possible only through Akhlaq's own knowledge and practical experience.

Revival

Bashir Ahmad was a student not only of Akhlaq, but also a disciple of Ustad Sheikh Shujaullah, who had been taught by Ustad Haji Mohammed Sharif. In this way, the chain of transmission linked straight back through Patiala to the Mughal karkhanas of Lahore.

Ahmad's vision is one of a committed traditionalist: "As a responsibility to this department, I continue to engage in ways of enhancing awareness of this endangered tradition of miniature art."[22] Ahmad's commitment to the field is one of sheer dedication. His approach is conventionally more fundamentalist.

In the NCA's miniature painting department today, all students are obliged to master the styles of four schools of painting—Persian, Mughal, Pahari, and Rajput—by copying the paintings from each school. The students are only allowed to experiment in their composition for their thesis work, undertaken in the last six months of their three-year training. While the use of the copy in today's orthodox program is authoritarian, the concern illustrates an awareness of the potential dividends from relating the traditional to the modern.

Bashir Ahmad is genuinely respected for his teaching of the technique. In his view, it is the key factor rooting the practice to a traditional method based on Persian origins. At the same time, it is the very obsession with maintaining the myth of the *ustad* that limits his tolerance of experimentation. This has set up a tension with practices that, in his view, deviate too far from the norm. The majority of the students are deferential to both dogma and their *ustad*; as one final-year student put it; "we have done no history of miniatures because Bashir *Sahib* gives us all the information we need: how the Mughals started, the different schools, how to tell the difference between originals and copies."[23]

The ways in which a Westernized educational process may generate conflict with traditional practice can be presented through the dynamics between the orthodox revivalists and the experimental re-inventors. These two factions are the outcome of the two very different approaches taken by Akhlaq and Ahmad. They represent clearly the notion that recoveries of traditional forms always have paradoxical aspects: reactionary and resistant.[24]

Conceptual and Formal Differences

The split between the two discourses around miniature painting appears to be widening. One is inspired by Akhlaq's belief in diffusing the method of the miniature into contemporary painting, and the other follows Ahmad's determination to keep it autonomous. The diversity of approaches within the miniature painting department, however, is also its strength.[25] The most interesting work today is being developed by students who have learned to read both discourses with critical distance. As they become teachers, the more dogmatic pedagogy is going through changes, and it is those changes that have informed the works in this exhibition. For the artists of the *Karkhana* project, for example, the delicate issue of "quality" is not simply about rigorous drawing, which is the fundamental requisite for good miniature work; it is about a conceptual vision, where perception contains a "thought element."[26] The key to the transformation lies in a joint radicalization of both form and content.

The differences in the quality of work made by those in the experimental group and those in the orthodox group were manifested clearly in an exhibition in 2000 at the NCA. Curated by Bashir Ahmad, the work selected revealed excellent copies of paintings from the Mughal, Persian, and Kangra schools; medieval style narratives; panoramic landscapes; "assignment" scenes of college life; vignettes of family and friends; local urban landscapes; and some abstract compositions based on geometry and pattern. The majority of these works appeared to fulfill the academic requirements of skillful technique, they were duly spectacular and responded to the public expectations of the familiar Mughal style. To judge from the general response, these paintings were highly admired objects, and sold well. The same exhibition represented only a few examples of work from the experimental group. Their themes were radically different. Issue-based, observing and commenting, they explored a variety of social issues in both the local and global arenas. Their subjects ranged across a wide terrain, from fundamentalism to family feuds. Because of this, their appreciation was slower in coming.

Many of the miniatures from the revivalist or experimental school are made by women artists, who have become bolder in illustrating the ongoing legacies of *purdah* (seclusion and the practice of veiling) and gender hierarchy. These narratives, including family constraints, unequal rights or sexual violence, all focus on male-centered *izzat,* or honor.[27] The subjects treated by the male artists in the group over the past five years revolve principally around military rule, nuclear policy, feudalism and political corruption. Both genders are preoccupied by the consequences of American hegemony, not simply through the war-mongering in Afghanistan and Iraq but through the intense "glocalization" of a culture influenced greatly by this imperialism: frantic consumerism, drug addiction, gun-running, McDonaldization and silver-screen machismo.

The tools of these artists are of parody and satire. Techniques and imagery are appropriated intentionally from indigenous and Western art history. Their appropriations from various miniature schools are with the intention of replaying them critically. Juxtaposing fragments from Mughal or Pahari miniatures with Western imagery, for example, signals a concern with both local and global issues. The assumption is often made in postcolonial critique that indigenous resistance to globalization only targets Westernization, but these works reveal that such strategies can operate in reverse. Mimicry as a tool of subversion has been well illustrated in postcolonial literary studies[28] as well as feminist psychoanalysis, but needs more attention from art historians.[29]

Miniature painting has a long history of transnational collaborations and visual eclecticism, and the repeated fable that hybridity signals postmodernism is seen as absurd by the new miniaturists. Collage, layering, juxtaposition and fragmentation of the narrative all serve their aim to re-invent the miniature. Rather than a supervised album promoting its patronage, these collective works resemble the surrealists' *Cadavre Exquis* or a "mail-art" work from the Fluxus codex.[30] The works of the *Karkhana* group have a comparable lightness of being which immediately communicates a sense of the artists' enjoyment of their practice. Each artist addresses specific themes through a visual vocabulary, which shares roots, and extemporizes by way of individual sets of signs and gestures. Interferences or inter-references have been made through subtle, often comical modifications of shading, pattern repeats, or graffiti-like flicks of the *qalam* (brush), almost caressing the previous offering. By intensive looking, the viewer can recognize the differences between the artists—detecting the contrasts of touch, texture, and titillation.

Conclusions

The works produced by this experimental group reveal how a hybrid pedagogy arising from a fusion between traditional oral transmission and a postcolonial art-school training has resulted in technical excellence and has encouraged experiment. This example contributes towards deconstructing the oriental (and orientalist) myth that a protected patriarchal transmission is a fundamental requisite for the continuity of a traditional art form. In her study of the miniature as a metaphor for interiority, Susan Stewart describes how the sensation of nostalgia is often overwhelming, due partly to the epic style of narrative, which is fantastic rather than rational.[31] Whereas such an arrested time and space suits the orthodox conception of miniature painting as romantic, the often-disturbing content of the radical miniatures places them clearly inside actual, shifting time. It is this actuality that upsets the orientalist concern with fixing the "other" into a timeless frame.

The reflection of the *Karkhana* group of artists on current social issues empowers them to be free from the "trap" of the copy. Their rejection of the authoritarian model has led to their work being seen as polemical by more conservative forces where there is often a deliberate mis-reading or a refusal to read their content properly. This may be a facet of the "blind eye" syndrome—a common reaction to provocative culture by neo-conservative ideology, which is based on a suitably ambiguous reasoning. Consequently, the provocative work is either declared to be inauthentic because of its "contamination" from sources that derive from globalization, or its content is simply not read. Both responses neatly avoid the acknowledgment of a subversive element in the content.

This consensual preference for what is seen to be traditional is worth a comparison with the reductive opposition of modernity and tradition, attributed to the orientalists and to the nationalist activists. This is now being replayed in the tension between the revivalists and the re-inventors of miniature painting. Resistance to either modernity or colonialism was not created out of exclusivity or cultural difference in the reductive ways pictured by some historians. There is far more overlay and interlapping in both movements of reform and revival than most reports will vouch for, since most representation re-invents by reduction.[32]

The actual practices employed in the *Karkhana* project reject the orthodox discourse on tradition as an invented one—one that is based on a false consciousness through denial of historical change. The artists' work reveals their consciousness of a practice that is historically situated—one that brings knowledge through dialectical reflection and, with this project, dialogical collaboration.

Notes

1 Aisha Khalid, interview with Hammad Nasar, *Herald* (Pakistan), March 2003.

2 Johannes Fabian, *Power and Performance* (Wisconsin: University of Wisconsin Press, 1990), p.6.

3 Eric Hobsbawm & Terrence Ranger, eds., *The Invention of Tradition* (Cambridge: Cambridge University Press, 1983), p.1.

4 B.N. Goswamy and Eberhard Fischer, *Pahari Masters* (Zurich: Artibus Asiae & Museum Rietburg, 1992), p.94.

5 Gauvin Bailey, *The Jesuits and the Grand Mogul: Renaissance Art at the Imperial Court of India 1580-1630* (Washington D.C. Smithsonian: Freer Gallery of Art. Occasional Papers. 1998), Vol.2., p.30; L. Bressan, "Mughal-Christian Miniatures," in Khalid Ahmed, ed., *Intercultural Encounters in Mughal Miniatures* (Lahore: NCA Press, 1995), p.24; Moti Chandra, *The Technique of Mughal Painting* (Lucknow: The U.P. Historical Society, 1949), p.24.

6 Sadaf Naz, discussion with the author, December 2002.

7 Nusra Latif Qureshi, discussion with the author, December 2003.

8 Thomas Macaulay, "Minute on Education," in Theodore de Bary et al. (comp.), *Sources of Indian Tradition* (New York: Columbia University Press, 1963), p.11.

9 Nelson Graburn, "Ethnic and Tourist Arts Revisited," in Phillips & Steiner, eds. *Unpacking Culture* (Berkeley: University of California Press, 1999), p.352.

10 Sir Richard Temple, "On the Subject of Exhibitions and Schools of Art and Design in India," Memorandum, Govt. of India Home Department, 1874, India Office papers, London.

11 Havell argued that there was an incapacity among Westerners to understand the spirituality of Eastern aesthetics "...it shines brightest at the point where we cease to see and understand it." E. B. Havell, *The Ideals of Indian Art* (London: Fergusson, 1911), p.2.

12 Nazish Ata-Ullah, "The Making of the Miniature: An Overview," in *Contemporary Miniature Paintings from Pakistan* (Fukuoka, Japan: Fukuoka Asian Art Museum, 2004).

13 Jalal Uddin Ahmed, *Art in Pakistan* (Karachi: Pakistan Publications, 1962), p.111.

14 Ibid., p.16.

15 Ibid., p.54.

16 Ibid., p.1.

17 Quddus Mirza, discussion with the author, December 2000.

18 Victor Turner, *The Ritual Process: Structure and Anti-Structure* (Chicago: Aldine Publishing, 1969).

19 N. Ata-Ullah, "The Making of the Miniature."

20 Akbar Naqvi, *Image and Identity: Fifty Years of Painting and Sculpture in Pakistan* (Karachi: Oxford University Press, 1997).

21 Shahzia Sikander, *Conversations with Traditions* (New York: Asia Society, 2001), p.68.

22 Bashir Ahmad, *Portfolio Preface.* Exhibition of Miniature Painting (Lahore, Pakistan: NCA Press, 2000).

23 Mariam Hashmi, discussion with the author, December 2002.

24 Juergen Habermas, "Modernity: An Unfinished project," in Hal Foster, ed., *Postmodern Culture* (London: Pluto Press, 1985), pp.3-15.

25 N. Ata-Ullah, "The Making of the Miniature."

26 Ludwig Wittgenstein, *Philosophical Investigations* (Oxford: Blackwell, 1968), p.193.

27 Saira Wasim's series on honor killings is one example of this.

28 Homi Bhabha, *The Location of Culture* (London: Routledge, 1994).

29 Luce Irigaray, *This Sex Which is Not One* (Ithaca: Cornell University Press, 1985).

30 Fluxus was a 1960s group of international artists with a Dadaist take on globalization. Their common theme was chance and they used cardboard or matchboxes to send their miniature-sized "mail art" through the post.

31 Susan Stewart, *On Longing* (Durham and London: Duke University Press, 1993).

32 Sugata Bose and Ayesha Jalal, *Modern South Asia: History, Culture, Political Economy* (Lahore: Sang-e-Meel, 1998), pp.109-25. Also Tapati Guha-Thakurta, *The Making of a New 'Indian' Art: Artists Aesthetics and Nationalism in Bengal, c. 1850-1920* (Cambridge: Cambridge University Press, 1992), pp.147-84.

Postcards to Empire: The Politics of Resistance in the Karkhana Project

Hammad Nasar and Anna Sloan

The six Pakistani artists who contributed to the *Karkhana* project are bound by a drive to engage publicly with contemporary political concerns. For each, the rights of the individual subject—whether artist or citizen—in the face of state control, recrimination, and physical force has formed a central and recurring theme. As displayed by the set of comparative paintings in *Karkhana: A Contemporary Collaboration*, all six of the project's participants were already addressing a broad range of political topics before their major collaborative effort began in 2003. Prior to the project's inception, members of the circle had explored subjects as diverse as the practice of "honor killing," Pakistan's political merry-go-round, the collective memory of colonialism, and India and Pakistan's nuclear testing duel. Some chronicled contemporary events, such as the power grab that placed General Pervez Musharraf at Pakistan's helm in 1999, while others addressed broader, historically grounded issues, such as the ubiquitous presence of state-sponsored propaganda.

Their collaborative project took themes established earlier in their careers to a new level. While each of the artists had already shunned the duress posed by state power, religious proscriptions and, in some cases, familial expectations, their commitment to truth telling would face an even bigger challenge in the wake of September 11, 2001. The events that followed the attacks on the World Trade Center would divide opinion and intensify extremist policies around the globe. The ensuing "War on Terror" would consolidate a new network of geo-political alliances and spur a military initiative of unchecked power and jurisdiction. It would also draw together distant localities onto a newly configured world stage; and incidentally, it would bring together the personal realities of the six artists, resident at the time in Australia, Pakistan, and the United States. These three nations, allied by their governments in the "War on Terror," were suddenly linked within a political network of global scope, despite the protestations of many of their citizens. The proximity of the military attack on Afghanistan and its spillover into Pakistani territory prompted members of the *Karkhana* circle, such as Khalid and Qureshi, to turn resolutely toward the contemporary political arena. The effect of the "war" on Pakistan's domestic situation and foreign policies also impelled the artists to unite as a group, both in face-to-face gatherings in their Lahore studios, and across two oceans via the Internet and postal service. Ultimately, it channeled their energies into collective expression. Part performance and part protest, the *Karkhana* project can be viewed as a series of postcards—a riposte to imperial aggression from disparate sites on the globe.

The six participants' shared perspectives on the catalytic events of 2001 and 2002 laid the groundwork for *Karkhana's* powerful imagery. But the act of resistance manifest in the project originates not only from the visual content of the twelve paintings, but also from the processes by which those paintings were made. By privileging the group as well as the individual, and the aesthetic as well as the conceptual, the process contributes to a radical act—one that defies the precedent of South Asia's "traditional" courtly miniatures. By choosing to deviate from many of the logistical practices and methods of imperial Mughal workshops before them, this modern karkhana represents a sharp turn from the convention of state-sponsored arts patronage. In particular, the process devised by Muhammad Imran Qureshi exploded the once static hub of the Mughal atelier into a series of diffuse sites. The peripatetic nature of the new karkhana shuns the symbolic potency of the imperial capital, which had once imbued Mughal paintings with the hegemonic authority of the center. The implications for the present day are obvious, and the project thus resists both the centralizing tendencies of the contemporary art world and the centrifugal force of international politics.

In their selective use of contemporary technologies and materials, the *Karkhana* artists highlight the unmistakable impact of globalization in the twenty-first century. At the same time, their use of an international courier company demonstrates their refusal to position themselves in a "pre-modern" or "Third World" context, rather than in the hybrid, transnational world they traverse in reality. Their artistic choices resist the tyranny of binary categories, which might force them to choose between "this" world and "that" one, between modernity and tradition, and between the preservation of local identity and global participation. Perhaps most importantly, given the categories constructed in the wake of September 11, 2001, they refuse to be pigeonholed into either of two newly contrived camps: those "with us" or "against us."

Darmiyan: "In Between"

Artist Aisha Khalid was in Amsterdam finishing a residency at the prestigious Rijksakademie when the World Trade Center's twin towers fell in New York City. Soon, she, like millions of others, tracked reactions to the event in the European print media and television programming. There, and in the United States, pundits, politicians, and journalists responded to the attack by reiterating long-standing clichés about Muslims and the Islamic world. Most notably, television screens, magazine covers, and newspapers reproduced a set of visual images that have a durable place in European and American art history: crowds in the "Arab street," despotic rulers (represented in this instance by Saddam Hussein and the Taliban), and veiled women.[1] The image of the *burqa*, which Khalid used frequently in her work to address complex negotiations between the self and society, became a global icon signifying women's oppression and simplistically implicating Islam as its root cause. Much of Khalid's work, both then and now, addresses the dissonance between "Eastern" and "Western" readings of visual signs, examining the political motivations that underlie particular readings (Fig.1). Her persistent use of the *burqa* image explores the role of

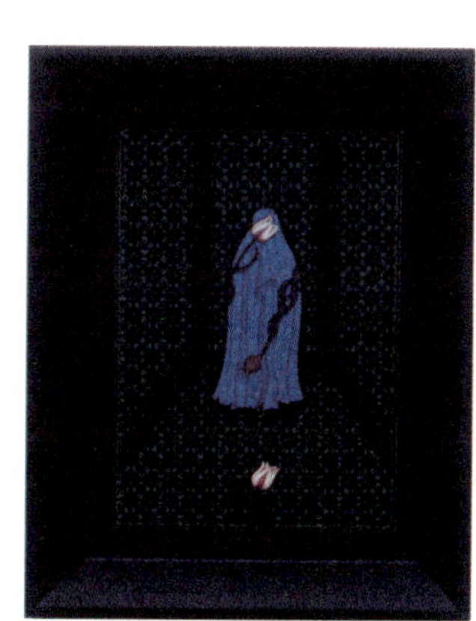

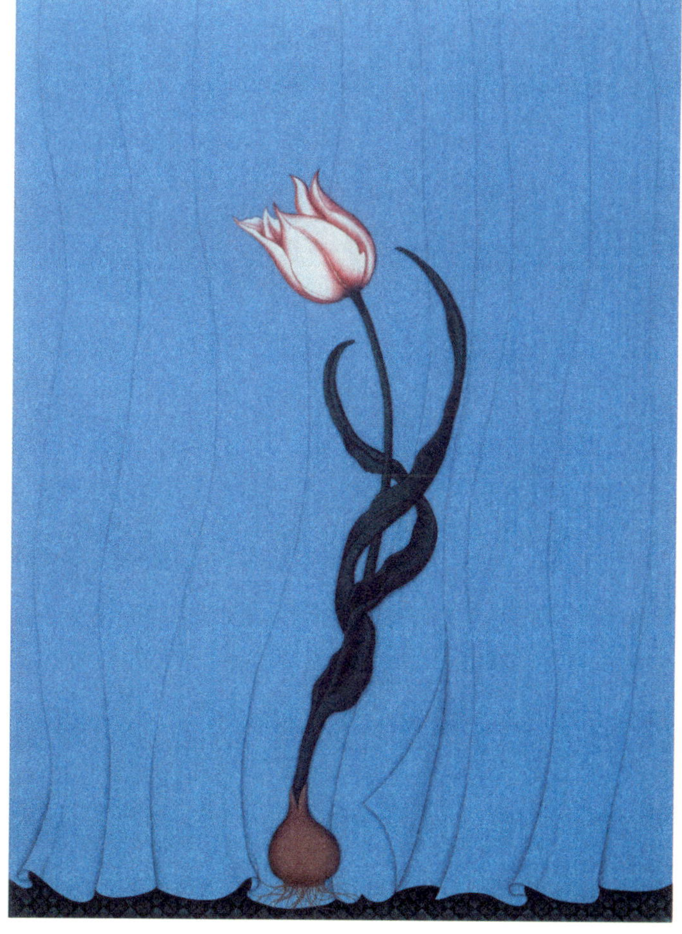

Figure 1
Aisha Khalid
Ongoing Conversation III, 2003
Opaque watercolor on *wasli* and illustration board; artist's frames
24.5 x 18.2 cm and 69 x 50.2 cm (9 1/2 x 7 and 27 x 19 3/4 inches)
Courtesy Corvi-Mora, London

Figure 2
Saira Wasim
The Battle for Hearts and Minds, 2004
Gouache, tea wash, lead, gold leaf on illustration board
9 1/2 x 6 1/3 inches (24 x 16 cm)
Collection of Mr. and Mrs. Indar Pasricha, London

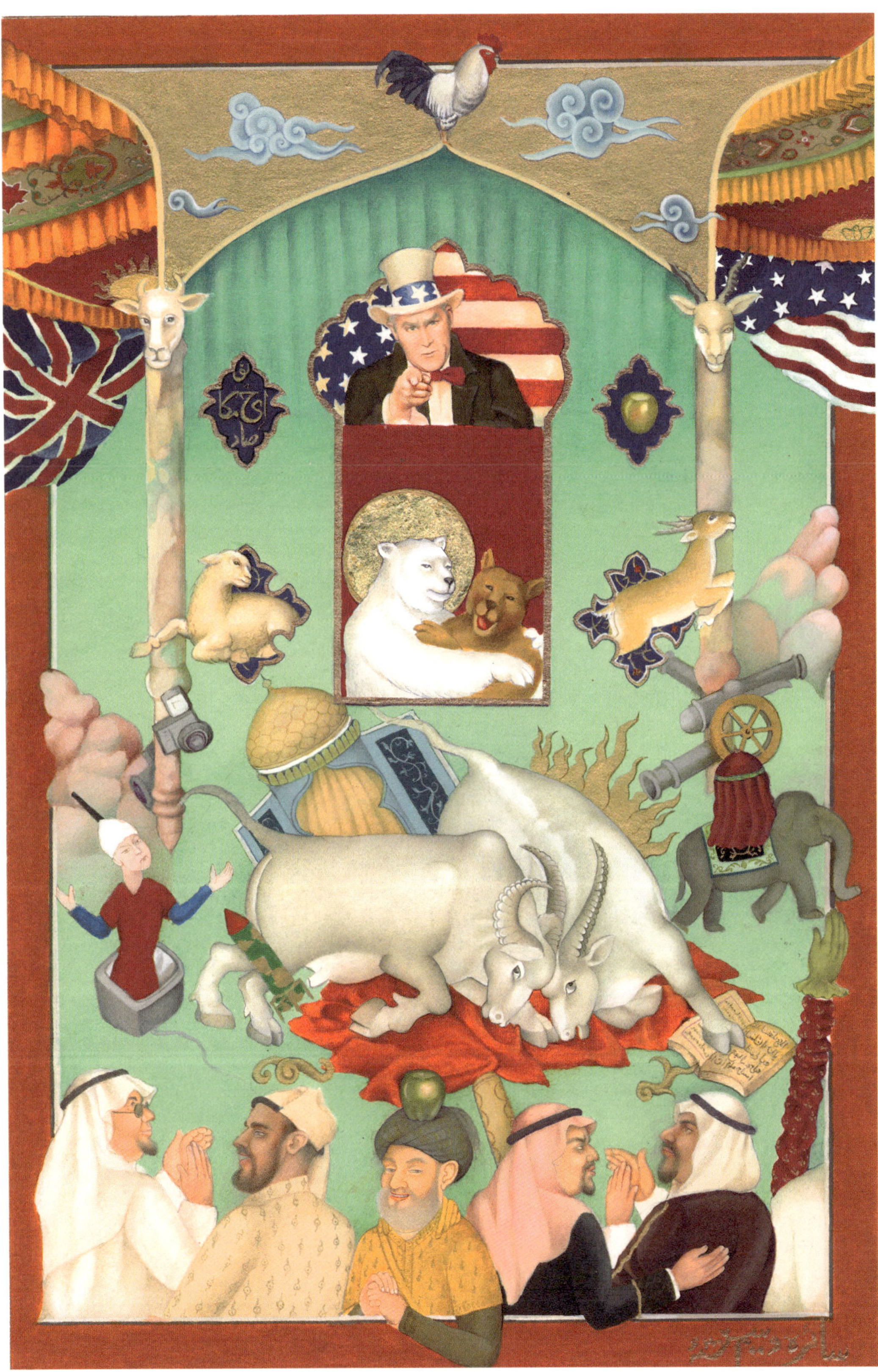

appropriation in constructing meaning.[2] In its most recent manifestation, the motif highlights the Western media's exploitation of women's bodies to legitimize the invasion of Afghanistan in the name of "liberation." In late 2001, reeling from the prospect of a US military retaliation on Pakistan's border, and estranged by the representation of a monolithic and repressive "Islamic culture" in the transatlantic press, Khalid decided to return home to Lahore.

As she watched the Western media monopolize images of the Muslim world, Khalid became increasingly determined to regain their authorship. She and Qureshi gathered a group of artists in the city of Lahore and organized a workshop called *Darmiyan* (In Between). The workshop was part vigil and part protest. Acknowledging that the loudest voices in the global arena articulate extremist positions (religious conservatism, unbridled consumer capitalism, isolationism, neo-imperialism), the group sought to give expression to a political middle ground. Its name, chosen to reference the situation of liberal Muslims trapped between dueling fundamentalisms, also suggests the position in which Khalid was placed during her residency at the Rijksakademie. As geopolitical rhetoric began to divide citizens into the binary "us" and "them," Khalid's own position became precarious outside of her homeland. Having been invited into one of Europe's most prestigious cultural institutions, she was thrust into the role of the "other" by the public discourse following the attacks in New York City.

Darmiyan articulated the need for conceptual nuance in the face of new pressures to conform to binary positions. Sidestepping false dichotomies such as "East and West" or "tradition and modernity," the workshop's participants sought to honor the inherent hybridity of personal, cultural, and political identities. The "middle ground" that artists sought in *Darmiyan* might be viewed as a painterly *jihad*, if one considers the term's primary meaning, derived from "the Arabic root meaning 'to strive' or 'to make an effort,' which refers, in first instance, to an inward spiritual struggle to attain perfect faith."[3] That most now associate the term *jihad* almost exclusively with violent strains of fundamentalist Islam has much to do with the rhetoric surrounding September 11, 2001. Just two decades earlier, the CIA and the US State Department were celebrating the Taliban's resistance to the Soviet invasion of Afghanistan as an example of *jihad*'s secondary meaning: "an outward material struggle to promote justice and the Islamic social system."[4] The impetus behind *Darmiyan*—the will to forge a new political course in line with an authentic set of human identities—would soon be channeled into the *Karkhana* project, which, in turn, would translate the collective experience and new political struggle into a monumental collaborative performance.

Problems of Interpretation

Khalid's personal response to her time in Amsterdam reflects broader perceptions shared by all six artists. Among these is their recognition that the contemporary political quagmire is grounded in misunderstandings. In different ways, their individual work examines the particularly problematic nature of the images, as they are fashioned in state-sponsored propaganda and the mass media. Though the public is often led to accept that "seeing is believing," their work acknowledges the omissions, acts of filtration, and outright distortions that characterize both media representations and propaganda. Perhaps more significantly, they address the particular facets of visual images and their reception that allow such distortions to be so readily absorbed by viewers. Among their targets are the seductive power of beauty, the absence of contextual knowledge or inquisitiveness, and the challenge of interpreting visual ideas across cultural divides.

If the visual world is suspect, it is also their chosen platform. As if fighting fire with fire, the artists often appropriate historical and contemporary images—employing vehicles such as collage, pastiche, iconoclasm, and graffiti—and subvert predictable readings. Despite the problems of interpretation incurred in presenting work to a transnational audience, each artist has chosen to exhibit internationally. Each has developed a no-holds-barred approach to representation, which begs active interpretation and frequently ushers viewers across cultural boundaries in the process. Saira Wasim, for instance, combines visual motifs from Mughal, Italian Renaissance, and Neoclassical painting with imagery from Pakistani films, popular media, and the circus, requiring her viewer to traverse a wide repertoire of cultural references (Fig.2).

Like the Mughals before them, many of the artists use meticulous details and complex coloration to draw the eye through the assortment of individual signs within a given painting—in essence, training their audience to look at a painting for an extended duration. If the desired response is not elicited, the viewer may even become the butt of a joke. Nusra Latif Qureshi's paintings, for instance, often include passages of Urdu text illegible to those who don't know the language or its Persian script.[5] Her use of complex historical references, too, offers one level of information to "insiders" and another layer to those with only a superficial or external knowledge of Pakistan's history and culture. By manipulating access to her images, Latif highlights more pervasive problems of misinterpretation, and in the process, these modest acts of subversion reclaim authorship of the "us" and "them" binary.

Writer and curator Salima Hashmi has described the visual vocabulary of the new miniature as a coded language, one that requires its viewers to *read* paintings carefully, as if they were texts. For an assortment of reasons, the twelve paintings of the *Karkhana* series are among the most challenging examples of the genre. Motifs contributed to the project by each of its six participants represent shorthand versions of visual ideas expressed more fully in their individual works. Over the last decade, each has developed a distinct visual vocabulary drawn from a wide array of sources, including Mughal and Rajput ruler portraits, colonial photographs, the contemporary mass media, personal memorabilia, and maps. Their relationship to these sources varies as well; and because the artists frequently use subversive techniques, borrowed material can be difficult to recognize and interpret in its new context. In keeping with a concept of politics based upon the validity of subjective truth and the dispersal of authority, they contain

Figure 3
Hasnat Mehmood
Profile of King in Orange, 2004
18 1/8 x 18 1/8 inches (46 x 46 cm)
Gouache, tea wash, lead on *wasli*
Collection of Lekha Poddar, New Delhi

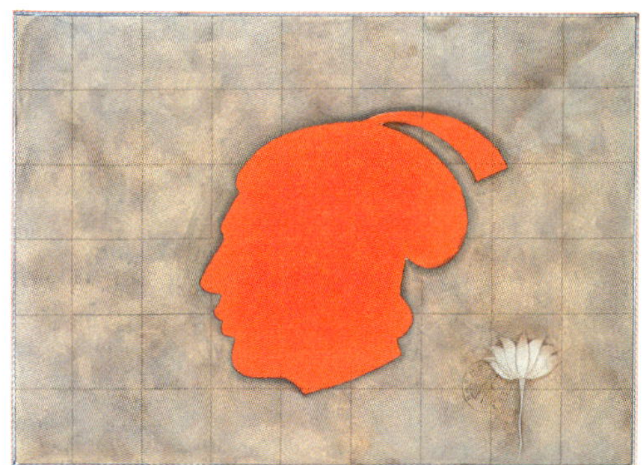

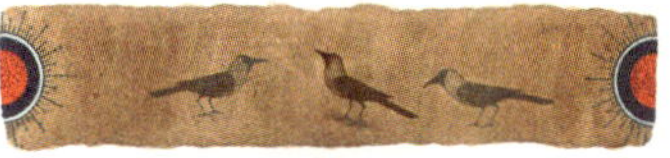

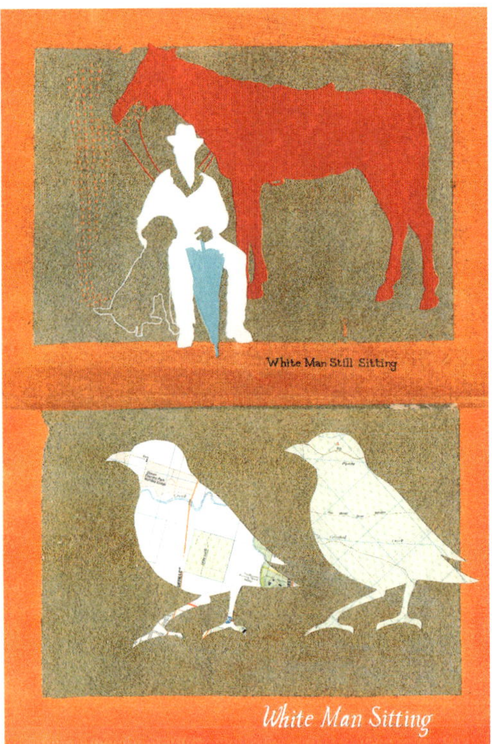

Figure 4
Nusra Latif Qureshi
White Man Still Sitting, 2002
Opaque watercolor, collage on *wasli*
15 5/8 x 10 5/8 inches (39 x 26.6 cm)
Collection of Nan Fleming

Figure 5
Muhammad Imran Qureshi
Missile is a Missile, 1999
Opaque watercolor, tea wash, collage on *wasli*
9 1/2 x 9 1/8 inches (24 x 23 cm)
Collection of Naazish Ata-Ullah, Lahore

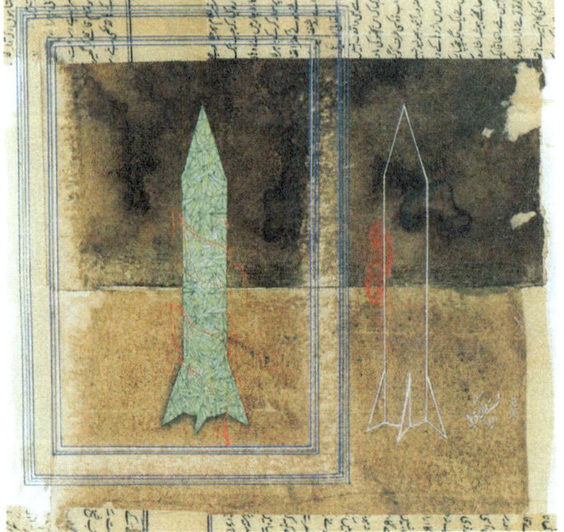

multiple layers of imagery. As a result, the *Karkhana* paintings are more densely coded than those made single-handedly by any one of the project's contributors.

At their core, the *Karkhana* paintings record a visual dialogue—a series of responses, both aesthetic and conceptual—that unfolded over several months. To follow that conversation in the finished artworks, one must perform an archaeological analysis of the picture surface, differentiating one layer of paint from another, and tracing discrete units of communication. In certain places, signature motifs or stylistic tendencies announce the contribution of a given artist. Yet, it is only with a close inspection of overlapping forms, erasures, and marginal notes that a viewer may construct the succession of related ideas that unfolded on the surface of a single picture. It is these formal relationships that bear the project's conceptual logic and political agenda.

The King is Dead, God Save the King

In response to Pakistan's history of autocratic and, at times, foreign hegemonic rule, three of the artists contributed a series of rulers' portraits to the *Karkhana* paintings. Conditioned by their training in historicist styles, Hasnat Mehmood, Nusra Latif Qureshi, and Saira Wasim offered allusions to Mughal imperial portraiture. Mehmood's silhouettes suggest the strict profile of princely figures and emperors depicted in Mughal and Rajput paintings (Fig.3). At the same time, the motif is sufficiently undifferentiated to stand for the iconic portrait of any ruler. The ruler portrait, often reproduced in series in his own paintings, appears repeatedly in the *Karkhana* paintings, "branding" them with an iconic imprint. The replicated image emerges as a visual theme in Latif's work as well. As opposed to Mehmood, however, Latif traces select contour lines from paintings of princely couples or British colonial photographs (Fig.4). These contour drawings present hollow, ghostly figures, suggesting the transcendent—and potentially sinister—power of images. Like Mehmood's opaque portraits, Latif's depiction of leaders strips them of visual details and identifying features. They stand in for all rulers past and present, and for the distance between the conceit of imperial images and the truth of authentic identity.

Qureshi takes the critique of the imperial image even further in a series of paintings that substitute the silhouette of a single missile for the formulaic profiles that once set the standard for Mughal royal portraits (Fig.5). In this motif—which he carried over into the *Karkhana* project—Qureshi's agenda is expressed with his trademark iconoclastic wit: in these phallic "portraits" he displays an emperor with no clothes at all! Like Qureshi, Wasim brings a subversively playful attitude to the ruler's portrait. Her imagery caricatures the gestures and iconography of Mughal allegorical portraits, substituting contemporary figures such as George Bush for the historical figure of the emperor.

If Mehmood and Latif's two-dimensional portraits suggest that rulers are essentially interchangeable, Wasim references the same notion by depicting world rulers in masquerade or in the thick make-up and costumes of circus clowns. In other instances, she uses the apple motif from the William Tell game to signify a political force or figure—perhaps a "bad apple"—that may be removed, but will readily reappear in another guise. In Wasim's individual paintings these jocular elements set a decidedly burlesque tone. By contrast, in the *Karkhana* paintings they contribute a hint of satire to more severe imagery. Like Latif, Wasim reflects upon the visual mechanisms that have sanctified imperial propaganda in the past and the present. In one of the paintings, for instance, her depiction of Pakistani general and head of state Pervez Musharraf riding a missile lampoons the contrived nature of Mughal allegorical portraits as well as their counterpart in the contemporary political "photo op" (Karkhana 9, p.89).

Talha Rathore uses the portrait in a manner apart from the other five artists. While her cypress trees and map motifs (Fig.6) appear parallel to Qureshi's symbolic "portraiture" and cartographic practices, her contribution is drawn more directly from personal life experience. Eschewing the obviously political, she references the Persianate form of the cypress tree and New York subway maps as metaphors for the separation, nostalgia, and sense of otherness that she felt upon arrival in the United States. Within the context of the *Karkhana* project, Rathore's visual elements insert references to subjective experiences that intersect with the larger global patterns addressed by her five collaborators.

The quiet force of Rathore's wistful cypress trees is matched by the impact of her needlework, which she applied to several paintings in the series (Karkhana 1, p.57 and Karkhana 3, p.65). The visceral power of needle and thread introduces complex notions of captivity and constraint to the paintings, often eliciting a strong response from her collaborators, who felt compelled to cut the bonds she made. In *Karkhana 8* (p.85), she joined in the satire—using orange thread to tie together Wasim's burlesque figures: a comment perhaps on the arbitrary banding together of friends and foes in the "battle for hearts and minds."

From Imperium to Imperium

On one level, Wasim, Latif and Mehmood are conducting a meta-analysis of the imperial image. On another level, they are performing an act of historical revision and post-colonial reclamation. Latif highlights significant omissions in the historical record by leaving out select details from appropriated images. In some cases, she, like Rathore, privileges a subjective version of the historical record, foregrounding the role of female figures in courtly scenes or marginalizing the position of British colonial rulers within a given composition. At the same time, her work acknowledges the persistence of collective memory.[7] By copying motifs from British colonial photographs and rendering them through partially obstructed contours, Latif evokes the "ghostly traces" that remain in the post-colonial era as indelible reminders of an imperial age.

Having developed in the context of a Mughal miniature "revival" at the National College of Arts (NCA), all six of *Karkhana's* participants have had to consider their own position vis-à-vis the weight of "tradition." For Wasim, historical styles and contemporary political content co-exist in humorous juxtapositions. Her satirical appropriation of past practices is matched by Qureshi's irreverent response to the techniques and materials of historical miniature painting. His tendency to thoroughly deconstruct the traditional miniature's pristinely burnished surface both conceptually and literally defies the expectations formulated by collectors, curators, and scholars. By adding collage elements to the *wasli*, sanding away its surface, and bringing marginal scribbles into its central picture surface, Qureshi demystifies the medium, liberating it from revivalist tendencies. His idiosyncratic use of historical details, such as the formulaic styles of foliage that once distinguished schools of courtly painting, is also anything but "traditional." Qureshi extracts the eye-shaped leaves found in early courtly paintings, and transforms them into cobalt blue circles reminiscent of a gun's sighting mechanism or bull's-eye targets. These acts of transformation suggest that the miniature must be applied to contemporary life and to immediate concerns. Liberated from the conditions of state-sponsored patronage that once restricted Mughal painters' expressions, members of the new *karkhana* have seized the opportunity to deviate from traditional formulae. For these six artists, "tradition" need not be conservative, and "modernity" need not obliterate the past.

Far from abandoning the lessons of the past, each of the artists uses collective memory and personal history to shed light on the present. The context of the NCA and the post-colonial predicament at large have made the artists acutely aware of the relevance of the past in contemporary life. From such a deeply historicist perspective, the present political realm can only be filtered through a historical lens. The group's exhaustive study of imperial images and political propaganda reveals unmistakable patterns, and visual tropes such as the imperial court setting are reiterated to hint that hegemonic powers will prefigure one another indefinitely. For each artist, these fixed patterns also provide a potent target for parody and have summoned a humorous tone, perhaps most memorably in Wasim's construction of "mutant mullahs"—an amalgam of myth, dogma, prejudice and technology (Karkhana 3, p.65 and Karkhana 12, p.101).

Where, and to whom is the group's grand scale parody directed? Trompe l'oeil stamps—masterfully rendered by Mehm-

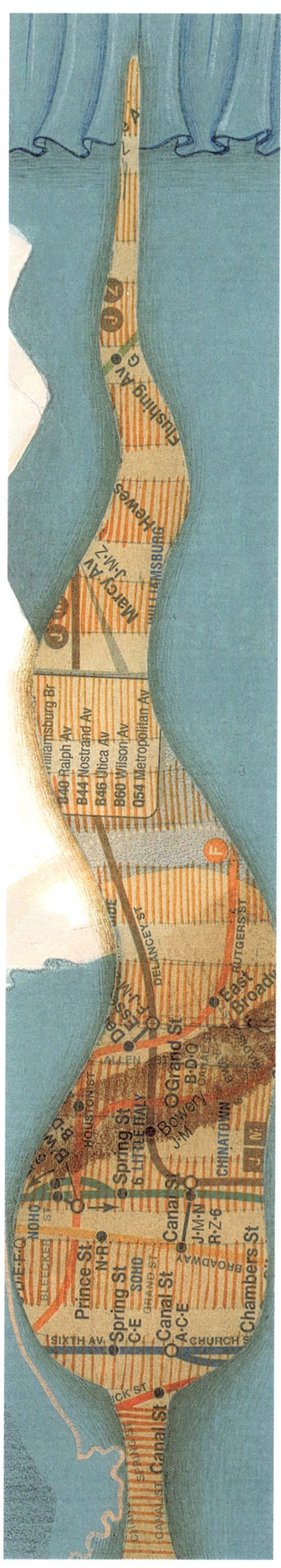

Figure 6
Karkhana 7 (detail), p.81

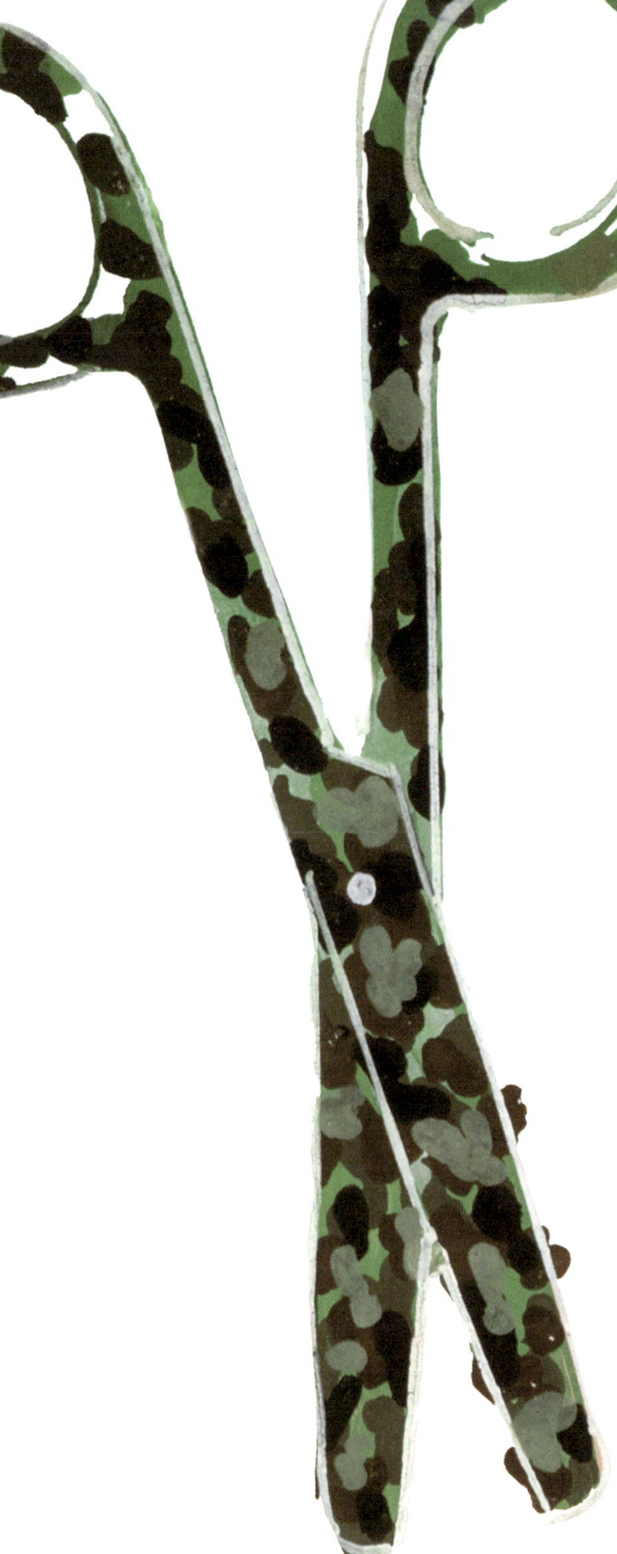

ood, and "endorsed" by Latif suggest an addressee. Mimicking nineteenth-century British kings, who disseminated their portraits around their empire on postage stamps as a reminder of their sovereignty, the *Karkhana* postcards return the message back to its sender. On one level, their addressee is the bygone British colonial empire; and on another, their recipient is Empire's latest manifestation: American neo-imperialism.

The Architecture of Resistance

The realm of the visual is just one of the formats that the *Karkhana* artists have used in their political resistance. The conditions they set for their collaboration—the project's materials and format, the use of an international courier service, the inherently democratic structure of their process, and the rigor of their craftsmanship—all contribute important additional elements.

Centuries ago, the Mughal *karkhana* dictated both the content and practice of painting. Its hierarchical structure limited individual artistic vision and prohibited any overt political criticism, while its bureaucratic structure controlled every element of working practice, from the materials used to the time spent on any given painting. Moreover, the imperial atelier gathered artists from around the globe to work within the confines of the royal capital. This consolidation of talent symbolized the centrifugal force of the Mughals' political hegemony. Paintings, therefore, articulated a vision of Empire through their content as well as their mode of production. The modern *Karkhana* experiment turned this symbolic potency on its head. As each artist was responsible for elements in all twelve paintings and for the finishing touches on two, the new karkhana positioned New York and Jhelum in an equal relationship. The project's multi-nodal, "rhizomatic" nature had no need for a hegemonic center. In this sense, the *Karkhana* artists have drafted a new *mappa mundi* of artistic influence.

On another very context-specific level, the new karkhana signifies a rejection of hierarchy and an assertion of democratic principles. It represents a deliberate rebellion against the system in which the artists were taught at the NCA. The school's miniature painting department, run by Ustad Bashir Ahmad along the lines of a traditional atelier, has actively sought to reinforce the hierarchical basis of the relationship between *ustad* and *shagird* (master and disciple). Qureshi, currently Ustad Bashir's assistant, has himself taught three of the *Karkhana* artists and yet, in the collaborative process, he worked on an equal footing with his former students.

Mughal predecessors received foreign paintings via the relatively slow processes of ocean trade, diplomatic envoys, and missionary activity; and yet, artists were able to exchange visual ideas readily within the immediate confines of the royal workshop. By contrast, the contemporary karkhana enlisted the shipping services of an international courier, and thereby located the project securely within context of current global markets. There is hardly a location on the globe where one can't send a package, dissolving (if only metaphorically) the borders, oceans, and politics that divide us. In the *Karkhana* project, the dissolution of borders is lent ironic potency when one considers two additional facets: the artists' nationalities (they are all Pakistani) and their selective use of technology. While Pakistani males find the process of applying for visas and being "processed" at airports made increasingly arduous, their labors—manifest for the *Karkhana* artists in their artwork—encounter no such constraints as they whiz around the world by courier. The *Karkhana* project bears witness to a unique global climate in which technology and the onset of globalization in the communication age have enabled us to overcome physical distance, while new barriers have arisen in place to reinstate the gulf between peoples and places.

Akin to the ironies that surround our new global divisions, it is worth considering the *Karkhana* artists' selective use of new and old technologies. In the project they decided to use *wasli* (layered hand-made paper, p.48), even though in their personal practices many use acrylic board and commercially-manufactured materials to make similar works. What is more, they chose a paper-based format, one that is "crafted" by hand, rather than a more easily transportable and less vulnerable format like digital or video media (both of which

Figure 8 (above)
Karkhana 7 (detail), p.81

Figure 9 (right)
Nusra Latif Qureshi
Specifications of Desire II, 2002
Watercolor, gouache, graphite on *wasli*
11 3/4 x 15 3/4 inches (30 x 40 cm)
Courtesy of the artist and Waqas Wajahat LLC, New York

are familiar to the *Karkhana* artists). This selective and willful rejection of technology reflects a critically aware practice in which technology is "anything but neutral."[8] In their choice of materials and process, it seems that the artists have intuitively responded to the fact that technology is often the means by which relations of economic and social power are perpetuated. And, finally, their choice of materials serves to counter a by-product of globalization—both past and present. All are aware that the tradition of painting developed in Mughal workshops was halted abruptly in the nineteenth century in the course of colonization, as the fashion for European photographic technologies replaced courtly painting and drawing. Their's is not so much a "revival" of tradition as it is an affirmative statement of craft's validity in the twenty-first century.

In choosing to accentuate the craft elements of their artistic practice—drawing, painting and even embroidery—the *Karkhana* artists attempt to reverse the Duchampian rejection of the aesthetic, and the contemporary drive toward speed and mechanization.

Conclusion

Karkhana, relying as it does on "traditional" fields of representation, and on the institutionalized art world to arrange exhibitions, fund catalogues, and even to pay the courier bills for its actualization, is not an activist demonstration but rather, a work of art. It is from this position, in fact, that it derives its political power—subverting elite institutions from within. It updates a historical form (the "traditional" miniature), which served one empire, in order to confront another. In their refusal to surrender the aesthetic in their art, the *Karkhana* artists use the very desire that their meticulously crafted and highly encoded paintings elicit to inject themselves into arenas where they would not ordinarily be granted access.

At the heart of the project is a challenge to commonly-understood notions of democracy and the collective. Making decisions is critical to the artistic process—and collaborative groups usually set out to make collective decisions. But in *Karkhana* the decisions remain individual. Democracy comes not from the fact that decisions are made collectively, but rather from the stipulation that everyone gets to make them—at least for a span of time during the production of each of the twelve works.

Critic Claire Bishop considers a democratic society to be one in which "relations of conflict are sustained, not erased."[9] The *Karkhana* artists, by rendering the friction in society (and indeed, within the group itself) visible, have done as much as any group of six artists could hope to do in showing society what democratic freedom looks like. With its mix of coded imagery and culturally specific references, the project raises multiple questions about power and the act of viewing: To what ends are images appropriated, altered, or commodified in the course of global exchange? What role do we play as viewers in a world increasingly constructed by visual images? These artists have laid down a challenge to make the viewer contemplate again.

Notes

1 In his now-famous explication of *Orientalism*, Edward Said traced these tropes in European literature. Many more recent studies have explored their manifestation in visual media. For a current set of statements on the trope of the veiled woman, with a full bibliography of relevant sources: David A. Bailey and Gilane Tawadros, eds., *Veil: Veiling, Representation, and Contemporary Art* (Cambridge, Mass: The MIT Press, 2003).

2 Khalid's use of the *burqa* motif was initially grounded in her own complex experience of Muslim womanhood. For a discussion of its evolving significance in her work, see Hammad Nasar, "From Conversation to Conversation," in *Acts of Balance*, ed., Salima Hashmi (Lahore, Pakistan: Sang-e-Meel, to be published in 2005).

3 Robert Wuthnow, ed., *Encyclopedia of Politics and Religion*, 2 vols. (Washington, D.C.: Congressional Quarterly, Inc., 1998), pp.425-426.

4 Ibid. The significance of the word *jihad* is centered in its root, which equates to the verbs "to strive" or "to struggle." Often casually translated as "holy war," its meanings within the *Qur'an* include spiritual allegiance, which one must hold before all others; the way to confront non-Muslims; and the way to conduct one's daily life as a Muslim. For a more detailed account: Moulavi Cherágh Ali, *A Critical Exposition of the Popular "Jihád"* (Delhi: Idarah-i Adabigat-i Delli, 1984), pp.166-8 and 171-92; Majid Khadduri, *War and Peace in the Law of Islam* (Baltimore: The Johns Hopkins Press, 1955), pp.74-82.

5 Interview with Anna Sloan, excerpted in *Tradition Unbound: South Asian Painters at Work*, video (Northampton, Mass., 2004).

6 Anna Sloan, *The Way I Remember Them: Paintings by Nusra Latif Qureshi* (Northampton, Massachusetts: The Smith College Museum of Art, 2004).

7 Ibid., pp.16-24.

8 John Roberts, "Collaboration as a Problem of Art's Cultural Form," in *Third Text*, Vol.18, Issue 6, (2004), pp.557-64.

9 Claire Bishop, "Antagonism and Relational Aesthetics," in *October* (Fall, 2004), p.74.

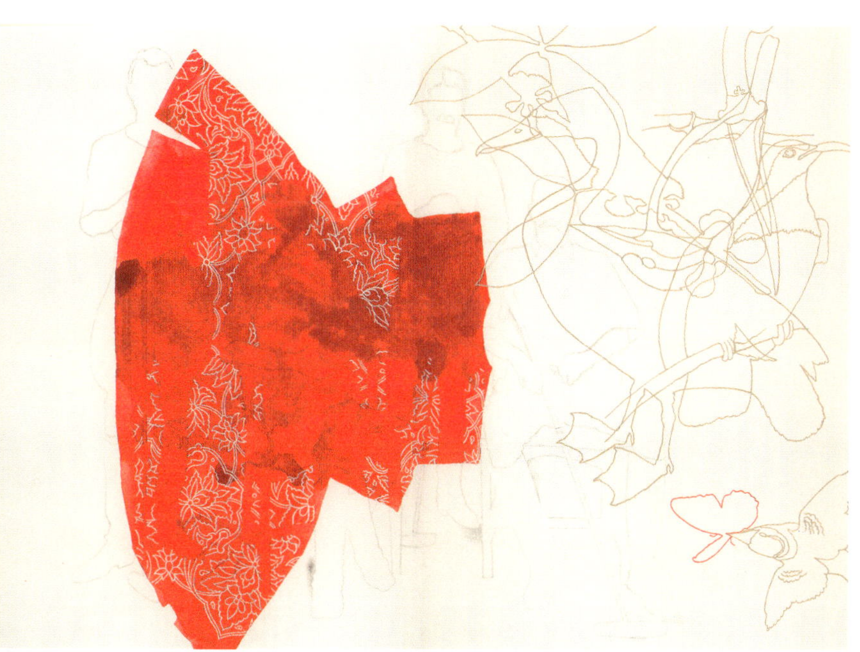

Journey's End: The Making of Karkhana

Salima Hashmi

"Chu qatra az watan-e-khesh
raft woh baaz aamad
Musaadefe sadafee gasht
woh shud yeke gohar."[1]

When the drop departed from its
native home and returned,
It found a shell and became a pearl.
Rumi

When Muhammad Imran Qureshi first mentioned the idea of the *Karkhana* project, it was envisaged as a working group in Lahore: artists together under one roof, moving their *waslis* (layered hand-made paper, p.48) from one to the other, an arrangement not too dissimilar to its Mughal-atelier origin. The discussion became more elaborate during the course of another collaborative venture, the *Darmiyan* (In Between) workshop held at Gallery Rohtas in Lahore in October 2001.

This took place in the aftermath of the US bombing of Afghanistan. Seven artists worked in the gallery space, producing a body of new work, fulfilling the obligation they felt to comment on the events engulfing their region after September 11, 2001. The title of the workshop, *Darmiyan*, was exactly where the artists felt themselves to be at that time—sandwiched between the hegemony of the mighty and the helplessness of the weak. It was at this time that Qureshi's concept of the "new" *karkhana* crystallized.

Qureshi was familiar with the concept of the Mughal atelier, where apprentices worked diligently under *ustads* (masters), who themselves collaborated in twos and even threes on the same imperial album. The sixteenth-century ateliers worked from pre-established designs, with the master correcting and improving the works—a process recorded in inscriptions accompanying the royal manuscripts. Intrigued by the notion of the subjugated individual artistic ego, which lay encapsulated in the past, Qureshi sought to revisit this aspect of the tradition. The subjugation or negation of self is a recurring theme in Sufi tradition, which works on myriad levels. The greatest of Sufi poets, Rumi, found his spiritual soul-mate in the mysterious wandering dervish Shams-e-Tabriz, who left him one day never to return. A desolate Rumi walked the world for seven years, until the truth dawned: "Why do you seek me in the four corners of the Earth, I am within you, look no further." With this realization came the finest of Rumi's poetry. We refer to this today not as the poetry of Rumi but as The Book of the Poems of Shams-e-Tabriz (*Divan-e-Shams*). It would be simplistic to read this as Rumi's pen name; surely the intent is different.

This dimension of collaboration brings it full circle, and while Qureshi may not have been thinking of these intricacies of the Sufi tradition, the ability to place full trust in those chosen to be in his circle is at the foundation of this *karkhana*. This way of working together reflects an intuitive understanding of the wider dimensions of traditional collaboration while raising a number of questions:

could there be a contemporary manifestation? Could one probe processes, investigate differences, possibly even invite collision on the way to collaboration? And would the works that came out of this be banal compromise, or edgy ingenuity?

Among the questions facing Qureshi, was that of the mobility of the artists he was most comfortable with. Within three years, most of them had moved to other parts of the world. The camaraderie they had shared in the Miniature Department at The National College of Arts (NCA) was now held together by the occasional exchange of emails and jpeg files. Collaborative paintings transferred through the services of an international courier seemed a logical solution. Qureshi's invitation to the five artists laid down no grand design, no thematic injunctions, and no "right way up" to approach the paintings. Each artist was free to pursue their own imagery, their own repertoire of mark-making and their own artistic agenda. The only stipulation was the *wasli's* standard size (approximately 11 x 8 inches) so that it could be easily dispatched by international courier. The project was underwritten by the promise of an exhibition at a venue in England, but it was held together by a more provocative proposition—the opportunity to touch base with one another in an unusually tangible manner.

In describing the Mughal karkhana, Ratnabali Chatterjee states: "In the Courts, the art form that prevailed depended very much on the world views of the ruling class of which the artist was a necessary member. The form developed out of the joint participation of the patron and the artist in the actual construction of the painting."[2] These new miniaturists consider and probe the questions that arise from a practice, which might otherwise have appeared obsolete. The splendor and security of the Court, the panorama of narrative content, the exquisiteness of medium and material, and generous deadlines all ensured a meticulousness of craft together with a subservience to a grand vision. In forming their *karkhana*, these artists took charge of what may traditionally have been passive or unquestioning roles—the largesse of the patron was internalized, and the authority shared, resulting in a personal stake in the outcome. Qureshi was careful to limit his role, for the most part, to that of a facilitator rather than a master or *ustad*.

The burden of history is not exclusive to the miniature painter. Contemporary artists everywhere grapple with myriad conventions, practices, imbibed usages and canons. For the painters of the *Karkhana* project, the rituals associated with preparation, and their delight in materials, is deeply embedded in their ways of living and thinking. Each of them, in their own way, has examined, copied and enjoyed the grandiloquence of the miniature tradition. Multiple narratives, compositional constraints and prescribed skills have been explored, employed, and subsequently resisted. Yet the rigorous training each of them has undergone is potent and the lure of what was familiar has persisted. Dispensing with what was almost second nature has involved sheer rebellion.

For Qureshi, the need to combat the stereotype of the miniature artist went back to his student days. Parallel to his studies in the NCA's miniature painting department was his presence in other studios, where he worked in acrylics and mixed media on board and canvas. When invited to exhibit his "miniatures" at the Bluecoat Gallery in Liverpool in 2001, Qureshi challenged many conventions. He combined plastic sheets with the *wasli* surface; he framed reproductions of miniatures alongside the "real thing"; he crumpled carefully made *waslis*, in his words, "to give the work a human presence and to demolish the barrier to touching the work."[3] In a genre for which remoteness seems intrinsic to its legacy, Qureshi's quest to establish intimacy presents challenges.

Qureshi has experimented with injecting personal meaning into traditional motifs. He lifts a plant form from landscapes in eighteenth-century Kangra painting and transforms it into his trademark symbol of love—the "love-foliage." He employs materials that could be considered banal, such as the ballpoint pen. He takes the risk of being misread, of diluting the intensity of his content, of weakening the delicacy of the surface. In this quest, though, Qureshi closes ranks with the painters of Kangra, Basohli, and Kotah, appropriating motifs imbued with romantic lyricism. He does this in a plausible unselfconscious manner speaking of a familiarity with a living, thriving tradition. He tempers political commentary and satire with a gentle understanding of human desires and failings.

Comfortable with the transitions and crosscurrents in his own practice, Qureshi was ideally positioned to initiate and propel the *Karkhana* project along its many journeys. Answering questions, expediting the clearing of roadblocks, easing any hiccups, Qureshi was able to take remedial measures, and simultaneously to stand back, allowing individual anxieties to work themselves out.

Karkhana 2 (back of *wasli*), p.62

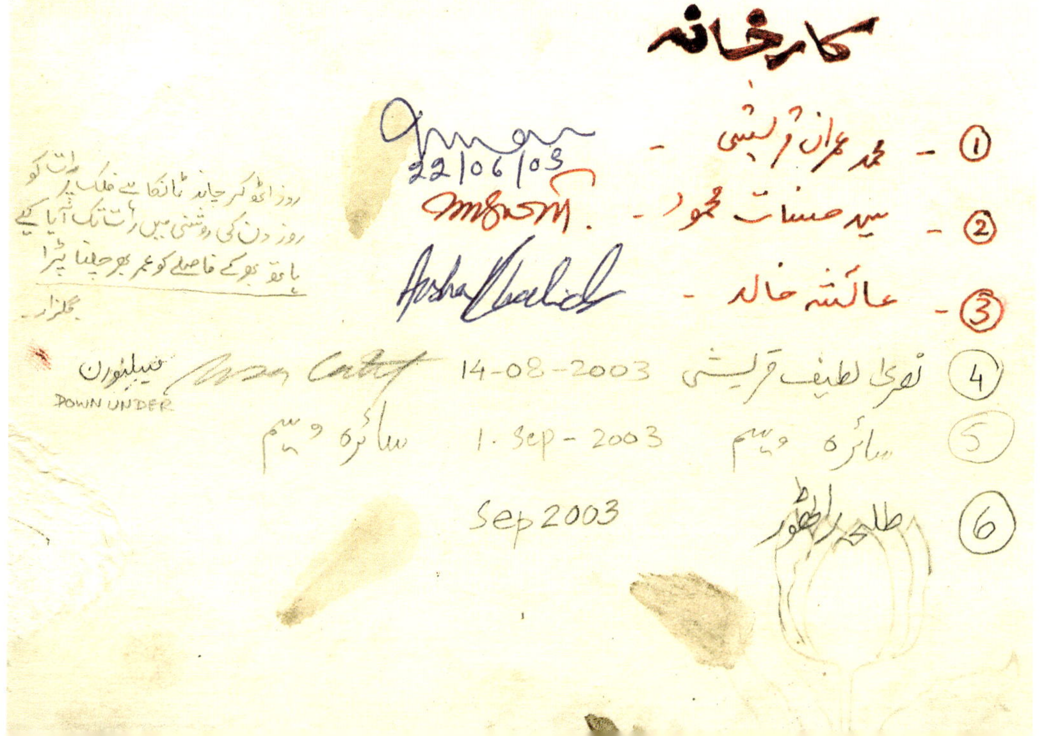

The instigator rather than the guru, Qureshi was nevertheless "the first among equals." But as the project proceeded, those among them who "dared" took turns at leadership. The strongest interventions came from Nusra Latif Qureshi, who emphatically removed and re-phrased parts of Hasnat Mehmood's handiwork.

The only guideline Qureshi had set for each artist was to manifest sensitivity to the integrity and soul of the work that arrived in the mail. Each artist could work in layers or alongside what had transpired on the surface. There was freedom to undo, to cover, to embellish, to add, and to transform the work. In one instance, a painting arrived folded in half, courtesy of the mailman's haste in pushing the packet through the mailbox. The work got a new life as the fold was underscored in paint and invited into the scheme of things.

Each artist commenced work on two *waslis*. Not surprisingly, these initiations referred to their own practice and were recognizable markers of their individual concerns. Qureshi and Aisha Khalid, although husband and wife, decided not to work in sequence in the process of the traveling paintings, to ensure parity in the encounter for all participants.

Qureshi initiated the first two works (Karkhana 1, p.55 and Karkhana 2, p.59), using the two motifs already identifiable as his own: the tailor's manual and the missile template. In Jhelum, Hasnat Mehmood's grid of postage stamps subverted the posed centrality of the missile (Karkhana 1, p.57). In Chicago, Saira Wasim filled the grid with images of a pulsating human heart, but only after Khalid in Lahore had rendered an undulating tulip in *neem rang* (half-colored technique, p.51) over the text, and Nusra Latif Qureshi in Melbourne had added a whisper of a layer in the form of a group of three polo-playing colonial gentlemen.

Latif's research studies in Australia introduced her to a new repository of British colonial photographs, a subject that had engaged her before she left Pakistan in 2000. Selecting images from this archive, she strips them gleefully of their regal context, undermining their imperious authority and reducing them to ghosts of their former selves. The images of the figures appear in these two works as reminders of once potent rulers—now tattered fragments among the many in the layers of history. Not content with letting ghosts be, the once-imposing colonial gentleman in *Karkhana 2* (p.61) was retrieved roguishly by Wasim in Chicago, who placed an apple on his head, and gave him a cherry for his nose. Talha Rathore in New York offered a recipe for co-habitation by enclosing both works in a block-printed border, the motif of which echoes Khalid's tulip bulb. Bringing the work to a finale with a border drew it closer to the conventions of the tradition—an effort, perhaps, at quiet compromise by the last artist in line.

The two works (Karkhana 3, p.65 and Karkhana 4, p.69) initiated by Mehmood commence with a regal profile in the form of a stamp, priced at one rupee and carrying the legend "King's Postage." Mehmood was captivated by the idea that unlike most Pakistani citizens, the artworks could travel effortlessly across the oceans without a visa. The meticulous stamp is a poignant reference to the rites of passage of the immigrant. The post office had its own plans for Mehmood's work, which arrived bent neatly in half for Khalid to work with in Lahore. Encountering the stamp on a near blank *wasli*, Khalid went along with the postcard idea. She worked on half the *wasli*, painting in her blue *burqa*-clad figure; a traveling companion for the prince. From Latif to Wasim, who added the subtly devilish priest with goat's legs, to Rathore, and back to Qureshi in Lahore, the painting retained a quiet demeanor. Qureshi fused the two halves of the work by adding the bullet holes or dots, as a compositional device,

Karkhana 1 (detail), p.57

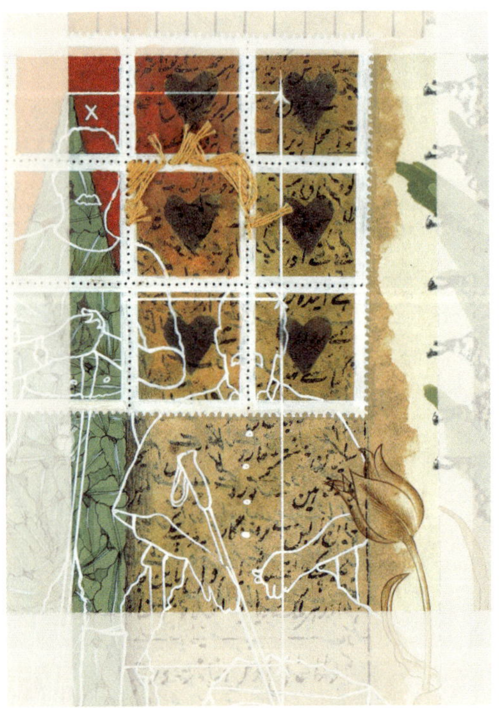

Karkhana 2 (detail), p.61

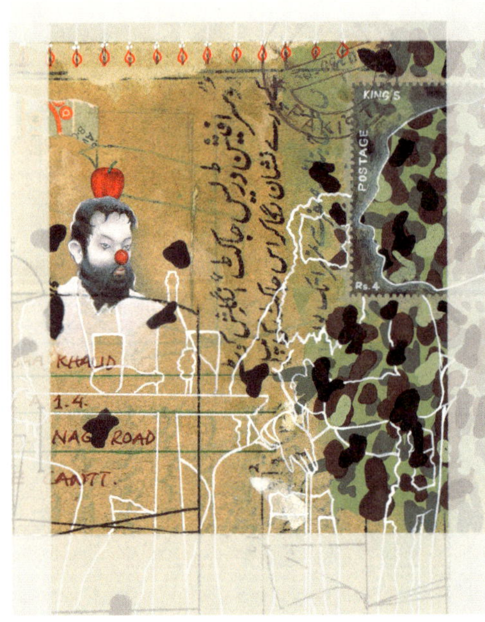

Karkhana 3 (detail), p.65

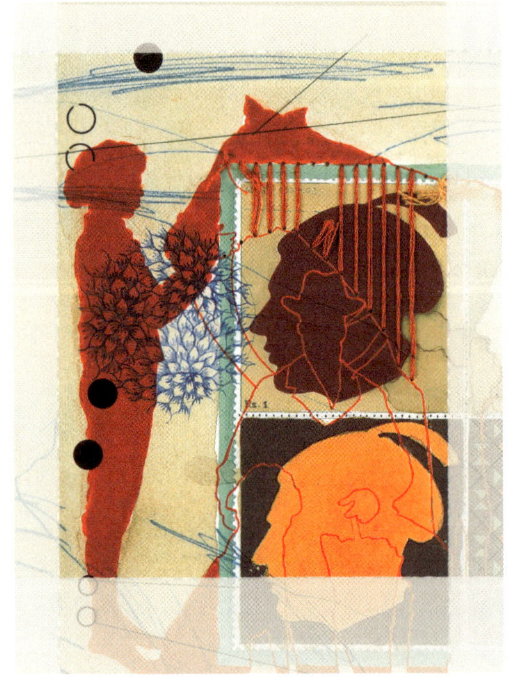

which brought Latif's shadowy intervention of the tiger hunt to the foreground. These signature dots of Qureshi's started out as a graphic representation of "rain drops" culled from Rajasthani precedents, and became cartographic markings as Qureshi traveled, crossing borders and oceans.

The formal and tightly-knit composition of *Karkhana 3* (p.65) provoked a very different response of some creative violence from Qureshi. Mehmood, Khalid and Latif had worked the stamp grid closely. Khalid had painted over one section of the grid and inserted an area of opulent pattern. Latif had rendered two layers, a gentleman in outline, his presence overshadowed by his native syce tending the mount beyond. She had also placed small red hearts into Khalid's dark palette. Wasim had filled in the outline figures protruding from the grid.

Rathore's response to this rather prim format was intuitive: using embroidery thread, she stitched across the surface, delineating the horse and claiming domestic intimacy. The New York experience—motherhood and loneliness—has been alienating for Rathore, almost smothering her gentle, introverted temperament. For her, the acts of piercing, decorating, and block printing have been extensions of the domestic processes of cooking, cleaning, mending.

Encountering Rathore's embroidery afforded Qureshi the opportunity to take further liberties. His final layer was playful, but also design conscious. He cut some of the threads, leaving them to wander across the surface and then with pen pressed over a carbon paper, he embarked on his own meanderings. His favored Kangra bushes, symbols of love, were accompanied by loose mappings—a reference to boundaries, and to journeys across continents and traversed territories. Halting the spontaneity, Qureshi then became the designer, editing the surface with carefully placed dots or bullet holes.

Khalid's authorship (Karkhana 5, p.73 and Karkhana 6, p.77) is clearly recognizable in the way the works manifest her preference for surface pattern—taut, dense and compact. This treatment of space, deployed in her personal practice to mark the domestic and intimate, is forced, in the *Karkhana* context, to become a public space where other artists are invited. But Khalid had left little room to maneuver and the *wasli* had become consumed by the rigidity of the geometry. Finding it difficult to intervene in such perfectly delineated space, Latif fell back on the gestural mark—a painterly intervention. Wasim resorted to ready-made stickers and Rathore to collage and rippling cypresses. Back in Lahore, Qureshi propelled a missile into the picture surface, its ominous arrival undermined by friendly ferns. Mehmood took his cue from Latif's shadowy groups, and added his brother's wedding photograph as an alternative ghost group. Appropriation of one another's imagery was already happening. Qureshi, deciding to take on the mantle of *ustad* briefly, later ripped this photograph out and repainted the *wasli*.

In *Karkhana 6* (p.77), Khalid's quilt was embellished with Wasim's stars and Rathore's collages, after Latif had violated its pristine spread with a stenciled dagger. The dagger's menace was diminished by the Kangra bush, "in blue, the color of love," explains Qureshi. Embarrassed perhaps by this lapse into sweetness, Qureshi reverted to the sharpness of black Letraset arrows, poised to strike at the heart of the Kangra bush. Or did they indicate its supremacy?

Mehmood added a wash of gold, bathing the *wasli* in a feeling of antiquity. The customary feature of the border is noticeably absent in most of the works, with the exception of the two initiated by Khalid. Her geometric dispensation held strong through to the culmination of the paintings. All the artists had embraced or succumbed to the memory of the

Karkhana 4 (detail), p.69

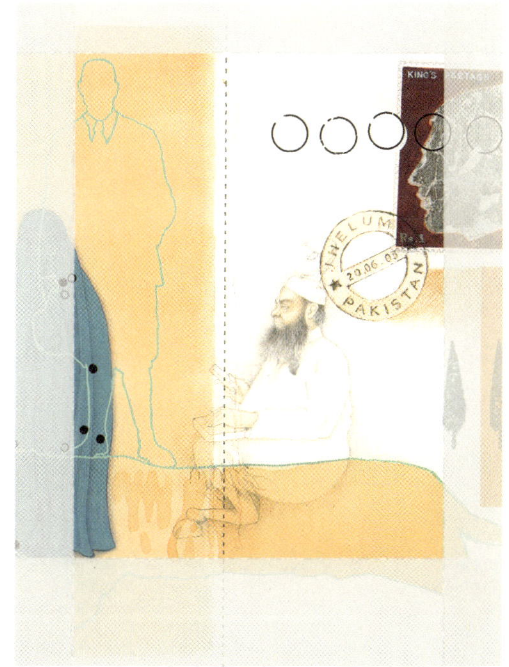

Karkhana 5 (detail), p.73

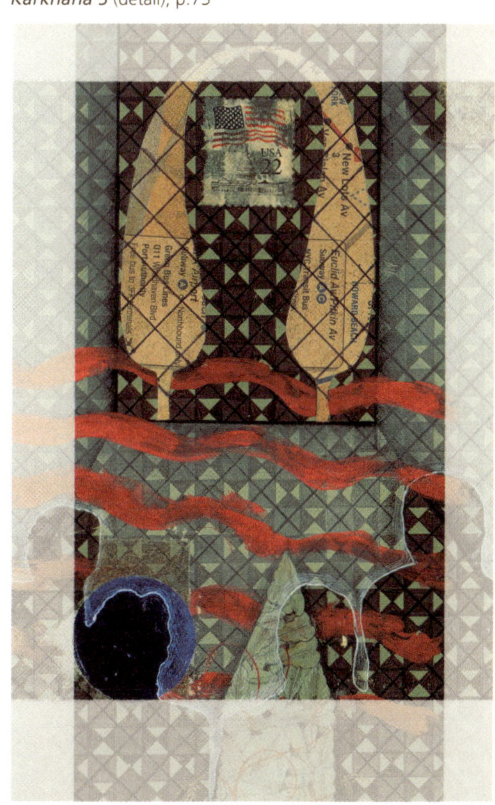

Karkhana 6 (detail), p.77

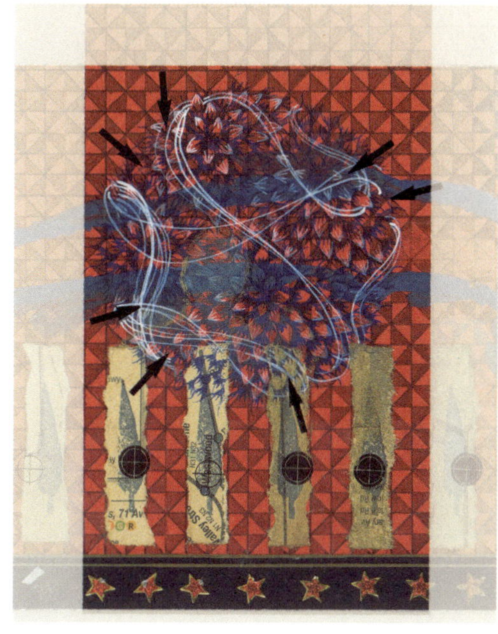

order they were schooled in. This is not surprising, given the layers of familiarity being built up in front of them.

In *Karkhana 7* (p.81) and *Karkhana 8* (p.85), Nusra Latif placed ceremonial tunics alongside romancing courtly couples. Wasim played with their official status, painting the figure of George Bush on one tunic, a mysterious clown-like figure onto the other, and then added two bearded figures. Among Mehmood's concerns is his interest in the image of the "primitive." Mehmood is taken with the physiognomy of the Neanderthal man, and the implications suggested by the dualities of nobility versus the brutish. The profile of this particular noble savage gains prominence in its proximity to Bush. Qureshi enhanced Bush's bow and arrow as he simultaneously etched in his Kangra bush. Khalid gave the work a proscenium curtain, a symbol she has employed in many works. The predominantly blue palette, nurtured by one artist after the other, suggests an intelligent striving for cohesion in a contentious and difficult painting.

In *Karkhana 8* (p.85), Khalid was the last artist on the *wasli*, and so restricted herself to patterning the *gao-takia* (bolster cushion) propping up two lovers. Rathore tied Wasim's figures together with apple-red thread, but also provided a proscenium of sorts—a collage of block-printed seedpods. In this painting, references abound to the domestic arts: embroidery, tassels and *duppatta* (scarf) edgings lead into the insertion of scissors by Qureshi (reminiscent of his missiles). Imagery from the domestic domain is something that Rathore, Qureshi and Khalid are all interested in, extracting from it playful meanings, which both refer to the past, and are metaphors for their personal experience. Alongside the shadowy wedding group, Mehmood could not resist a cheeky addition of a tiny signature scissor, homage to Qureshi's overpowering one.

Manuals, templates, stencils, pattern books and maps have all been used in their own body of work by most of the artists in the *Karkhana* group. The Mughal dress patterns that fascinate Latif stand alongside Qureshi's sartorial imagery. His own incorporation of a cheaply-printed tailoring manual is playfully subversive, inviting the viewer to question what is being "stitched up." As the artists referred back to their own individual vocabulary, the underlying assumption was that each understood the others' concerns. This did not hinder the spontaneity of the dialogue, nor did it imply a pre-conceived arrival. Quite to the contrary, it facilitated an unfolding of sub-texts, and the prospect of self-discovery. Each participant left traces of coded messages for the other.

Wasim's attention to detail and color was harnessed to the task of inventing social re-mixes and sardonic political narratives (Karkhana 9, p.89 and Karkhana 10, p.93). Her combination of photo-realism and kitsch can be startling when, in *Karkhana 9* (p.89) President Musharraf rides a Corinthian pillar. His accompanying Ghauri missile spews smoke in a delicate arabesque, courtesy of Latif. Mehmood picked up on Rathore's collages, introducing newspaper clippings, while Latif labeled Mehmood's crows and cocked a snook at Musharraf's bravado in a populist text. She then added a note for the curator on how the work should be presented. Her impishness in text is also apparent in *Karkhana 10* (p.93), where she itemizes each image, titling the work *Janaab ki Soorat* (His Majesty's Face), subverting the pomposity of lineage.

The artists seem to delight in their own fearlessness of approach, and the *Karkhana* works reveal how they have built on one another's ideas. Without setting definite rules, they were comfortable enough to take liberties—turning the work on its side or ripping up another's work. In one instance, Latif pulled out part of a collage pasted on by Mehmood and then painted the residual glue

Karkhana 7 (detail), p.81

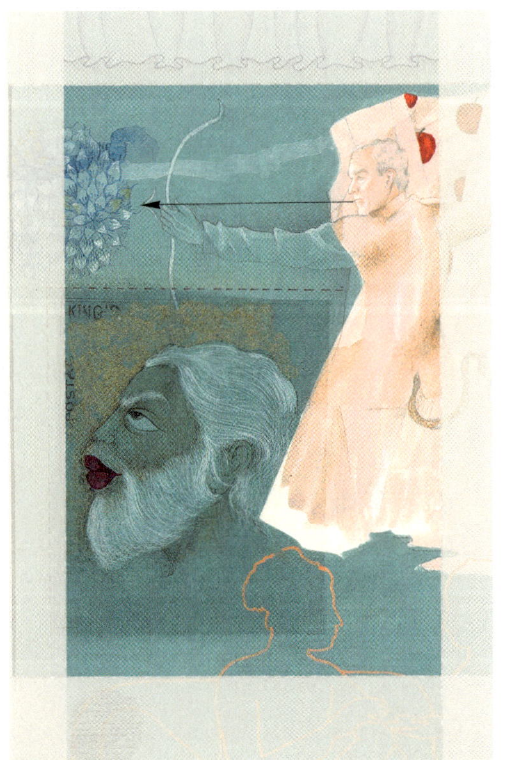

Karkhana 8 (detail), p.85

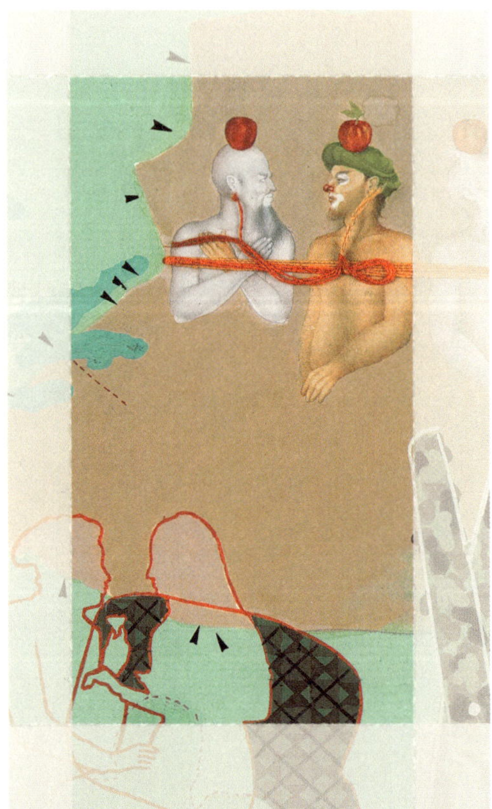

Karkhana 9 (detail), p.89

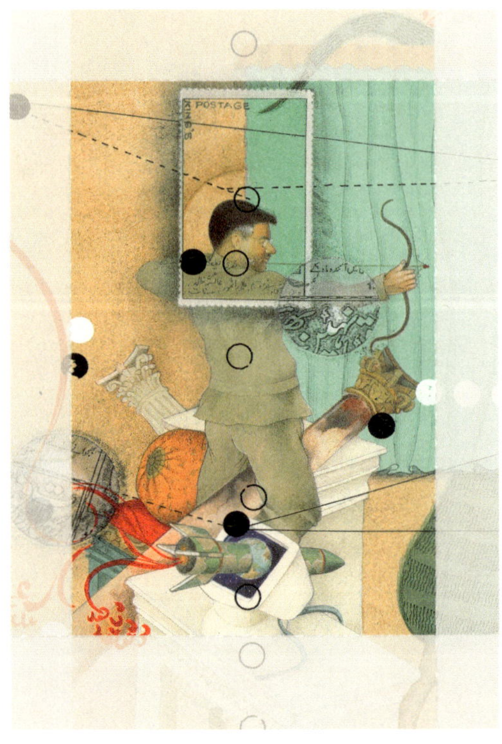

stains that were, after all, Mehmood's marks. Mehmood's "trademarks" seem in some instances less integrated into the fabric of the work than the others. His need to establish presence, for instance in *Karkhana 11* (p.97) may have had to do with being the youngest artist in the group. Qureshi, concerned with not crowding out the voices of others was, on the other hand, deliberately low-key. Some works are more successful than others in intertwining individual vocabularies, while others, such as *Karkhana 12* (p.101) are more circumspect about how different motifs co-exist. The emergent balance is often less engaging than the risk-taking, as is evident in *Karkhana 1* (p.57), *Karkhana 2* (p.61), and *Karkhana 8* (p.85).

The assumption that contemporary miniature painting refers primarily to the past or is engaged in a nostalgic, romantic revivalism is belied by the *Karkhana* series. In the context of revivalism in architecture, Romi Khosla states that less developed societies "are being encouraged to reject the modern agenda as a system of Western exploitation and culture and are increasingly advocating ancient futures."[4] The "quaintness" of traditional societies becomes an argument for retaining their otherness, and remaining petrified in their pasts. The "innocence" and supposed inability of these traditional societies to intellectually engage with modernism is emphasized, while their facility to entertain, charm, and ensure cultural tourism becomes a vindication of their purpose.

These artists were certainly not "advocating ancient futures." A multiple partnership that stimulated dialogue, and reinforced artistic relationships seemed possible, but it required daring exploration, almost a leap of faith, on the part of this group of practitioners. No one knew how the final paintings of the *Karkhana* group would turn out. During the five months of the project, each artist had the opportunity to muse on both process and purpose. Questions of authorship were pondered, and the artists gained fresh insight into the relevance of past practices. Each was energized by the *Karkhana* experience, and it became a catalyst for their individual practice. They had taken apart a powerful, legendary concept on their own terms. Individually, they interpreted their own involvement with the whole. Distances receded and advanced, issues were reiterated, stimuli seized upon. The concept of the historical atelier was reframed until it became a distant memory; only the basic *sur* (tune) of the *raga*[5] remained. It had acquired a fresh structure, a new melody.

Notes

1 Reynold A. Nicholson, ed. and trans., *Selected Poems from the Divani Shamsi Tabriz* (Richmond, UK: Cuyrconrzon Press, 1994).

2 Ratnabali Chatterjee, *From the Karkhana to the Studio: Changing Roles of the Patron and the Artist in Bengal* (New Delhi: Books and Books, 1990).

3 From an interview with Muhammad Imran Qureshi by Quddus Mirza, "The Miniature Work," News on Sunday, Pakistan (2002).

4 Romi Khosla, *The Loneliness of The Long Distant Future* (New Delhi: Tulika Books, 2002).

5 A *raga* is a group of musical notes that can be considered a base unit of a larger composition.

Karkhana 10 (detail), p.93

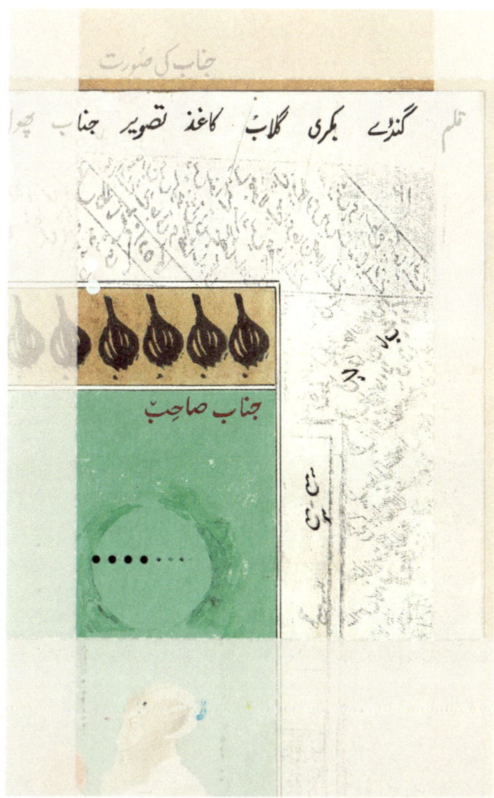

Karkhana 11 (detail), p.97

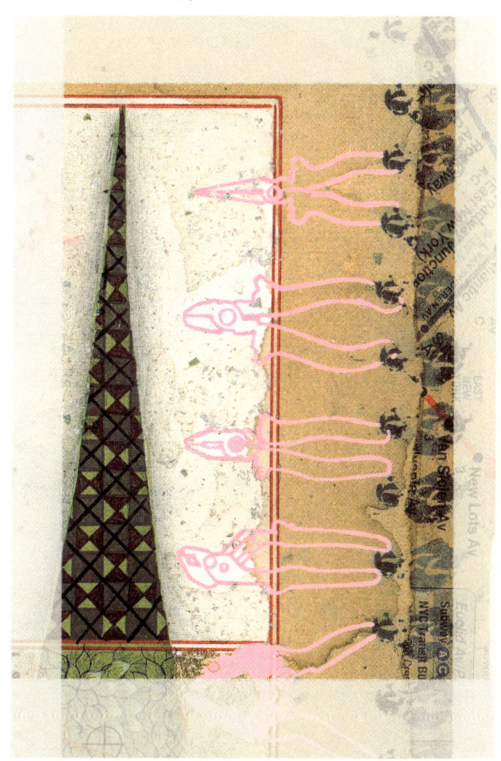

Karkhana 12 (detail), p.101

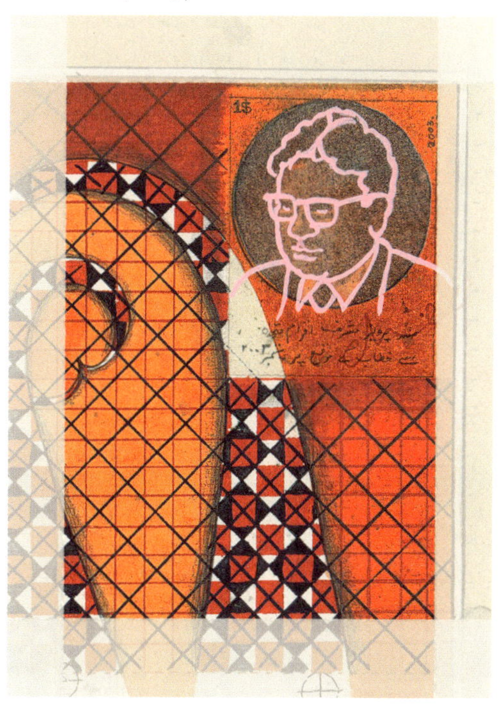

Innovations to a Timeless Practice: Materials and Techniques of the Karkhana Artists

Qamar Adamjee and Sandhya Jain

The art of the book occupies an important place in material culture across a wide geographic and chronological span. Illustrated books have always been highly prized as luxury objects. Much of their value derived from the precious materials, skill and labor required for their production, which often made royal patronage a necessity. The artists behind the *Karkhana* project, all former students of miniature painting at The National College of Arts (NCA) in Lahore, Pakistan,[1] have trained in practices that ultimately derive from Persian and Mughal painting. These were popular forms in their time, with traditional sources of patronage.[2]

The training process for miniature painting emphasizes drawing skills and highly labor-intensive practices. Its focus on retaining the so-called purity of the South Asian model (in terms of subjects and methods), where the boundary between art and craft is blurred, is now being challenged by contemporary artists.[3] These artists are interested in expanding the scope of an artistic expression that traces its roots to the sixteenth century and prides itself on highly-finished surfaces and methods. While they continue to use practices with a long, specifically Indo-Persian, history, they have combined these with techniques, processes and concepts more closely aligned to contemporary art practices.

The paintings from the *Karkhana* project retain the three basic elements of traditional painting in that they are relatively small scale (the largest painting measures approximately 8 x 11 inches), are works on *wasli* (layered hand-made paper), and are executed with ink and water-based opaque colors.

Wasli

Wasli, from the Persian word *vasl*, meaning union, is a thick support prepared by joining multiple sheets of paper using a wheat-based glue preparation (*layee*). Because of how it is made, it allows the artists to apply multiple layers of paint without causing the paper to warp. Paper in the sixteenth century was expensive, and not easily available. Usually made from cotton, hemp, or linen fibers, it had to be ordered directly from an expert paper maker. In a traditional *kitabkhana* (literally, "book-house" in Persian—a specialized term for the imperial workshop where books were prepared and collected), the project supervisor could choose to have the paper made into *wasli* directly by the paper maker, or by an in-house apprentice.

The making of *wasli* is a time-honored and time-consuming process in which three

Figure 1

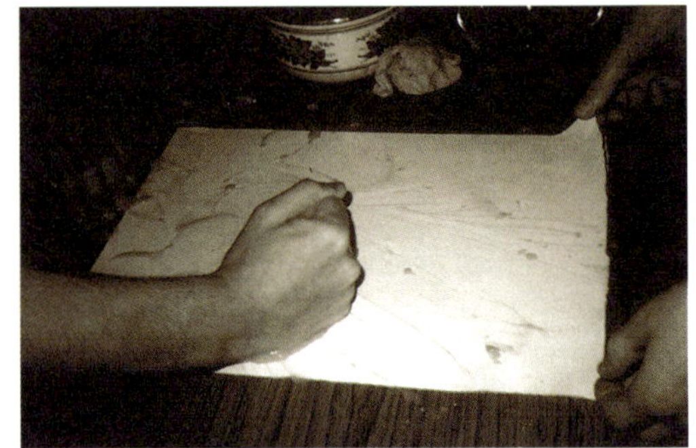

to four sheets of paper are pasted together with a surface sheet of high quality paper. Each sheet is applied over the other, with care taken to eliminate air bubbles that may be trapped between the layers (Fig.1). The composite sheet is then secured to a flat surface for several days to ensure even drying. It is then burnished with a large, round shell when fully dry to produce a smooth working surface.

All of the artists in the *Karkhana* project are able to make *wasli* in the traditional manner, and Talha Rathore and Muhammad Imran Qureshi do so for most of their paintings. The NCA recipe for *layee* calls for the addition of a small amount of copper sulfate to inhibit insect growth, although the ingredient is not mentioned in traditional recipes. In addition to *wasli*, commercially-produced drawing paper is used today. The surface sheet used for the *Karkhana* project, for example, was Canson CA Grain paper. To soften the off-white color of this paper, many of the *Karkhana* artists have stained the surface with tea (Fig.2), producing a beige color similar to traditionally hand-made papers. This has been preferred over white for centuries because it is easier on the artist's eyes. Turmeric, instead of tea, has been used by Hasnat Mehmood for the same purpose.

Figure 2

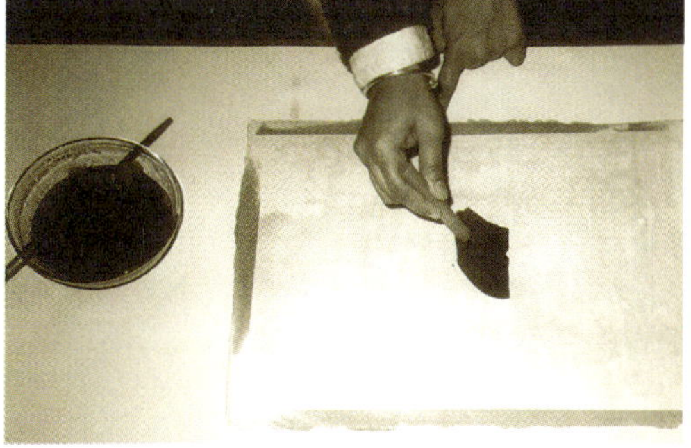

Qureshi returns to tradition, in a sense, with the use of paper torn from old Urdu manuscripts as his surface sheet. The paper from these old books is locally produced and often hand made, though of varying qualities. Qureshi's choice is determined by the relationship of the planned painting with the content of the printed text—Urdu poetry (Karkhana 1, p.55) or dressmaking patterns (Karkhana 2, p.59). The top sheet of found paper is abraded with sandpaper, varying degrees of which allow for different effects—when lightly sanded, the printed text on the surface is made to recede in the background and be subtly visible as a palimpsest; when repeatedly sanded, the upper layer of paper becomes so thin that the print on the reverse starts showing through, creating a mirror image of the text, and allowing for an interesting visual interplay.

Pigments

Two types of pigments were traditionally used in miniature painting: inorganic pigments, or "stone colors," made from semi-precious stones such as lapis lazuli or malachite, or from minerals such as vermilion and orpiment; and organic pigments, which were derived from plant or animal matter, such as indigo, carbon black, lac, and *gogoli* (cow urine). The inorganic pigments were prepared by being ground to a powder (Fig.3) and then levigated in water several times to separate particles of different sizes. When the particles were sifted to satisfaction, they were mixed with *safaida* (white pigment) to make an opaque pigment (Fig.4). Organic pigments, on the other hand, were dried, powdered, and then mixed with *safaida*. Both types of pigments were bound with gum arabic to make a gouache-like medium.[4]

Figure 3

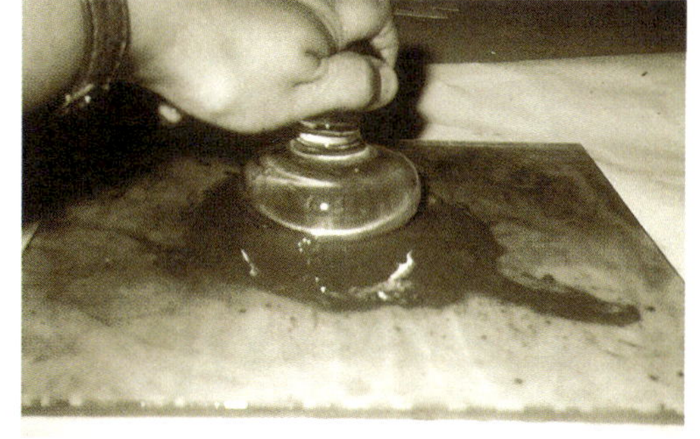

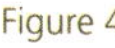

Many miniature paintings also had gold or silver leaf applied to them. The area designated for leaf was first covered with a thin wash of gum arabic. The metal leaf was then either laid down whole, or broken up and sprinkled to create a sparkling effect. After the binder was dry, the leaf was burnished to secure it to the paper and optimize its shine. This traditional method is still followed by artists today.

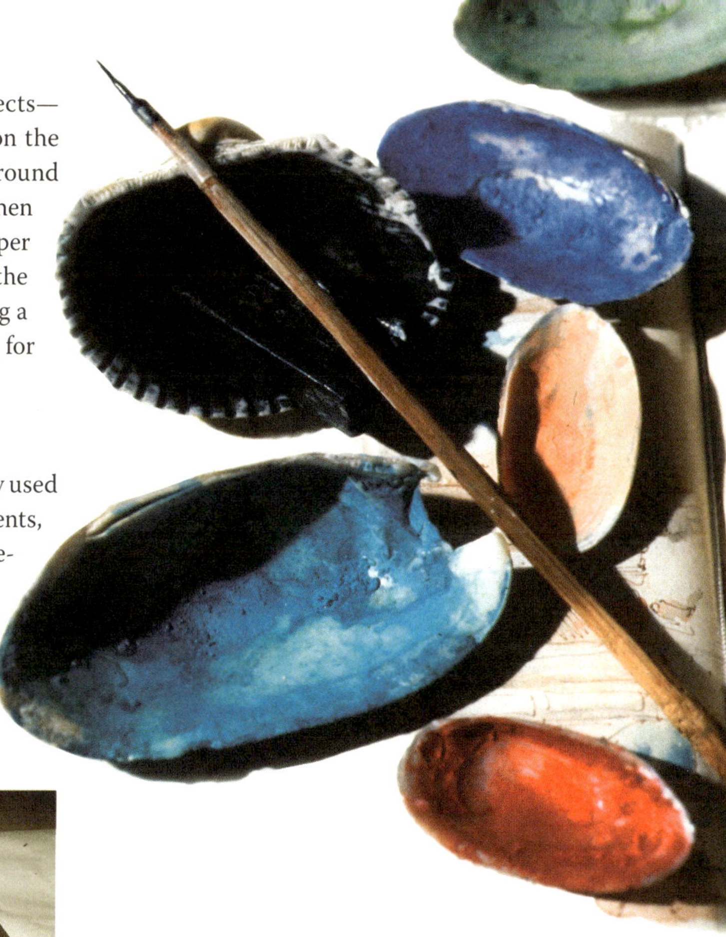

Figure 4

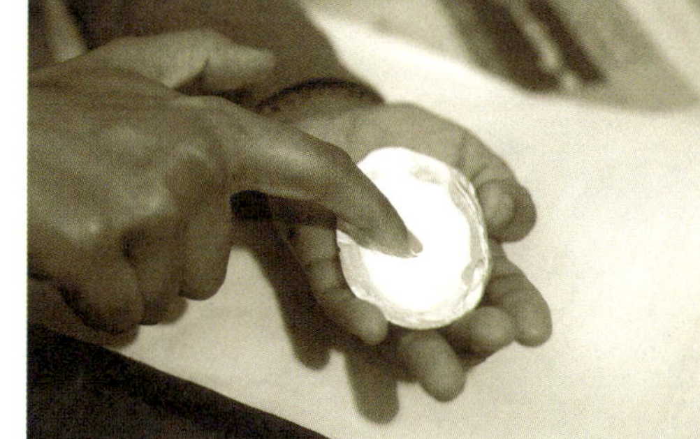

Figure 5
Karkhana 3 (detail), p.65

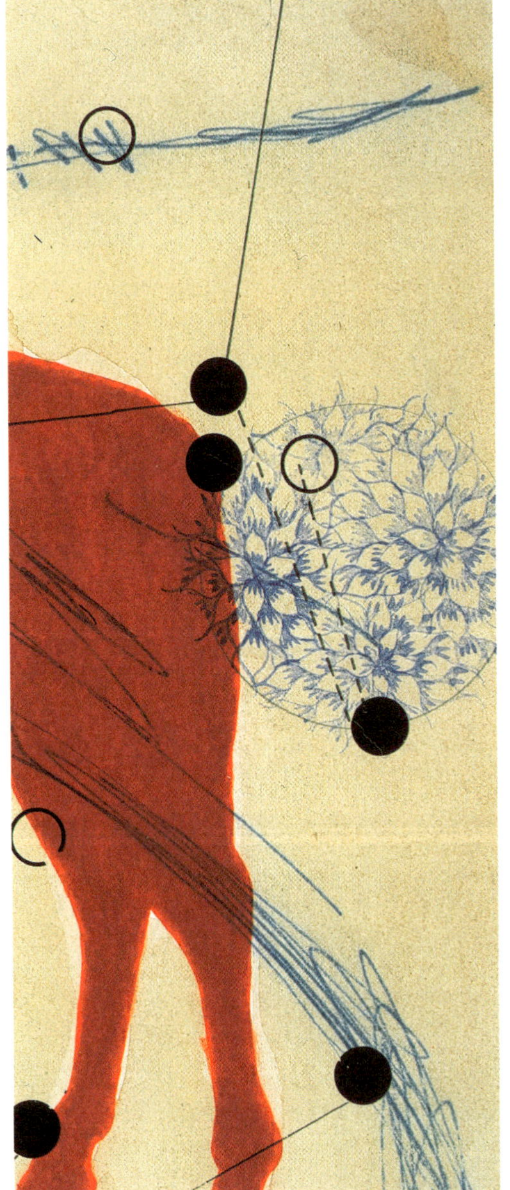

Figure 6

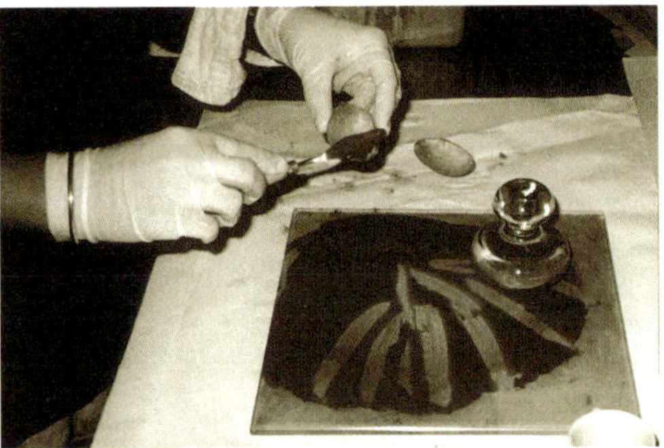

Instead of stone colors, many contemporary artists now use commercially-available colors in the form of poster colors or paint tubes as their source of pigment, but they purify them in the same laborious process of repeated levigation. To make opaque pigment, each color is mixed with a little bit of *safaida*, and all pigments are bound with gum arabic. In keeping with tradition, the colors are stored in seashells (Fig.6) instead of a European palette. Seashells were traditionally used because it was easy to store and reactivate the pigments in them. Also, the white of the shell interior is compatible with the *safaida*, ensuring that the pigment will not spoil. Painting in the miniature style involves working close to the *wasli* and using one color at a time. Seashells are conducive to this, fitting comfortably in the hand (Fig.4).

Modern pigments have now become an essential material for contemporary artists, and the *Karkhana* group have sourced and used them in innovative ways: Qureshi uses markers to draw the lines which connect his circles and dots, and carbon paper to draw his graffiti-like lines (Fig.5). Nusra Latif Qureshi typically uses acrylic paint in many of her works (Karkhana 6, p.77), whereas Rathore uses stamp-pad ink in the perimeters of her paintings (Karkhana 11, p.97, and Karkhana 12, p.101). Mehmood uses tailor's chalk in *Karkhana 5* (p.73) to create a halo around the outline of the audience and a ball-point pen to "check" postage stamps (Fig.9). Finally, in addition to the use of gum arabic as a binder, new adhesives include UHU gum and fixative, both of which are commercially available and synthetic. Gum arabic however, is still the binder of choice among the *Karkhana* artists for binding pigments and affixing metal leaf to the paintings (Karkhana 4, p.69).

Figure 7

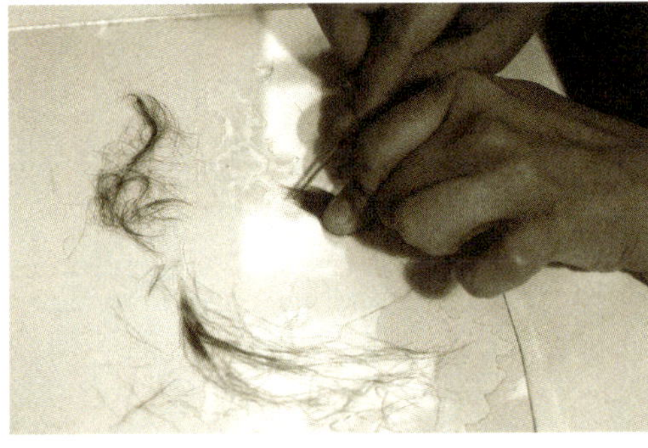

Brushes

Squirrel-hair paintbrushes are still often made by hand (Fig.7), and sometimes by the artists themselves. The process first involves selecting fine equal-sized hairs, their number depending on the desired thickness of the brush. These hairs are then tied together with thread, hardened with gum arabic, passed through a hollow straw of a pigeon feather—which serves as the ferrule and the whole secured to a sharpened bamboo shoot. Brushes used for color filling are made of a group of hairs, while those used for line work have a single hair extending past the main bulk of hairs. One or two such delicate brushes are used for each painting and then discarded. Today, good quality squirrel-hair brushes are commercially available in India, Pakistan, and in other parts of the world (e.g. France and New York City) and most artists, including those of the *Karkhana* group, use these rather than making their own brushes. In addition to squirrel-hair, these artists also use commercially-available sable-hair brushes.

Applying Color

Traditional methods for layout and color application continue to be practiced today. Historically the layout of each page was planned with the aid of margins and ruled lines that allocated space for the text, the painting, and the borders. A highly detailed under-drawing was executed with a fine pencil, over which a thin wash of *safaida* was applied. The barely-visible under-drawing was reinforced by dark, usually black, pigment and applied with a single-hair brush (Fig.8). Finally, the color was applied. There were several methods of color application in tradi-

Figure 8

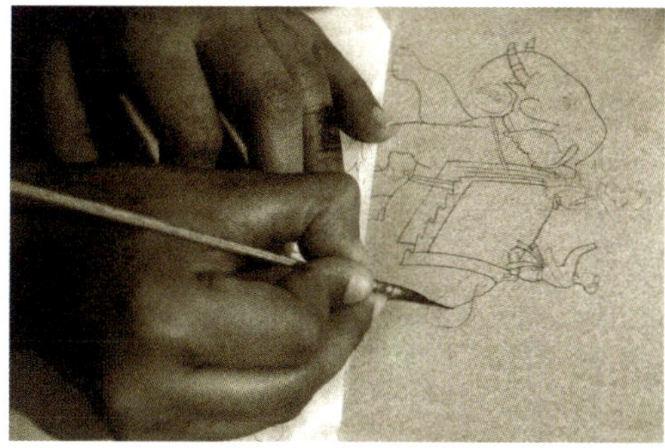

tional miniature painting. *Siyah qalam* (black brush) is a monochromatic form of painting in which the entire image is executed in a single color, usually black (Fig.10). Shading was achieved by carefully applying layers of transparent watercolor with a brush.When a *siyah qalam* painting has some opaque color, it is referred to as *neem rang* (half-colored). The technique most familiar to admirers of miniature painting today is *gudd rang*, in which the entire painting is rendered with gouache and burnished from the reverse to produce an enamel-like surface.

Innovations in Techniques and Materials

The works and individual styles of the *Karkhana* artists reflect a modern sensibility. They are comfortable using and experimenting with techniques, materials, and ideas foreign to miniature painting in conjunction with the older courtly traditional methods. One such technique, popular amongst the group, is collage, in which a design is created by adhering basically flat elements such as newspaper, wallpaper, printed text and illustrations, photographs, cloth and string to a surface. Different forms of collage are used in the *Karkhana* paintings. Found objects, such as the postal stamps applied by Latif in *Karkhana 5* (p.73) and *Karkhana 6* (p.77), are one type.[5] Mehmood introduces mechanical mediation into the collage process by photocopying his images (contemporary newspaper headlines, self-portrait, etc.) onto nearly transparent tracing paper, cutting them into different shapes in some instances, and applying them to the painting (Karkhana 9, p.89, Karkhana 11, p.97, and Karkhana 12, p.101). Because of the transparency of the tracing paper, these elements are not immediately discernible as collage. Rathore has glued strips of New York City subway maps onto the edges of the paintings, where they take the place of the highly decorated borders of traditional manuscript paintings.

Rathore also innovates with the traditional form of certain functional features in her paintings. For example, a *jadval* was used traditionally to frame the central image window on a painted page, and mask the physical join between the central window and the border. The *jadval* took the form of a series of variably sized bands of color and blank space outlined in black. Rathore uses rubber stamps, as can be seen in *Karkhana 11* (p.97) and *Karkhana 12* (p.101).[6] These motifs, which are laid partly on the *wasli* and partly on the pasted subway map borders, create a transition between the borders and the painting area. Rathore also uses sewn threads, which though not collage, are new to miniature painting (Karkhana 1, p.57, and Karkhana 3, p.65). In this instance, the practice generated a dialogue between the artists, as Qureshi responded to Rathore's interjection of a new medium by cutting the threads.

The processes of mechanical transfer used by the *Karkhana* artists in their collaboration are also new to miniature painting. Qureshi has used Letraset transfers to create circles and dots in many of his paintings (Fig.5). These motifs, commercially available on transparent paper, are placed facedown so they are in contact with the painting. The motif is then transferred by rubbing the paper with pencil or some other implement, so that the media is burnished onto the surface. In other paintings, Qureshi has placed photocopies of Urdu texts facedown onto the *wasli* and rubbed mineral spirits through them to transfer the text to the painting, resulting in mirrored text (Karkhana 10, p.93).

The *Karkhana* artists are no less innovative when conceptualizing the painting process, and each, in their individual way, is reassessing the theoretical framework of their chosen artistic medium. Qureshi is interested in the role of the artist in the miniature tradition. He has tried to create a transparency within a practice that stresses exquisitely-finished surfaces and where the artist would traditionally have remained virtually invisible. Historically, the mechanics of

Figure 9
Karkhana 11 (detail), p.97.

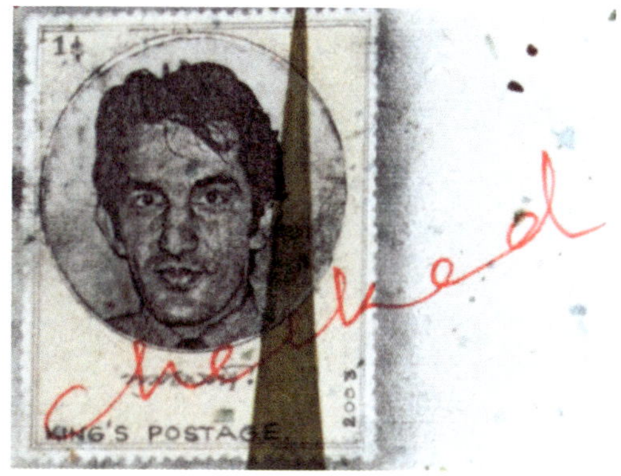

Figure 10
Jamil Naqsh
Seated Rider with Pigeon, (ca.1970)
Ink on *wasli*
12 7/8 x 8 3/8 inches (32 x 21 cm)
Collection of Arif Hasan, Karachi
Courtesy of the artist

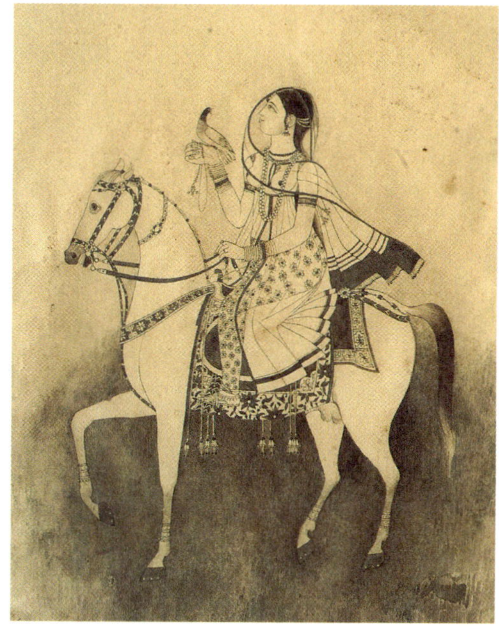

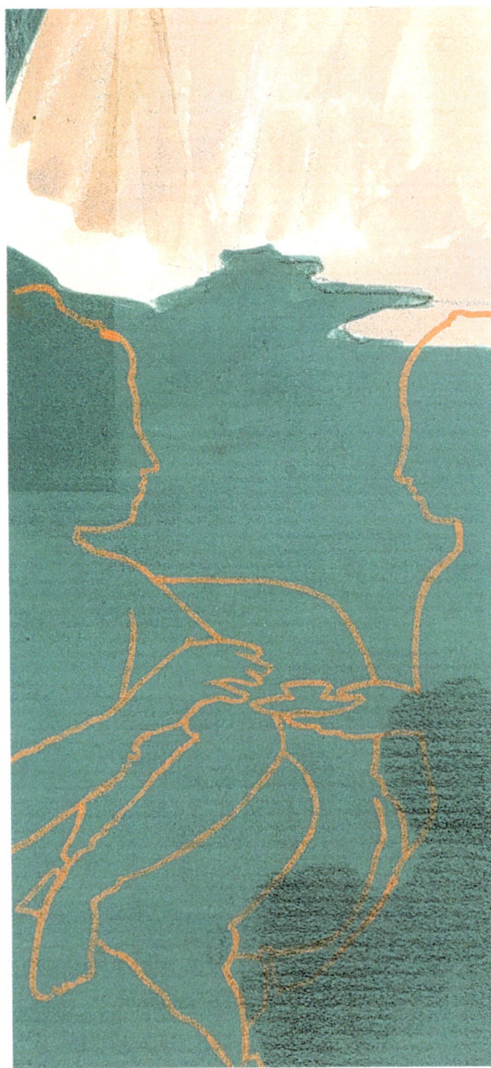

Figure 11 (above)
Karkhana 7 (detail), p.79

Figure 12 (right)
Karkhana 12 (detail), p.101

production were concealed beneath paint and behind decorative borders. Evidence of the artist's presence is important to Qureshi, and he indicates his own with loose brush strokes in the margins where he tests the shades of his colors or wipes off excess paint from the brush (Karkhana 1, p.57). These "digressions" become an integral part of his paintings and provide a subjective artistic voice alongside fine details within the picture.

Of the *Karkhana* group, Saira Wasim's interest in the highly-detailed, delicately-rendered, and carefully-finished painting form aligns her work most closely with traditional practices. Wasim begins each painting in the traditional way, planning the layout with margins and ruled lines and executing a highly-detailed under-drawing with a fine pencil before applying any paint. However, she does not intend to conceal these markings in her work, and instead offers the viewer a glimpse of the mechanics of this process. With this motivation, she frequently leaves areas of unfinished paint application in an otherwise skillfully-rendered image.

Aisha Khalid reverses the relationship between decorative motifs and the central image. Patterning is a strong decorative element in Persian and Indian painting, where it creates a sense of multi-faceted perspective and luxuriousness. In Khalid's work, patterning becomes the subject (Fig.12). The gridded, geometric patterns that Khalid creates are found typically on architectural decoration and tile work. By using elements from a different media, as picture fields or on vegetal forms, she alters their function and the viewer's perception.

Latif's interest, on the other hand, lies in reducing the painting process to the bare essentials. In her paintings she often uses outlined motifs that recall under-drawings (Fig.11). For instance, the pink pliers that appear in *Karkhana 11* (p.97), and Musharraf's portrait that appears in *Karkhana 12* (p.101). Through these contour drawings, she finishes her compositions with what was traditionally the preliminary step in the painting process. She may fill some of these outlines in with *gudd rang*, but this is not a necessary step in the completion of her work.

The miniature painting form, hitherto associated with a specific historical time and geographical setting, is being redefined and reinvented by the artists of the *Karkhana* group. By bringing transparency to the art-making process and introducing non-traditional media into the strictly paint-on-paper practice, they have contributed much to its reinvention.

By using materials such as acrylic paints, ballpoint pens, markers, Letraset transfers, found paper, and techniques such as collage, block print, stitching and photocopying, these artists have opened up new dialogues between art and craft; individuality and anonymity; the historical past and present reality; East and West; and modernity and tradition. By questioning the strictures of their training, they are successfully finding ways to make a traditionally-valued art practice relevant to their own context in the twenty-first century.

Notes

1 It is now widely accepted that the term "miniature" derives not from the small scale of the work but from the Latin word *miniare*, meaning "to color with red" (the adornment of books originally was executed in red, or minium). See Michelle P. Brown, *Understanding Illuminated Manuscripts: A Guide to Technical Terms.* (London: J. Paul Getty Museum and British Library, 1994), p.86.

2 The artists at NCA are trained in the styles of the Mughal, Rajasthan and Pahari schools (which include centers such as Kangra, Basohli, Guler and Mandi) of North India. While the overall techniques and materials of these courtly centers shared features of Persian painting, some were particular to the Indian context.

3 From a modern point of reference we call this painting "traditional." Historically speaking, it was the only form of painting across the Islamic world from the seventh to the eighteenth centuries distinguished by different schools of production, geographic locations, or dynasties e.g. Shiraz or Bukhara school, Mughal, Safavid, etc.

Both terms, "miniature" and "traditional," are used interchangeably in this essay to refer to a particular type of painting that originated in the form of illustrated manuscripts. For more information see Oleg Grabar, *Mostly Miniatures: An Introduction to Persian Painting* (Princeton, NJ: Princeton University Press, 2000); J.M. Rogers, *Mughal Miniatures* (London: Published for the Trustees of the British Museum by British Museum Press, 1993); Milo Beach, *Early Mughal Painting* (Cambridge, MA: Published for the Asia Society by Harvard University Press, 1987).

4 The use of the term "gouache" for courtly or traditional miniature paintings is misleading. Gouache pigments contain water as their binder, which is not the case for pigments used in miniature paintings.

5 There are other paintings in the *Karkhana* project that seem to have real postal stamps but which are actually mimicked with paint and collage elements (*Karkhana 1*, p.57; *Karkhana 11*, p.97; and *Karkhana 12*, p.101).

6 For more on the *jadval*, see Moti Chandra, *The Technique of Mughal Painting* (Lucknow: The U.P. Historical Society, 1949), p.66; Yves Porter, *Painters, Paintings, and Books: An Essay on Indo-Persian Technical Literature, 12-19th Centuries* (New Delhi: Manohar Publications, 1994), pp.59-61; Marianna Shreve Simpson, *Sultan Ibrahim Mirza's Haft Awrang* (Washington, D.C.: Freer Gallery of Art, Smithsonian Institution, 1997), p.63.

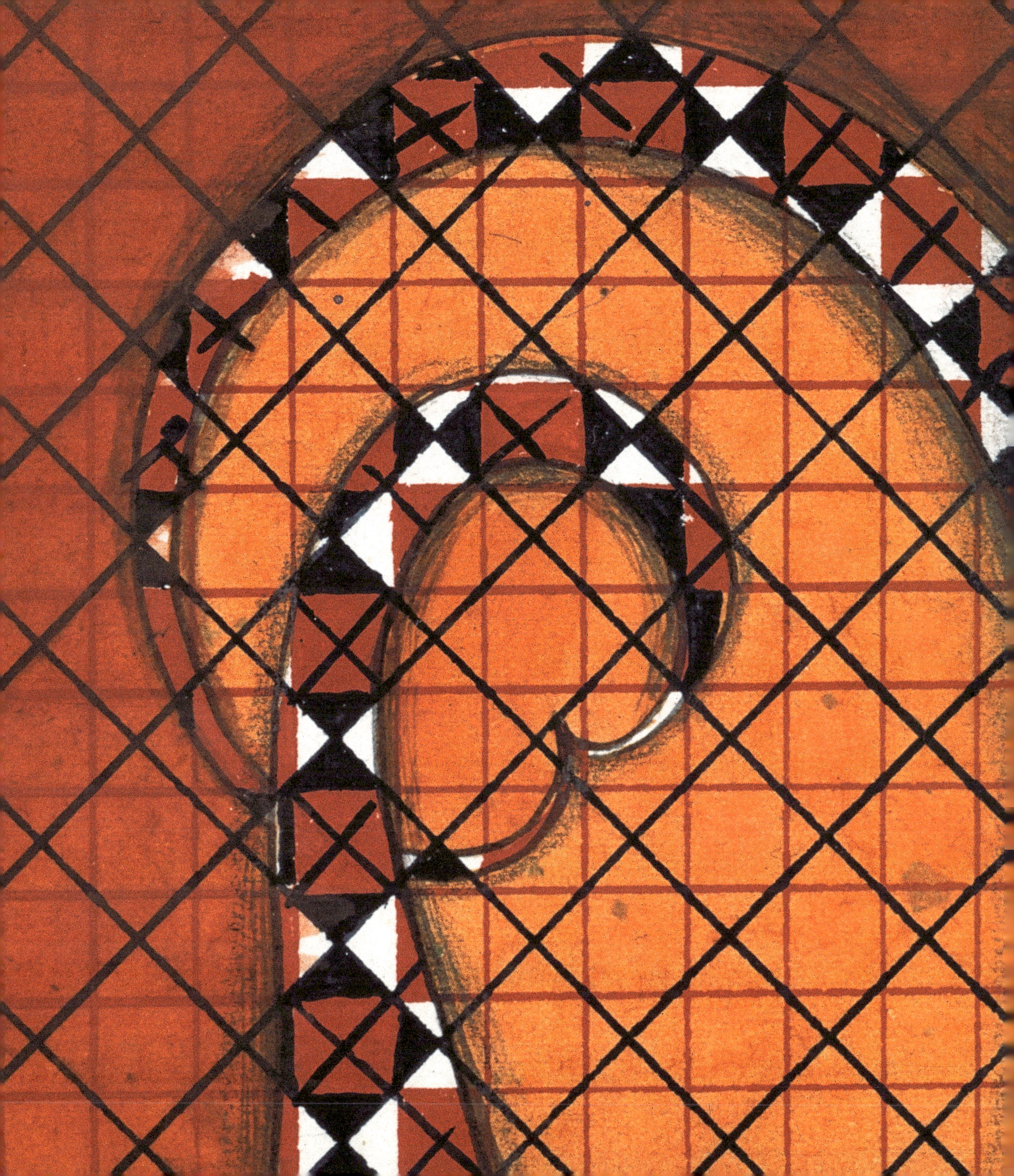

The Karkhana Project

The *Karkhana* works are untitled. They have been numbered in this catalogue for ease of reference.

The text accompanying the images is extracted from Salima Hashmi's (S.H.) essay. Text within quotes is transcribed from interviews with the artists conducted by Qamar Adamjee, Sandhya Jain and Hammad Nasar.

The photographic documentation of the interventions by each artist was done in varying conditions for their own records, and the colors and frames of the images vary. In a few instances the visual record of a particular intervention is not available.

Muhammad Imran Qureshi Lahore

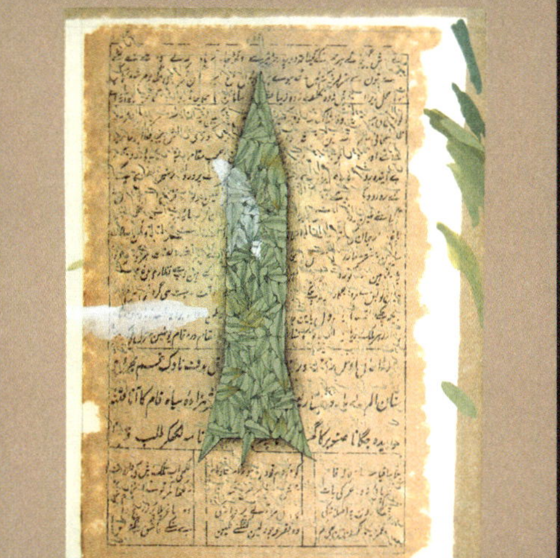

Hasnat Mehmood Jhelum

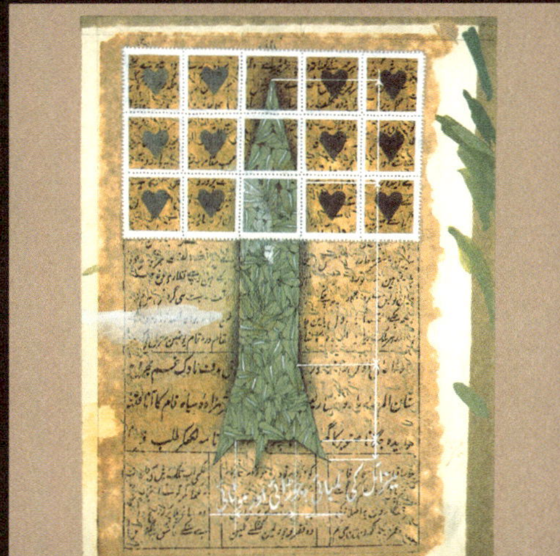

Karkhana 1

"I was tempted to do just a bit more. I had

Aisha Khalid Lahore

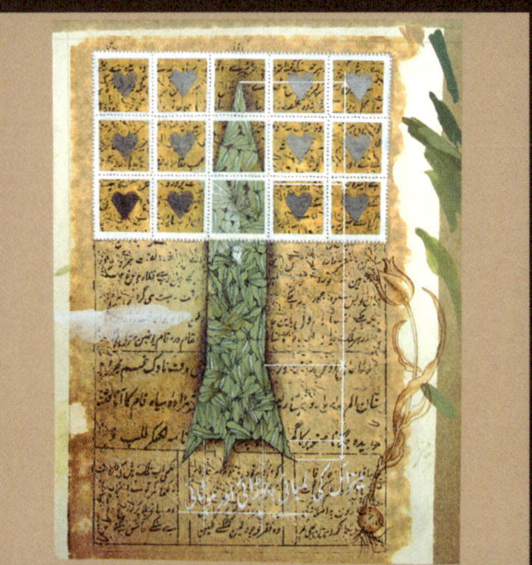

Nusra Latif Qureshi Melbourne

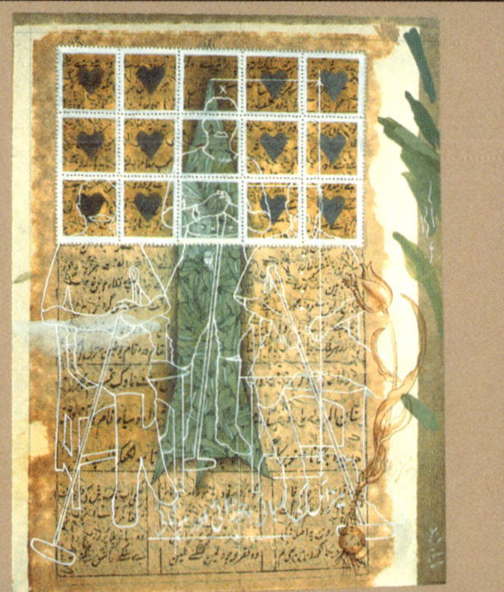

Saira Wasim Chicago

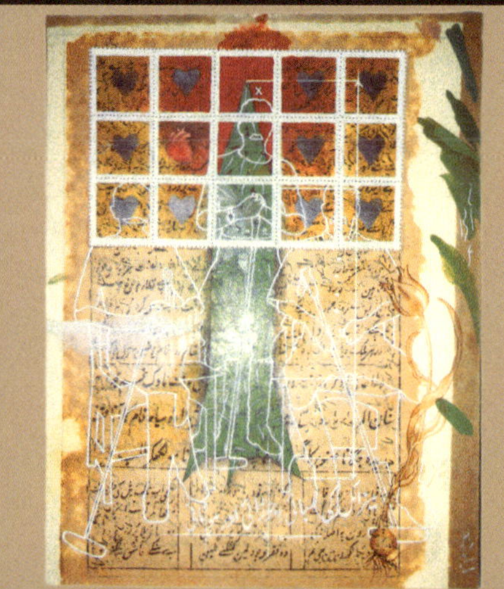

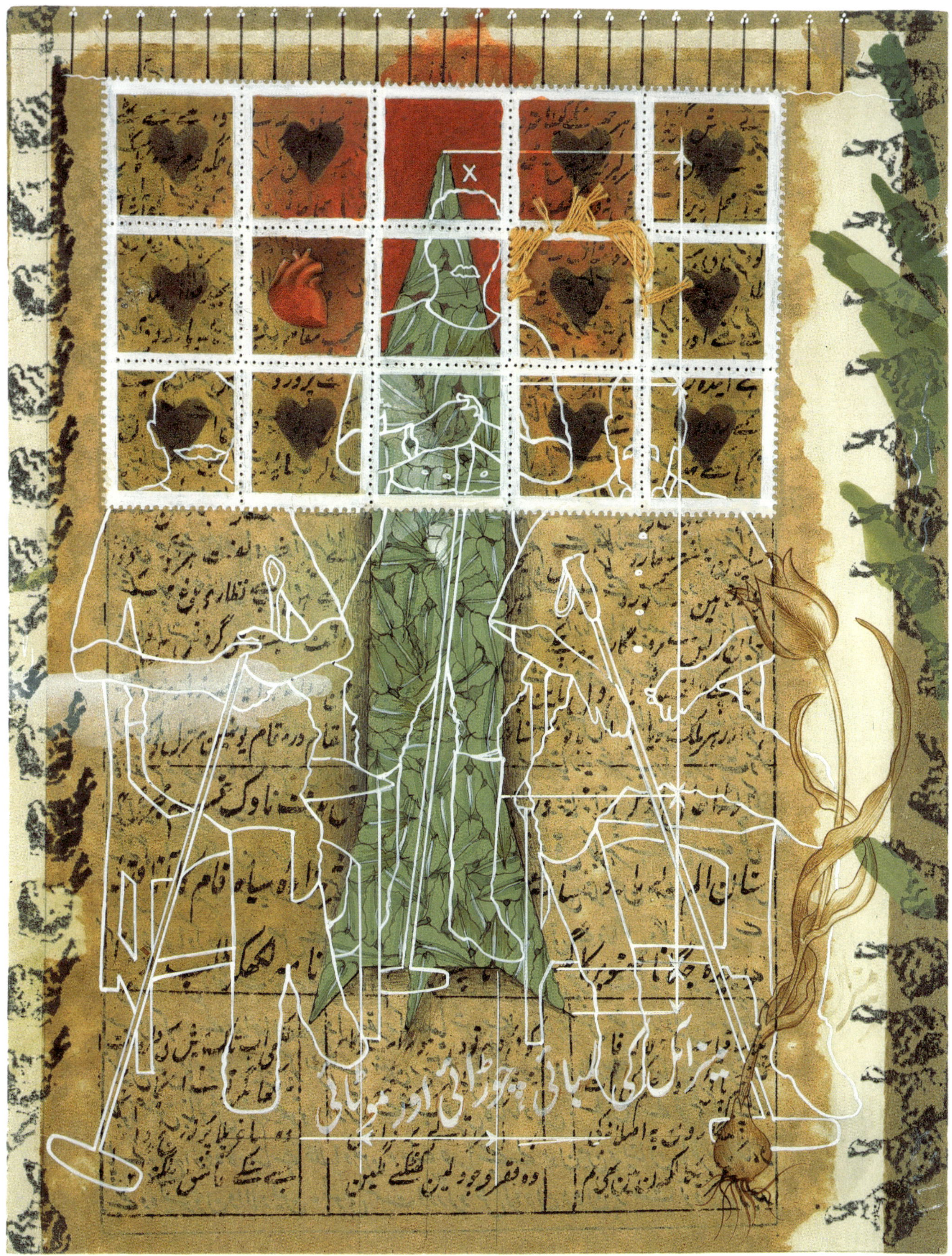
میری ناک کی لمبائی چوڑائی اور موٹائی

KARKHANA 2003

✓ → ① - Muhammad Imran Qureshi - [illegible]
21/06/03

✓ ② - [illegible]
26-06-003

③ - Aisha Khalid [illegible]

④ - Nusra Latif Q[illegible] 14-0[illegible]-2003

⑤ [illegible]

⑥ - Talha Rathore [illegible] 2003

Karkhana 2

Muhammad Imran Qureshi Lahore

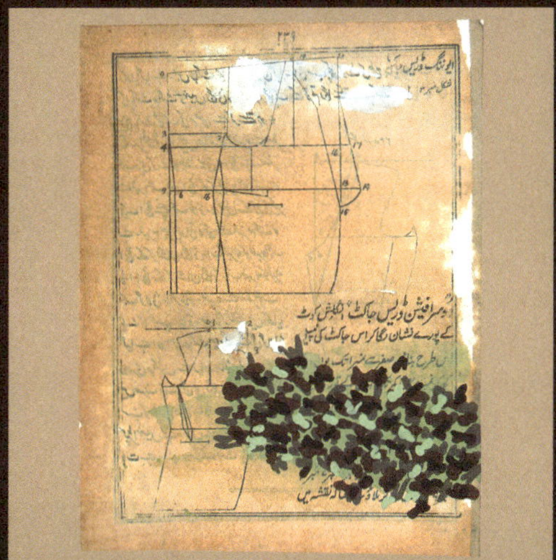

"I bought this Urdu tailor's manual from an old bookshop on a footpath in Lahore. Its headings and cutting patterns were loaded with political intent."

Hasnat Mehmood Jhelum

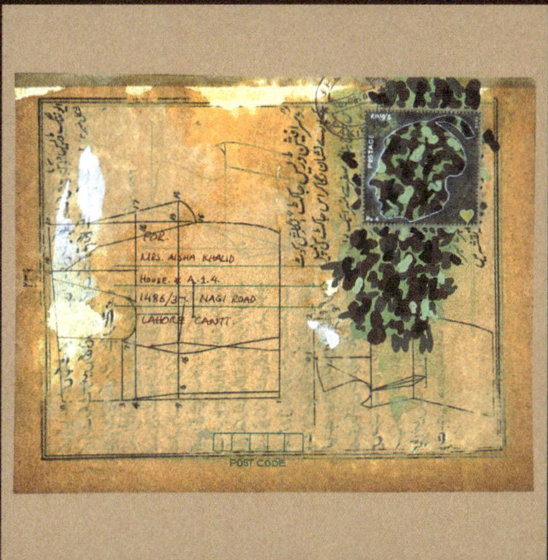

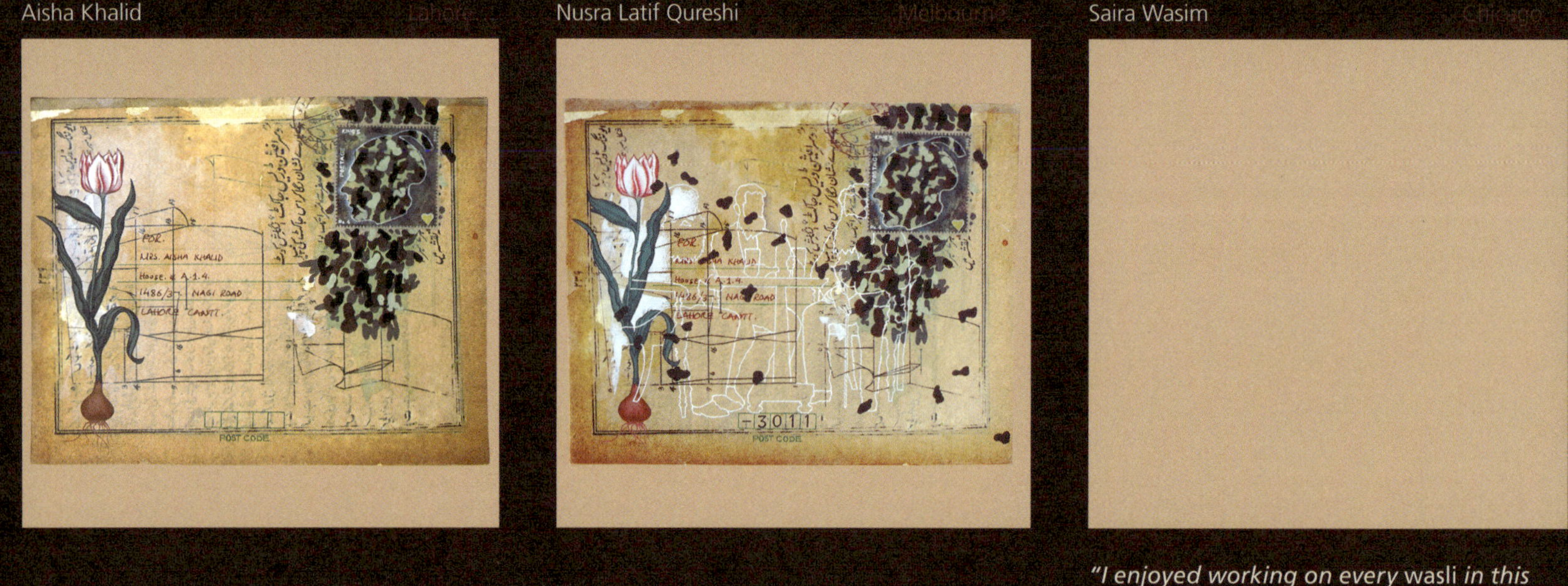

Aisha Khalid Lahore

Nusra Latif Qureshi Melbourne

Saira Wasim Chicago

"I enjoyed working on every wasli in this series, but as a student of Imran's, it was a special treat to be working on the two waslis he started."

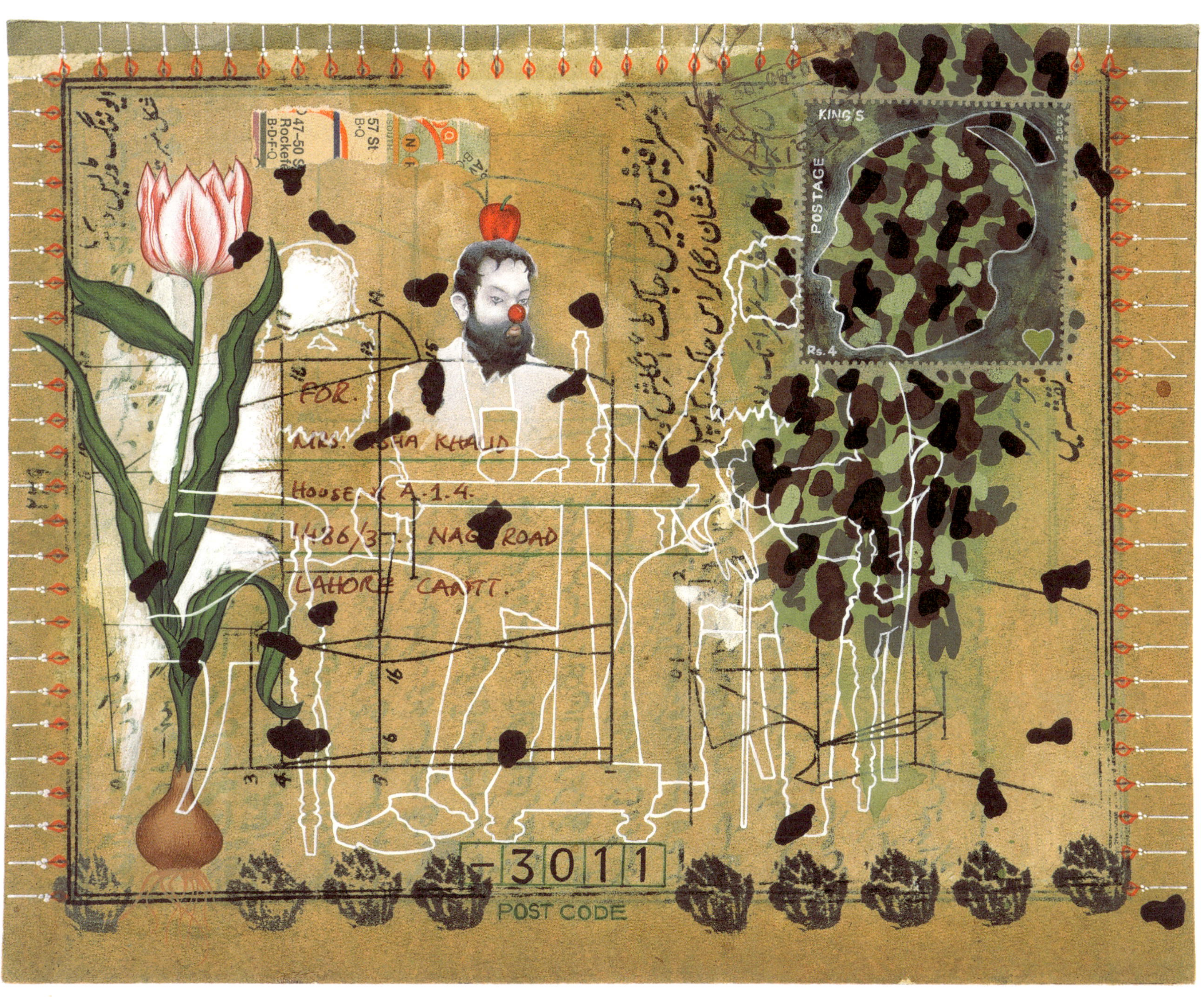
FOR.
LAHORE CANTT.
KING'S
POSTAGE
Rs. 4
3011
POST CODE

کارخانہ

① - محمد عمران قریشی - 22/06/03

② - سید حسنات محمود -

③ - عائشہ خالد -

26-06-03

Karkhana 3

Hasnat Mehmood Jhelum

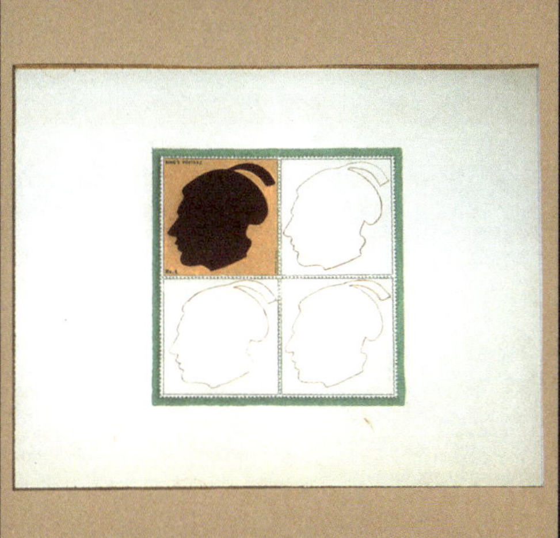

Aisha Khalid Lahore

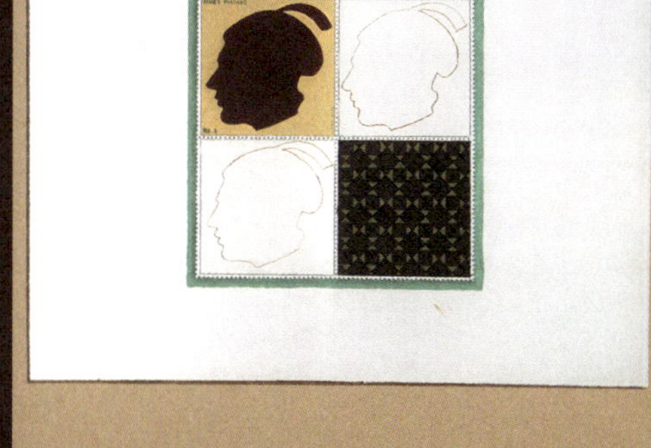

Mehmood was captivated by the idea that unlike most Pakistani citizens, the artworks could travel effortlessly without a visa. S.H

Nusra Latif Qureshi Melbourne

Saira Wasim Chicago

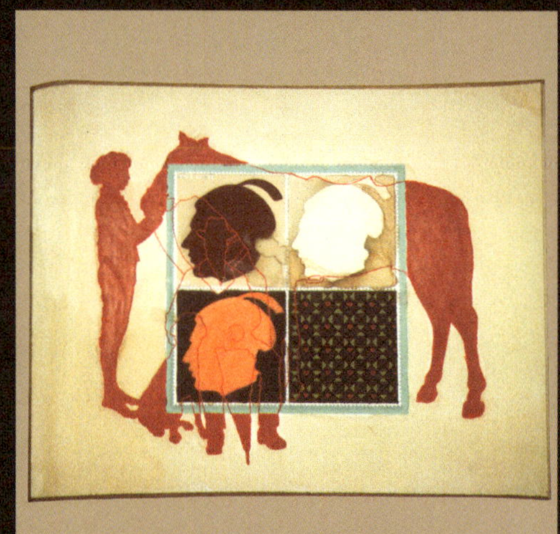

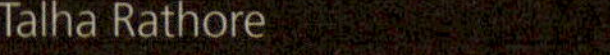

Talha Rathore New York

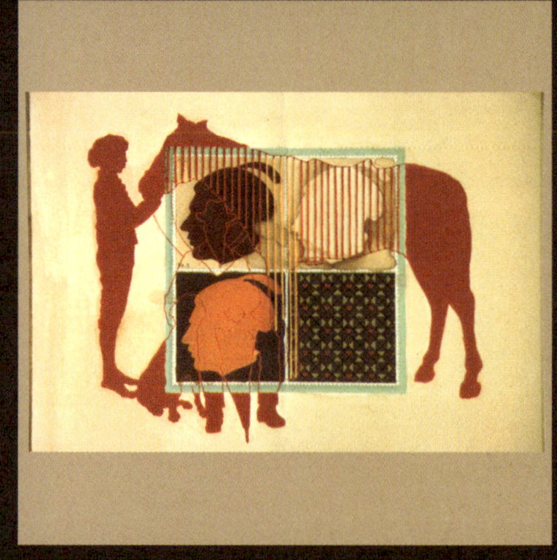

For Rathore, the acts of piercing, decorating, block printing have been extensions of domestic processes of cooking, cleaning, mending. SH

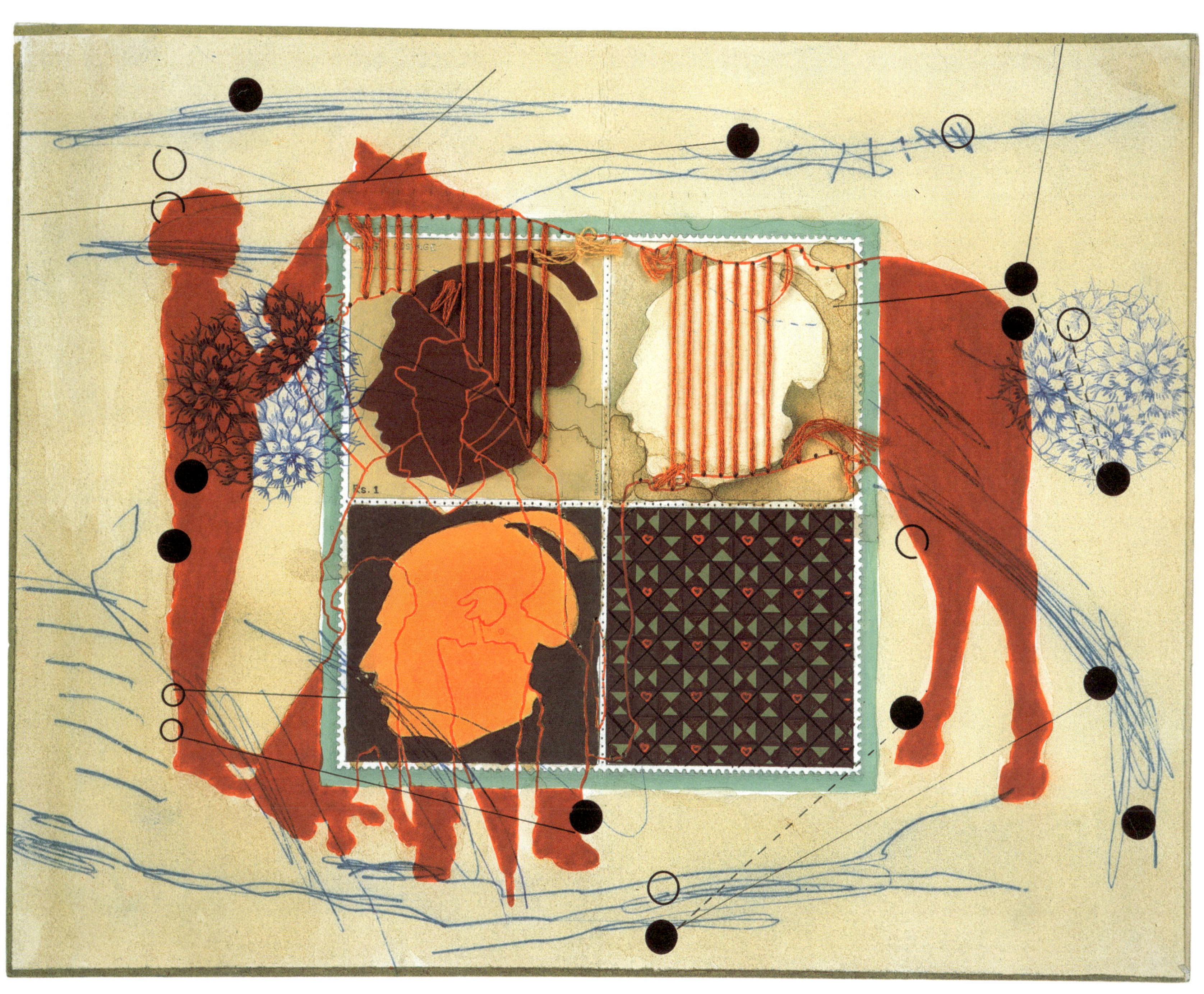

(1) Hashat Mehmood

(2) Aisha Khalid

(3) Nusra Latif

(4)

(5)

(6) Imran Qureshi 11/10/03

HASHAT MEHMOOD.
14-06-2003

Karkhana 4

Hasnat Mehmood Jhelum

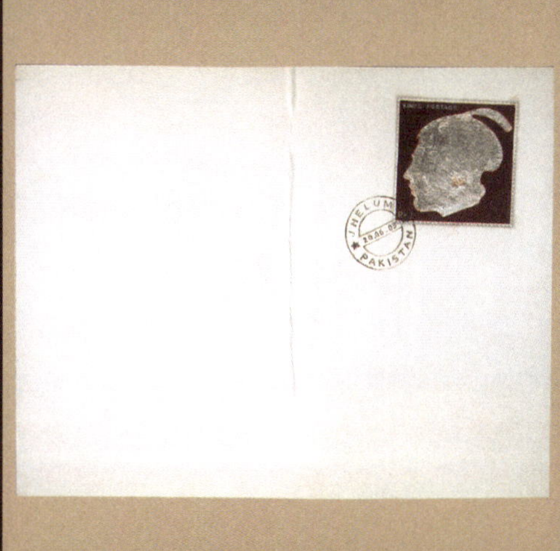

"Postage stamps are archives in themselves. I was using my stamp portraits to record the process of this karkhana."

Aisha Khalid Lahore

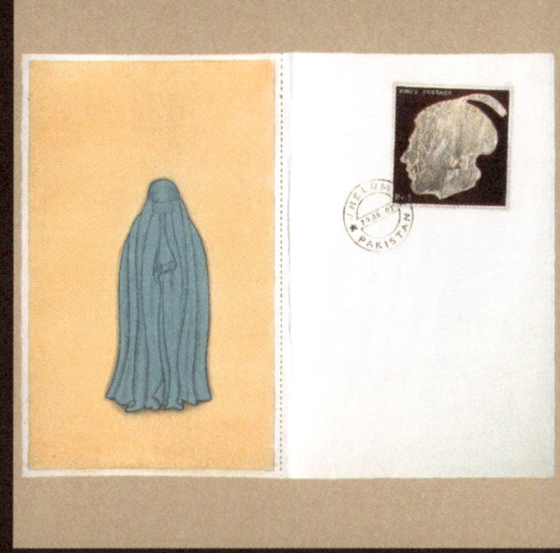

The post office had its own plans for Mehmood's work, which arrived bent neatly in half for Khalid to work with. S.H

Nusra Latif Qureshi Melbourne

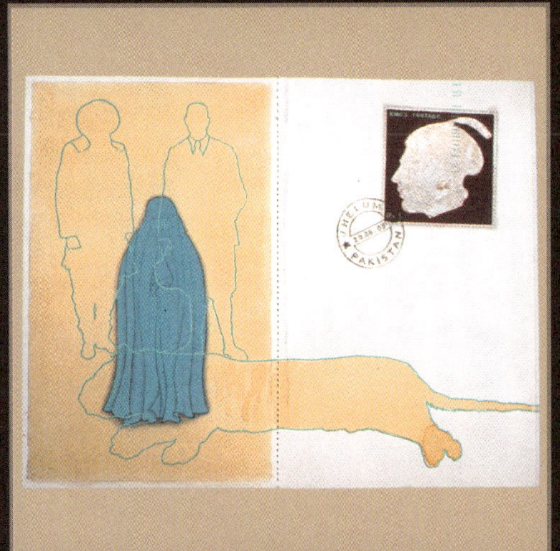

Saira Wasim Chicago

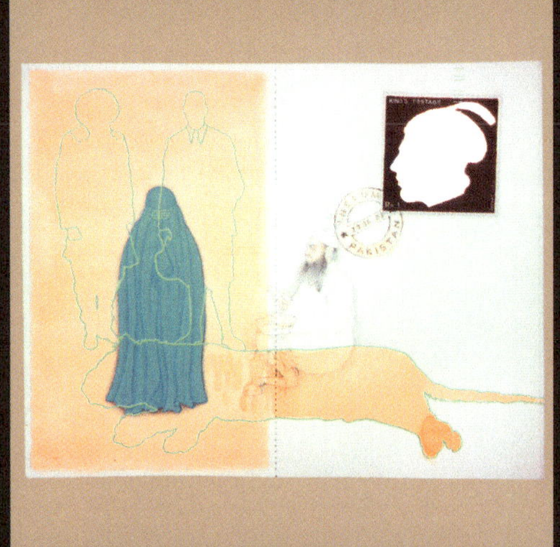

Talha Rathore New York

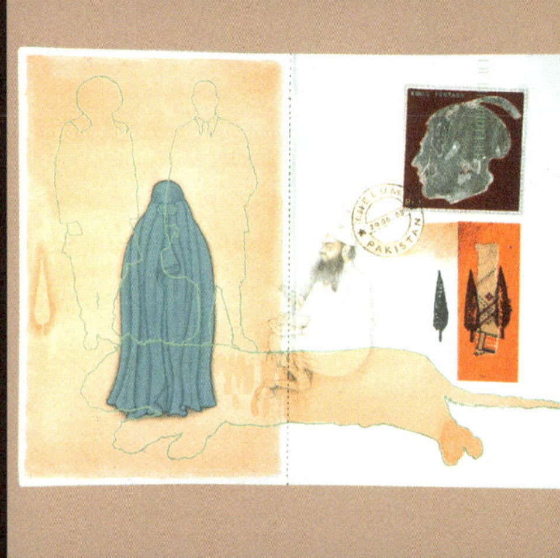

"This colonial photograph is one of my favorites because of its in-your-face arrogance and pomp. It is the presumed racial, political and cultural superiority that I am challenging by elimination of details."

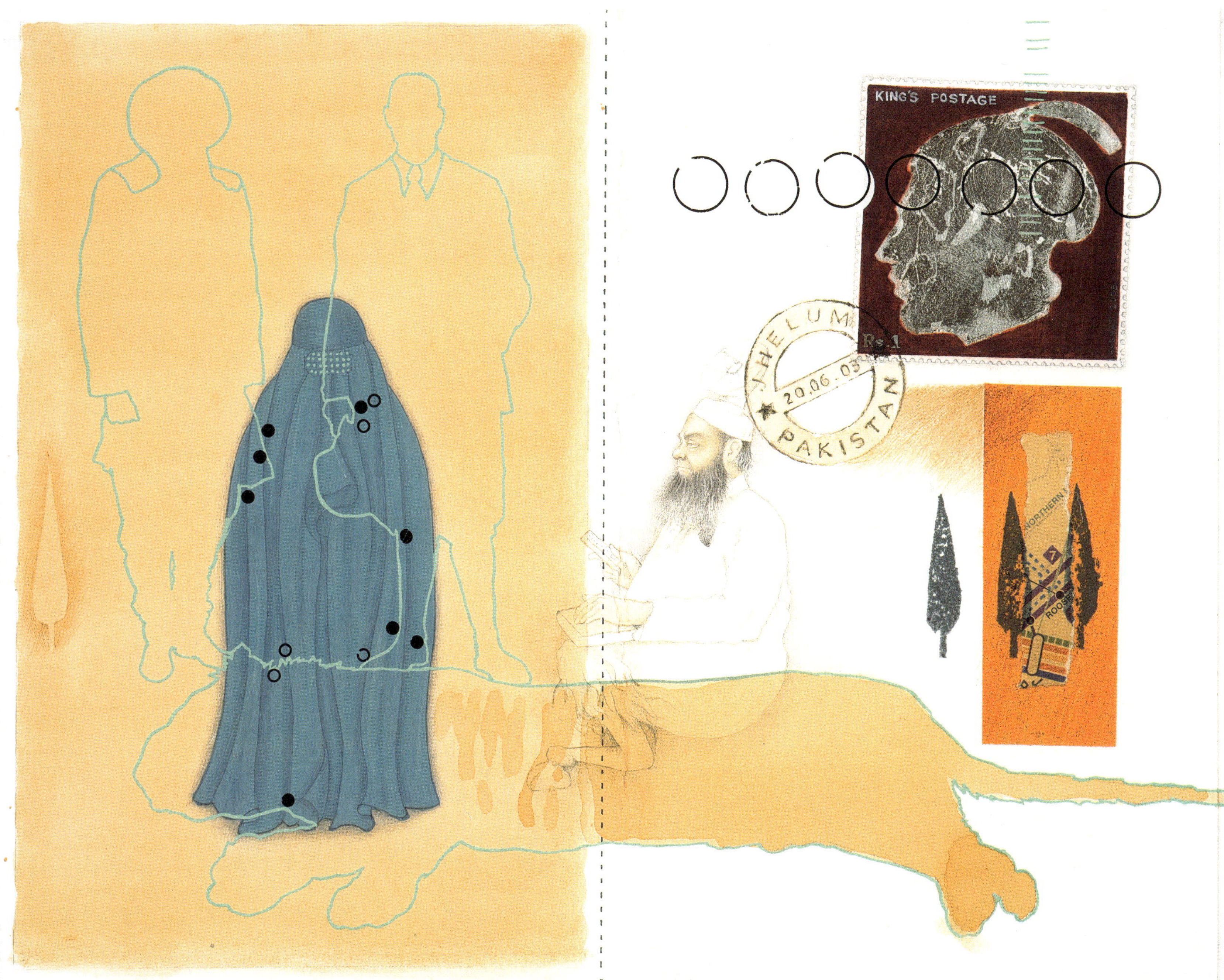
KING'S POSTAGE
Rs.1
JHELUM
20.06.03
PAKISTAN
NORTHERN

1. HASNAT Mehmood
2. Aisha Khalid
3. Nusra Latif
4. [illegible]
5. [illegible]
6. [illegible] 11/11/03

HASNAT MEHMOOD
18-06-2003

Karkhana 5

Aisha Khalid Lahore

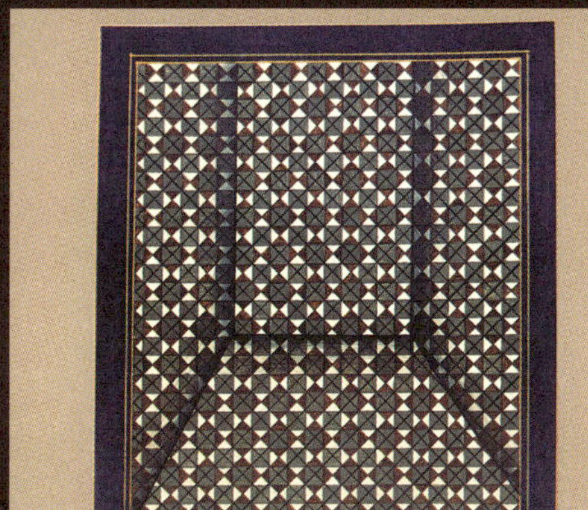

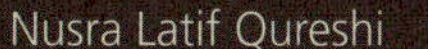

Nusra Latif Qureshi Melbourne...

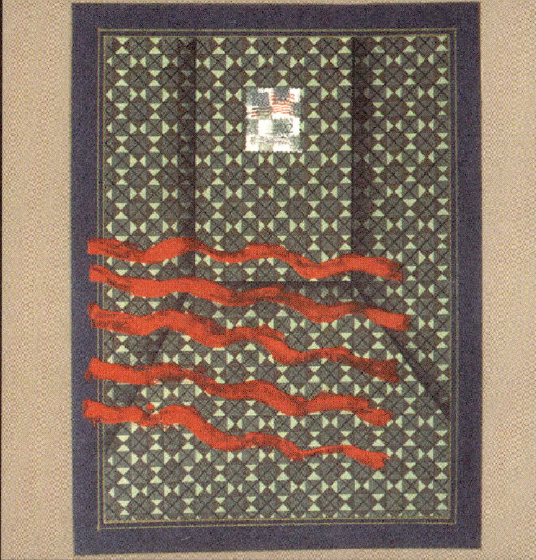

"It was the first painting of the project by another artist that I received. Working on or adding to another artist's work was quite intimidating and exciting at the same time."

Saira Wasim Chicago

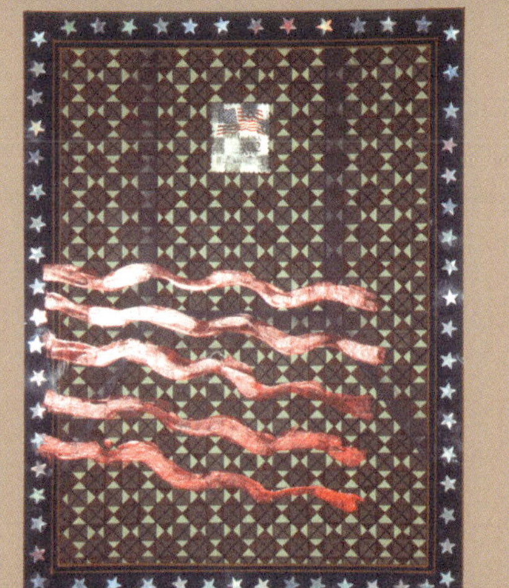

Talha Rathore New York

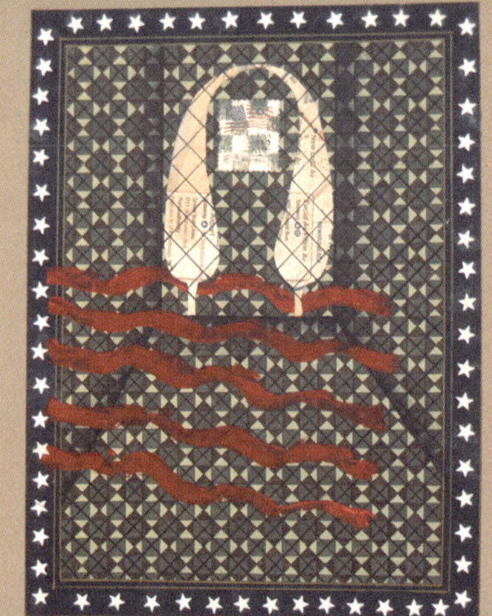

Muhammad Imran Qureshi Lahore

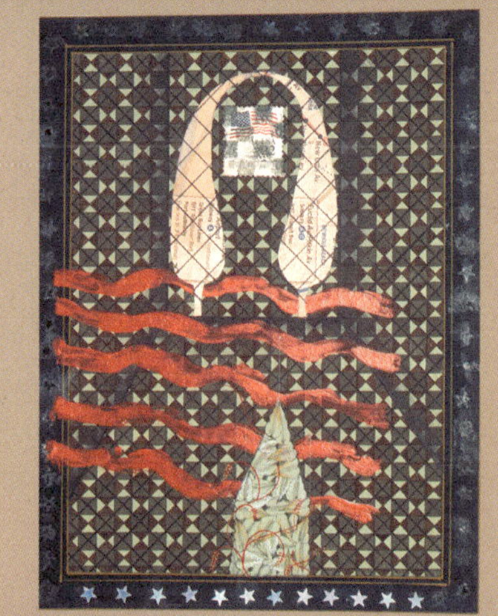

"There was hardly any space for me to step into Aisha's tiled rooms, so I just

"This geometrical tiled room is Aisha's pet image. I decided to make my pet image

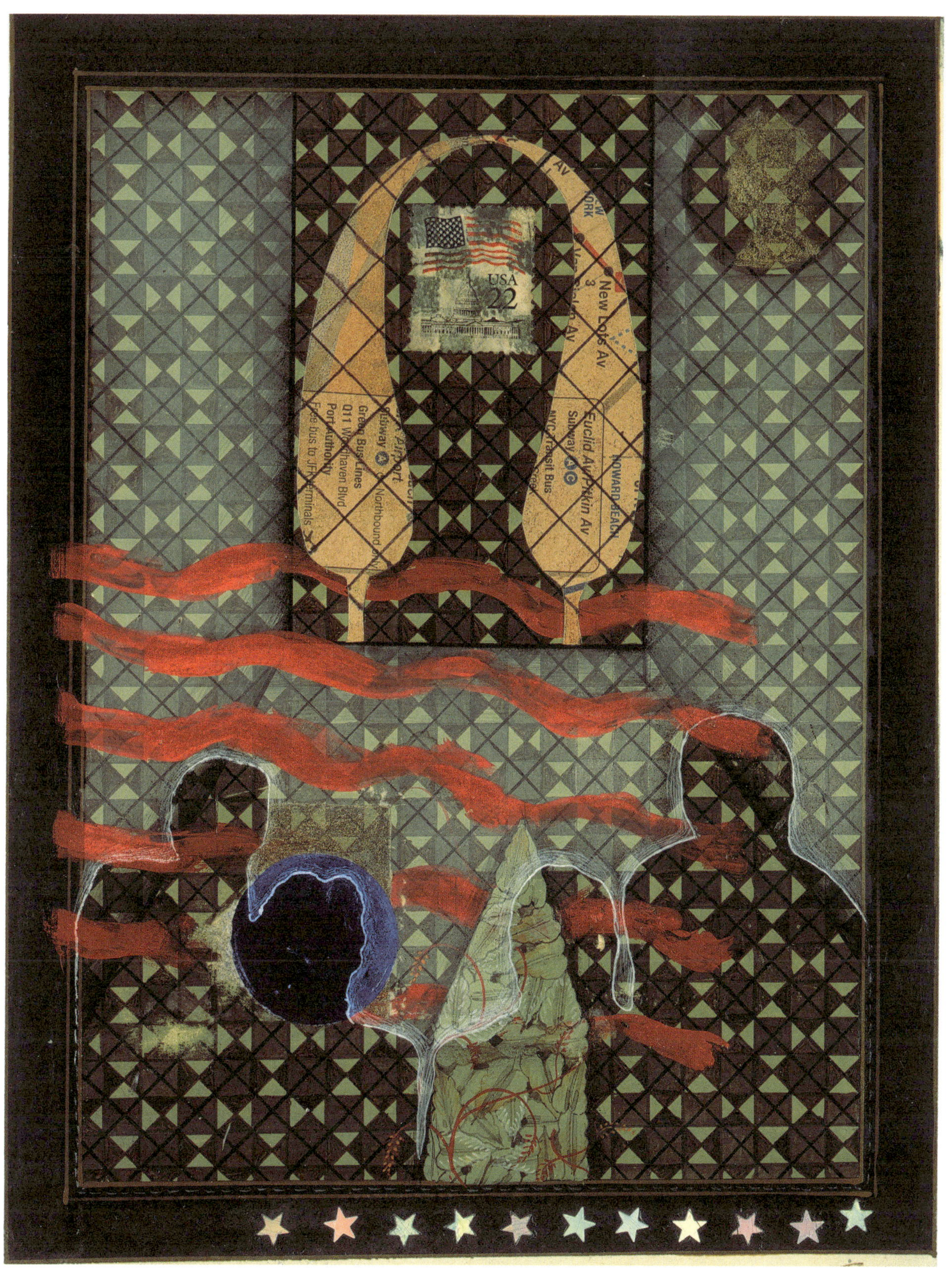
USA
22
New Lots Av
HOWARD BEACH
Northbound

KARKHANA 2003

1- Aisha Khalid

2 - Nusra Latif Qureshi — 24 July – 31 July 2003

3 –

4 –

5 – [illegible]

6 – [illegible]

2003

Karkhana 6

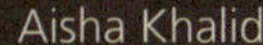

Aisha Khalid Lahore

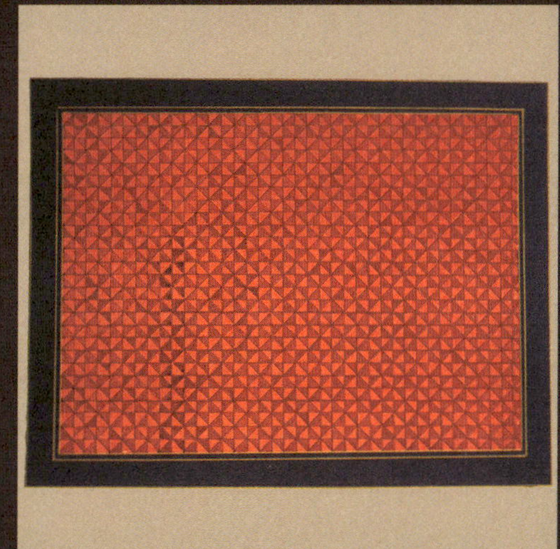

Nusra Latif Qureshi Melbourne

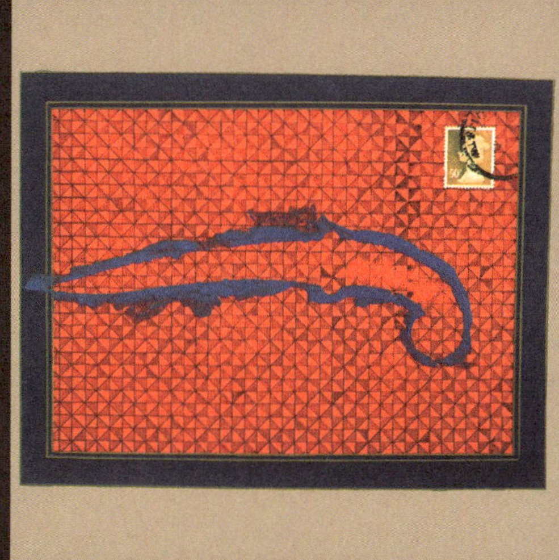

"I have all the usual associations of daggers with violence, sexual assault, abuse, penetration and men—its status as a symbol of honor for men."

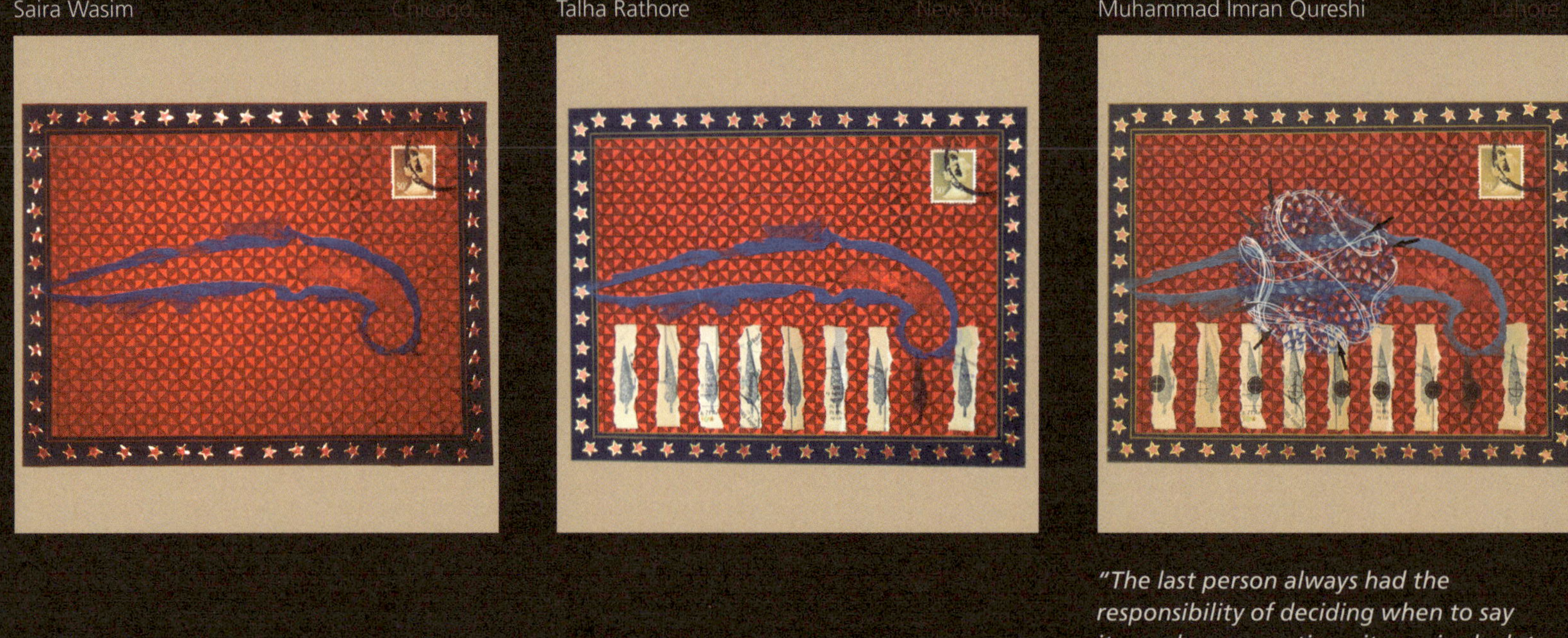

Saira Wasim Chicago

Talha Rathore New York

Muhammad Imran Qureshi Lahore

"The last person always had the responsibility of deciding when to say it was done: sometimes it required a lot more work, sometimes virtually nothing."

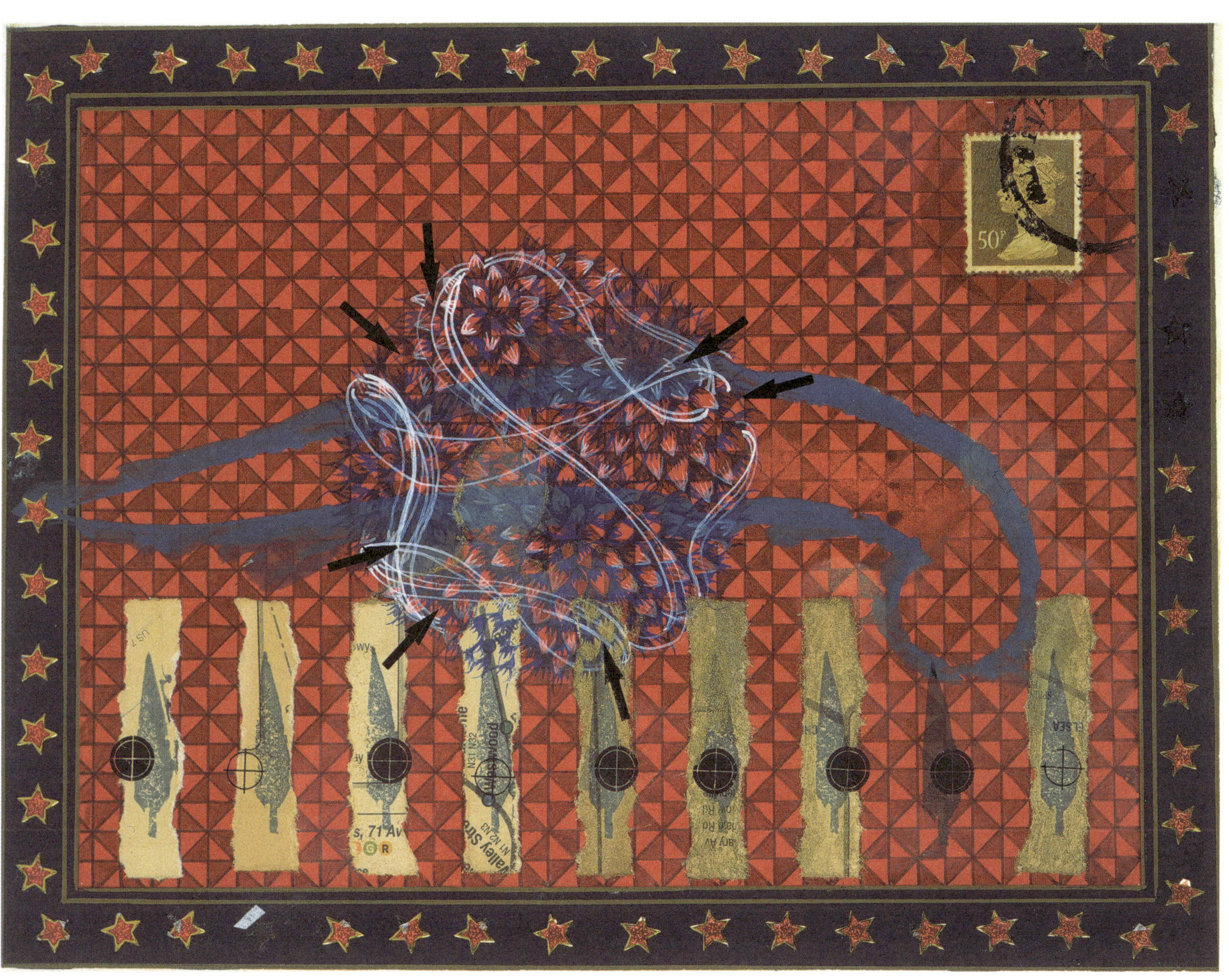
50p
s, 71 Av

KARKHAN 2003

1 — Aisha Khalid [illegible] June 03

2 — Nusra Latif Qureshi [illegible] 24–31 July 2003

3 —

4 — Talha Rathore [illegible]

5 — Imran Qureshi [illegible] 12/10/03

6 — Hasnat Mehmood — [illegible]. 14-OCT. 2003.

[illegible] 26 June 200[illegible]

Karkhana 7

Nusra Latif Qureshi Melbourne

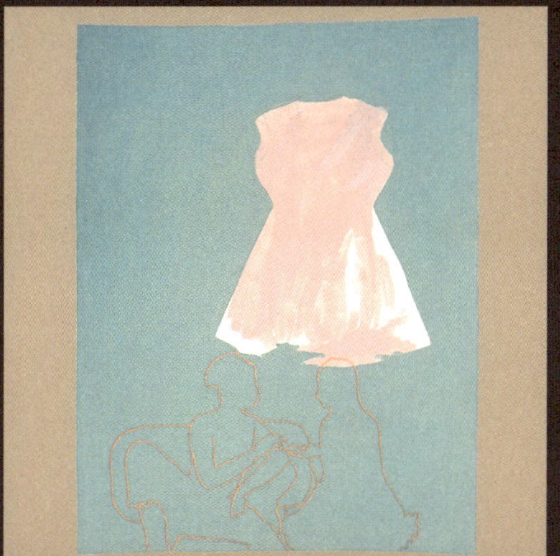

Saira Wasim Chicago

Wasim played with their official status, painting the figure of George Bush on one tunic. S.H

Talha Rathore New York

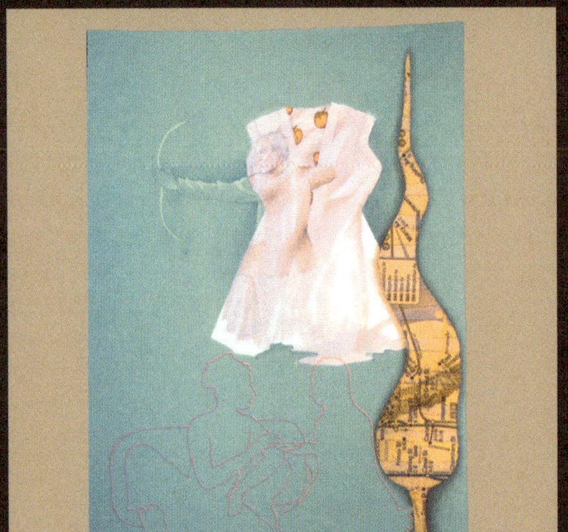

Muhammad Imran Qureshi Lahore

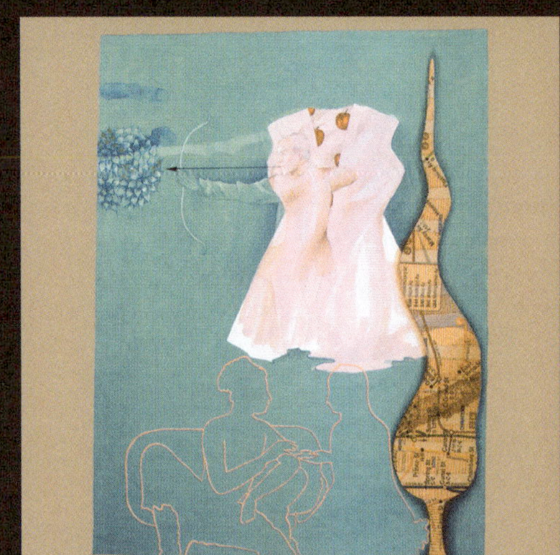

Hasnat Mehmood Jhelum

Mehmood is taken with the physiognomy of the Neanderthal man, and the implications suggested by the dualities of nobility versus the brutish. SH

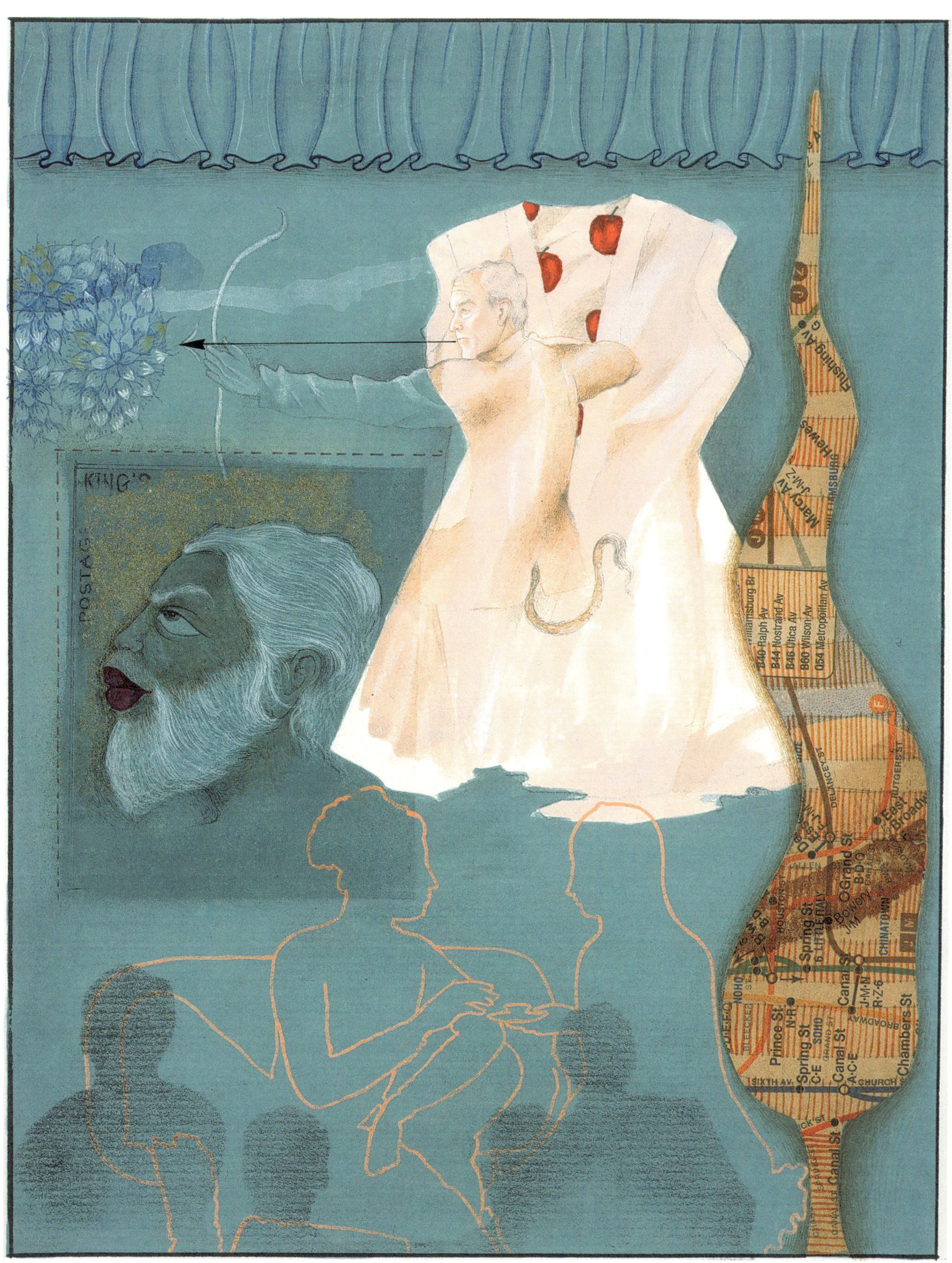
KING'S
Flushing Av
Hewes
Marcy Av
WILLIAMSBURG
Williamsburg Br
B40 Ralph Av
B44 Nostrand Av
B46 Utica Av
B60 Wilson Av
Q54 Metropolitan Av
DELANCEY ST
RUTGERS ST
East Broadway
Grand St
Bowery
CHINATOWN
Spring St
Prince St
SOHO
NOHO
Canal St
Chambers St
SIXTH AV
CHURCH
BROADWAY

14-OCT. 2003

Karkhana 8

Nusra Latif Qureshi — Melbourne

Saira Wasim — Chicago

Talha Rathore New York

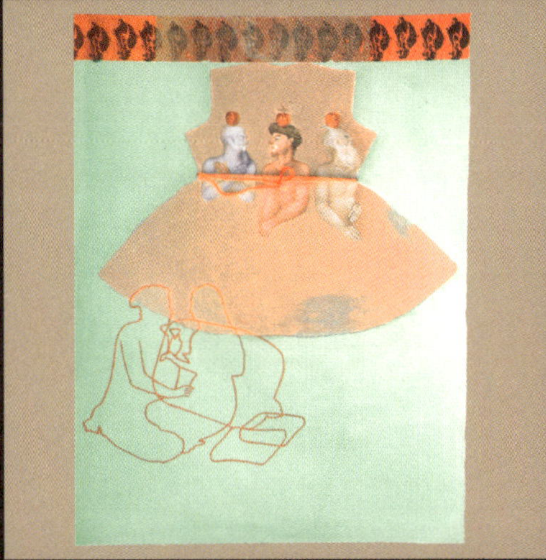

Muhammad Imran Qureshi Lahore

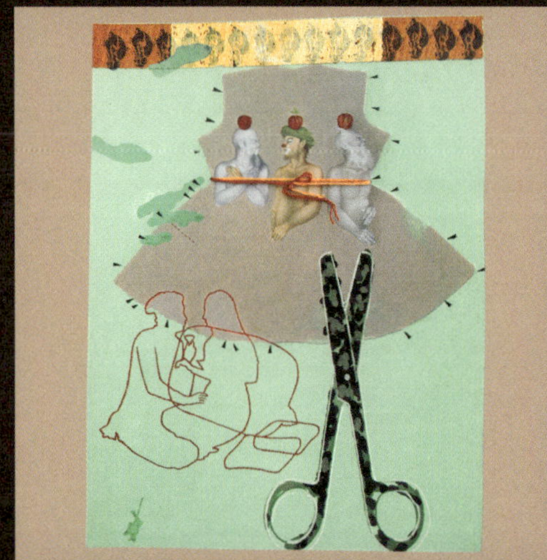

Hasnat Mehmood Jhelum

Alongside the shadowy wedding group, Mehmood could not resist a cheeky addition of a tiny signature scissor, homage to Qureshi's overpowering one. S.H

Aisha Khalid Lahore

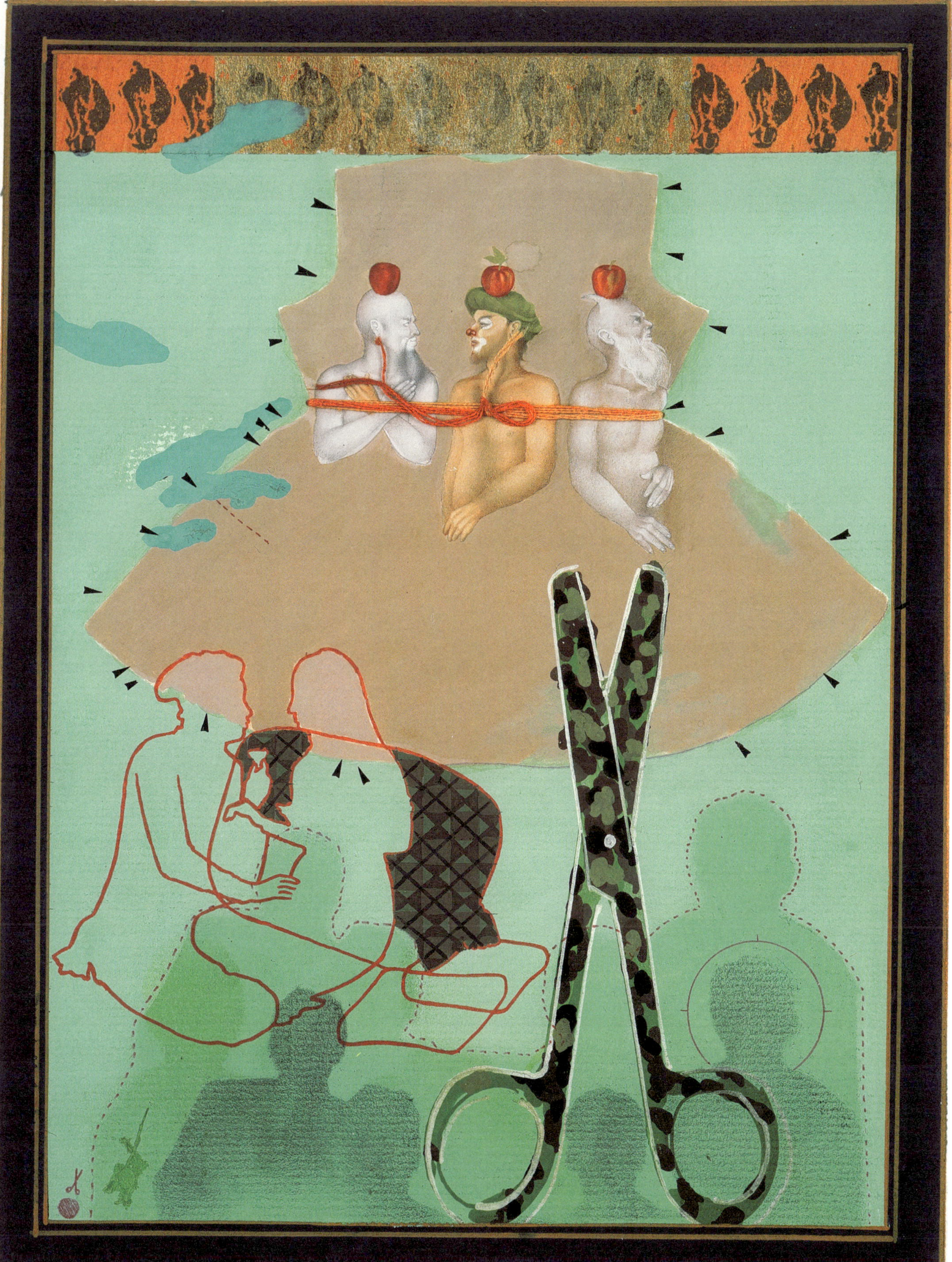

2 -

3 -

4 - [illegible]

5 - Hasnat Mehmood - [illegible] 14-OCT-2003.

[illegible]

Karkhana 9

Saira Wasim Chicago

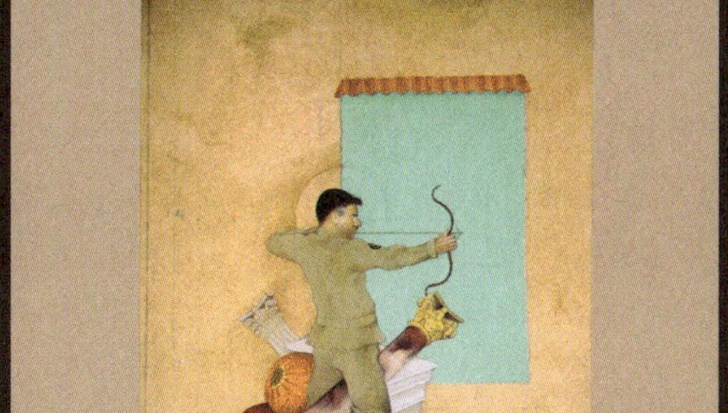

Talha Rathore New York

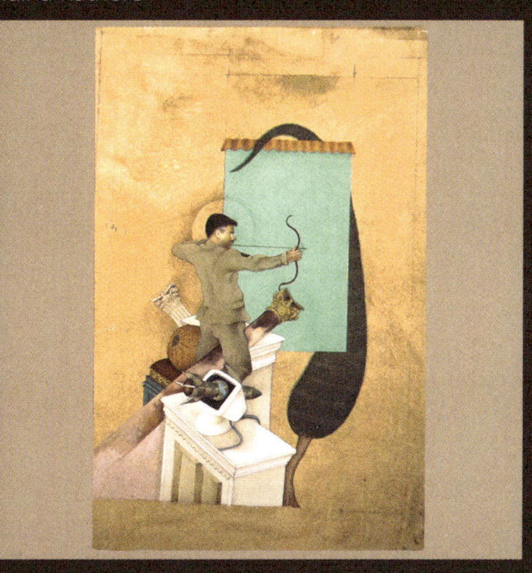

"When I received this from Saira, it already looked like a complete painting."

Muhammad Imran Qureshi Lahore

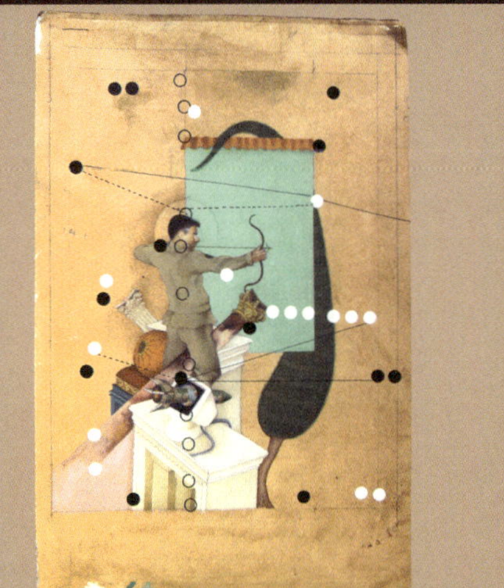

Hasnat Mehmood Jhelum

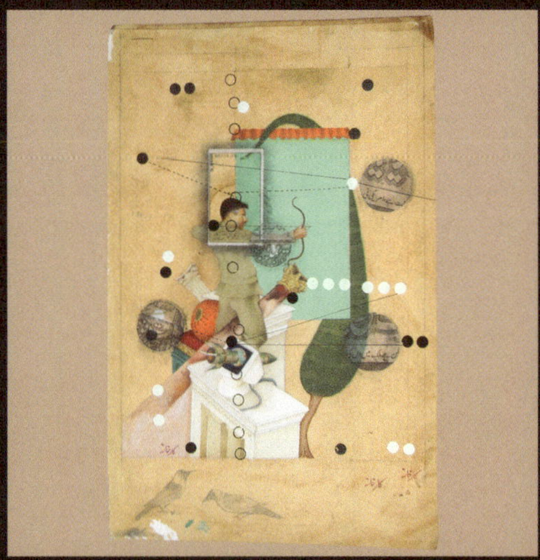

"It doesn't matter whether you understand the words or not, news headings are important only when they are printed, after that they just become words."

Aisha Khalid Lahore

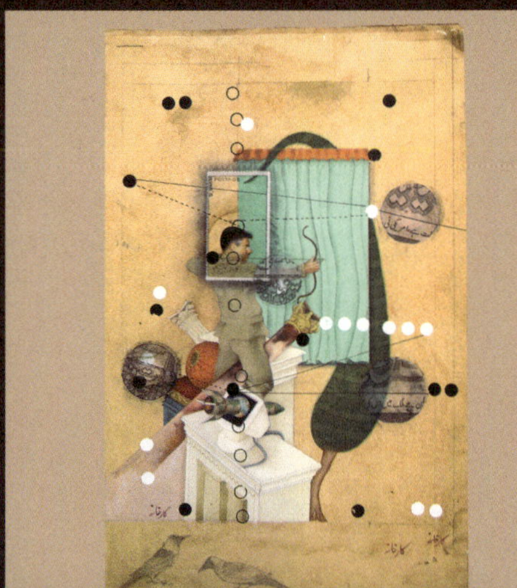

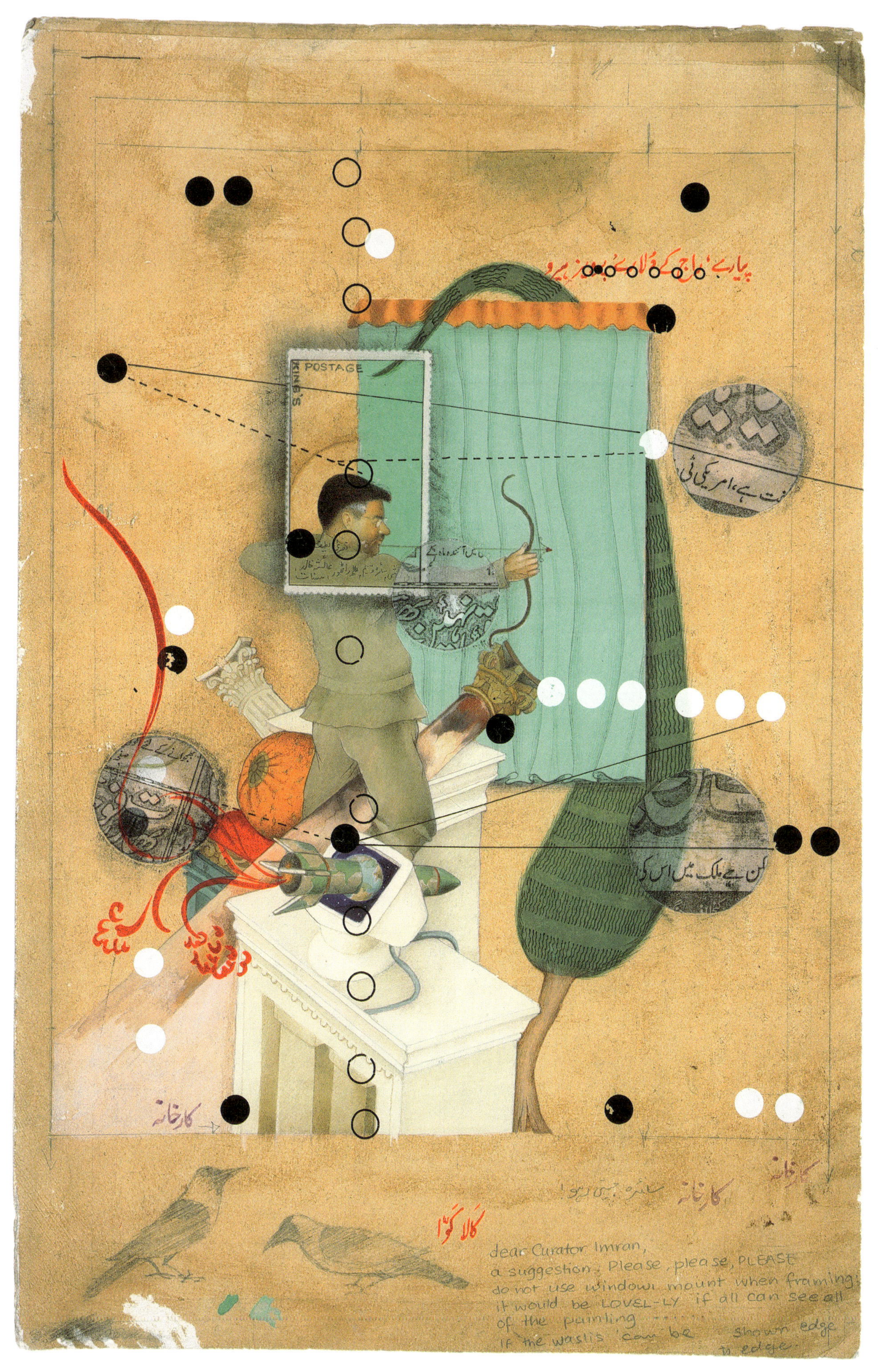
POSTAGE
KING'S
کارخانہ
کالا کوّا
dear Curator Imran,
a suggestion. Please, please, PLEASE
do not use window mount when framing;
it would be LOVEL-LY if all can see all
of the painting
if the waslis can be shown edge to edge.

(1) عمل
سائرہ وسیم جون ۲۰۰۳

(2) عمل: طلحہ راٹھور جولائی ۲۰۰۳

(3)

(4) OCT. 2003.

(5) oct. 2003

Saira Wasim Chicago...

Talha Rathore New York...

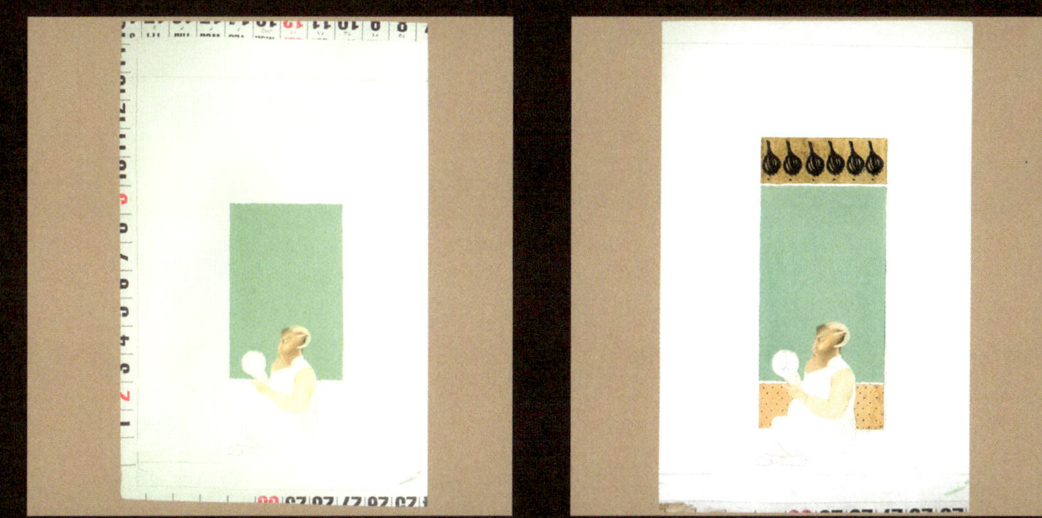

Karkhana 10

Muhammad Imran Qureshi Lahore

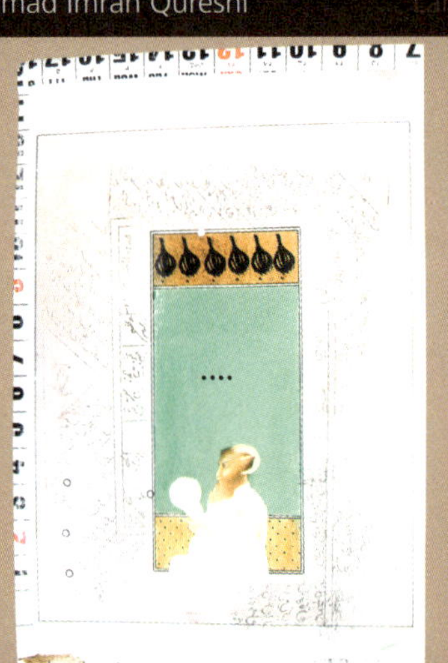

Hasnat Mehmood Jhelum

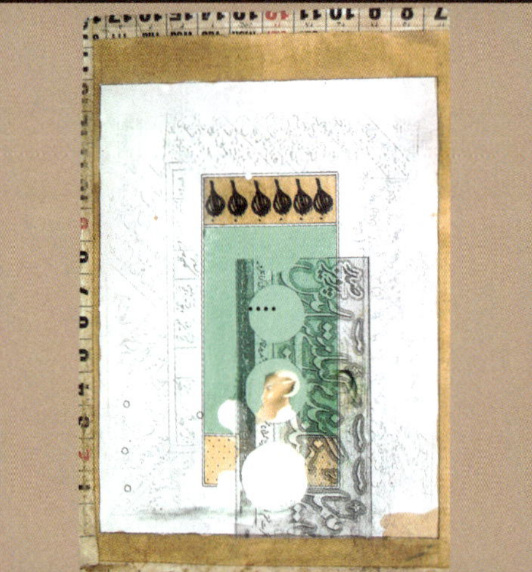

Aisha Khalid Lahore

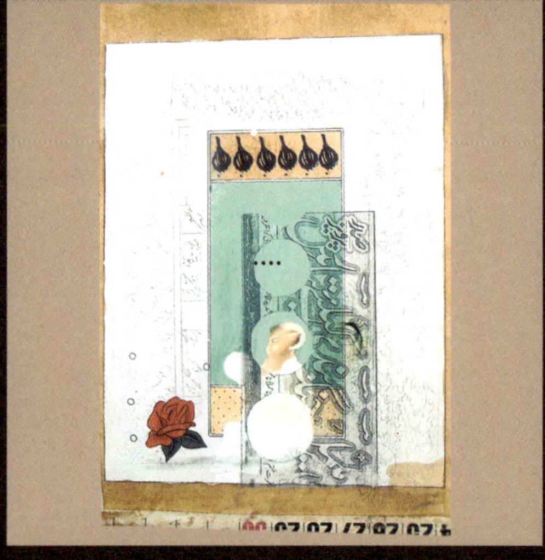

"I hated it because of the animal-like figure. At first I could not bear to work on it, but then I decided to paint something which would counteract how I was feeling."

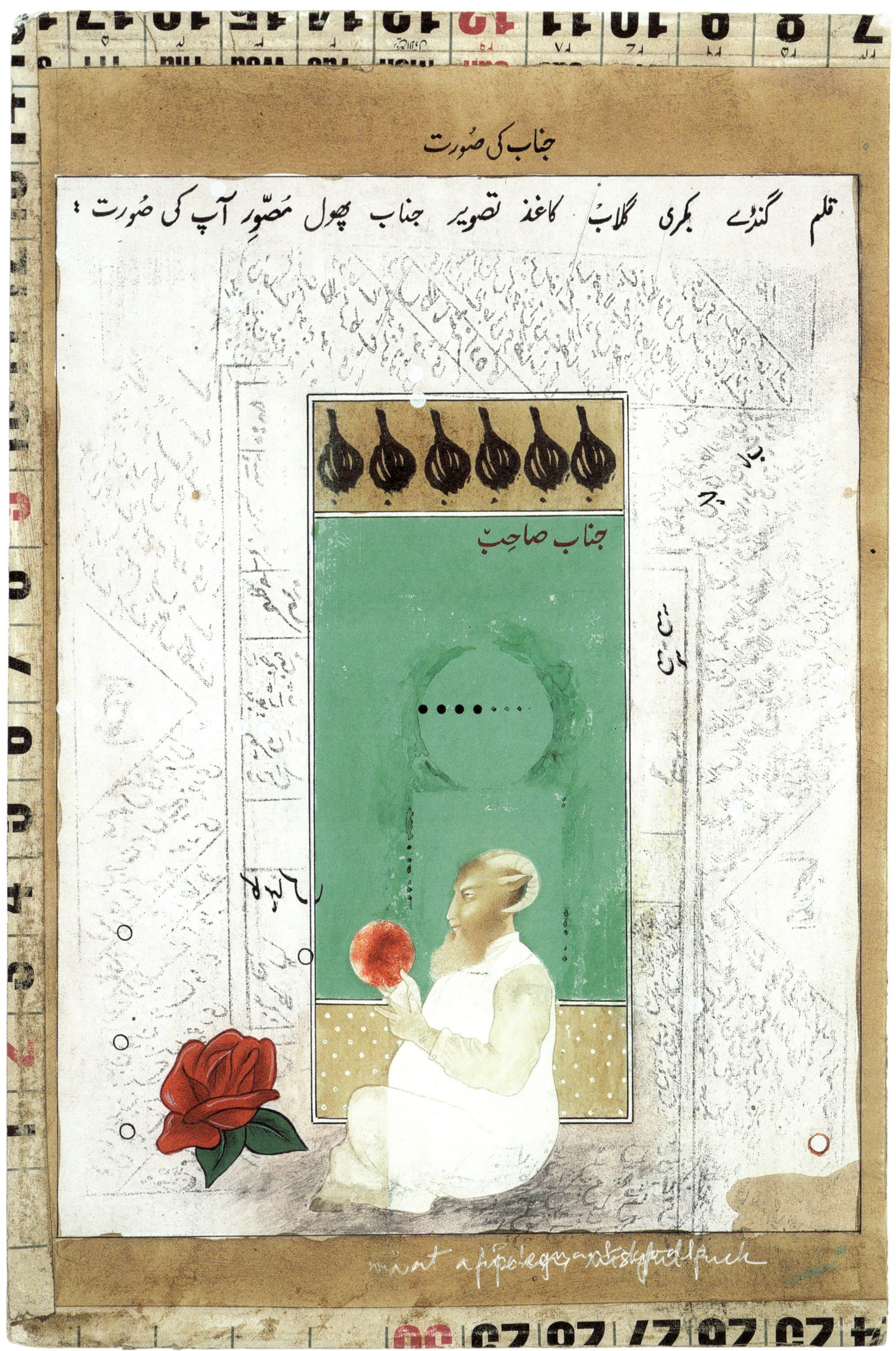
جناب کی صُورت
قلم گنڈے بکری گلاب کاغذ تصویر جناب پھول مُصوّرِ آپ کی صُورت
جناب صاحِبؒ

دل من مسافر من

Amean Qureshi
Sept: 2003

oct. 2003.

Yushin Khalid
oct. 03

Nusra Latif Qureshi
Finished 23 Oct 2003
Nusra Latif

Karkhana 11

Talha Rathore New York

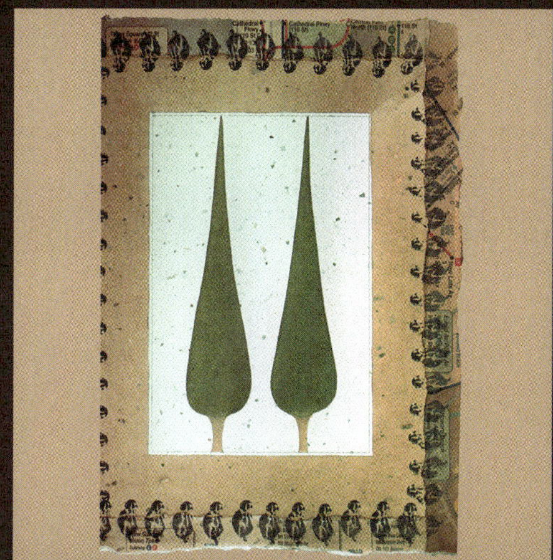

Muhammad Imran Qureshi Lahore

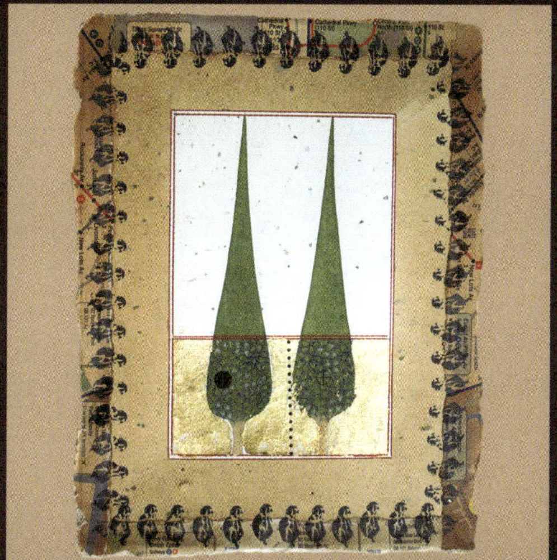

"The targets are Letraset transfers depicting one of the central themes of my own work—life and its destruction."

Hasnat Mehmood Jhelum

Aisha Khalid Lahore

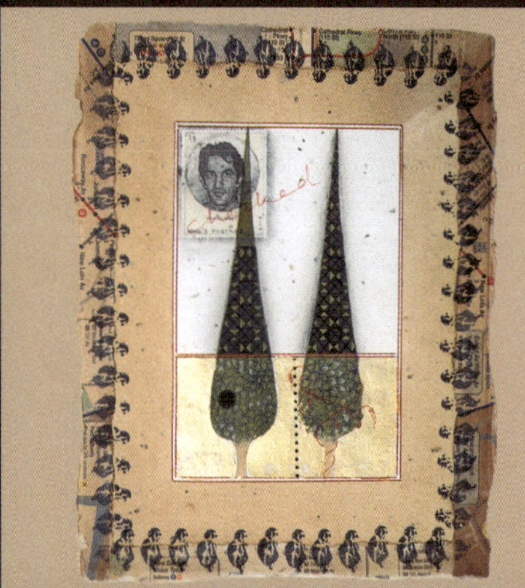

Nusra Latif Qureshi Melbourne

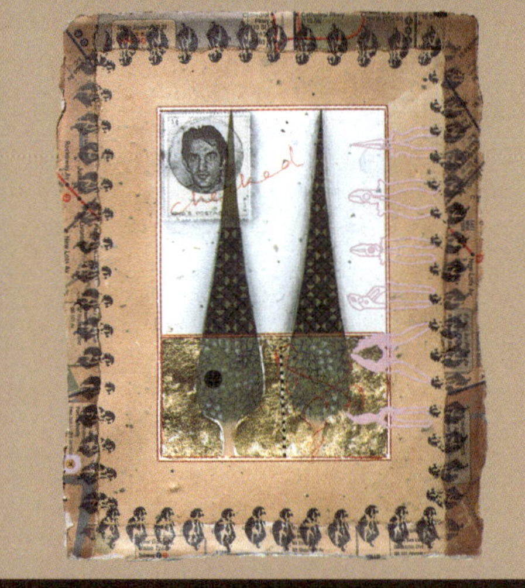

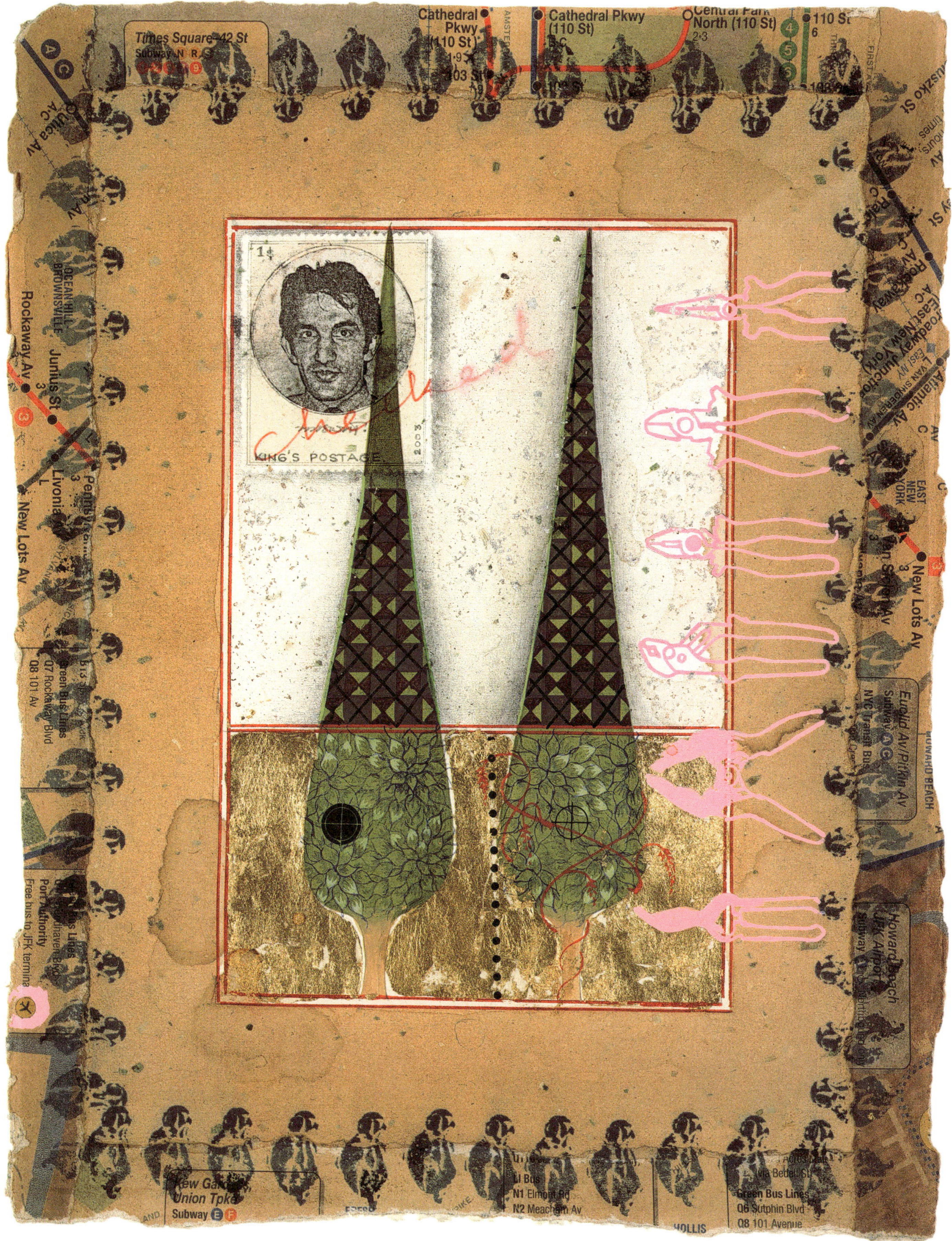

1. Talha
2. Iman Qureshi
   Sept. 2003
3. [illegible]
4. Fishat Khalid. oct. 2003
5. [illegible] Latif Qureshi [illegible]
6. Saira Wasim [illegible] recevied 28th.
   finished. 29th. oct.

Karkhana 12

Talha Rathore New York

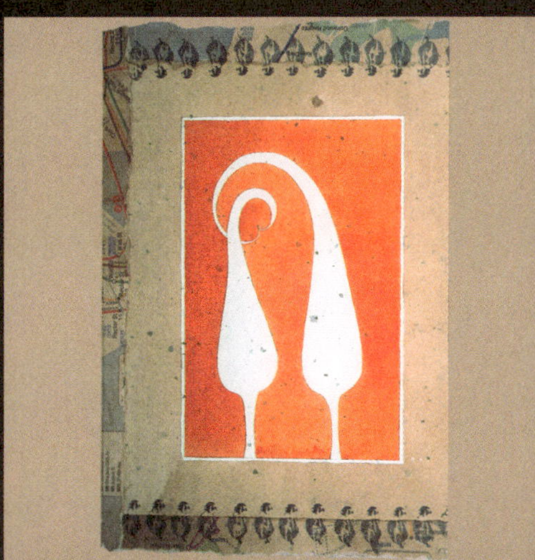

Muhammad Imran Qureshi Lahore

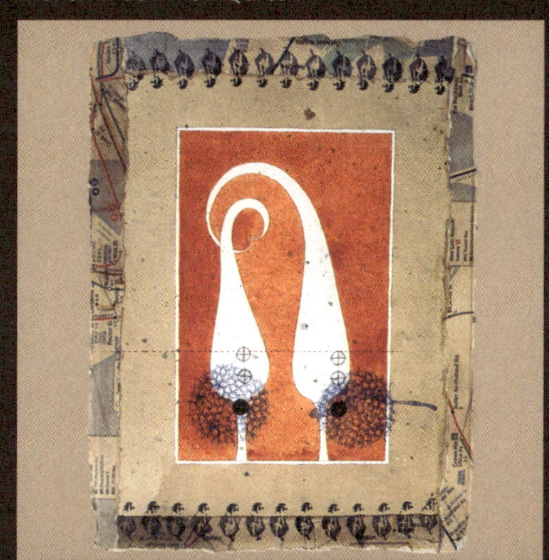

Hasnat Mehmood Jhelum

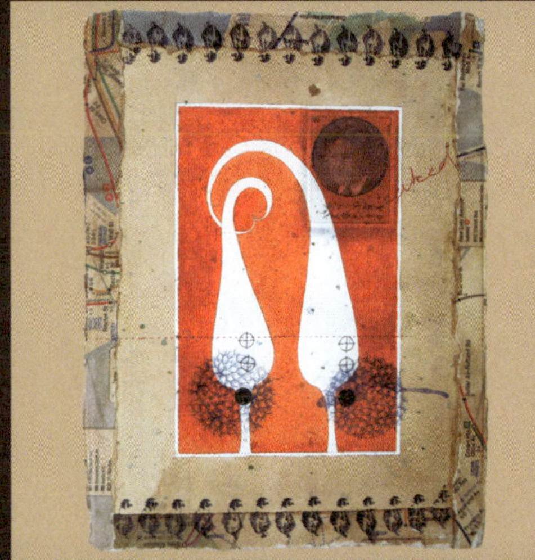

"Rulers are mostly the same, however different their appearance. I work with the idea of a generic ruler rather than one particular leader from history or the contemporary moment."

Aisha Khalid Lahore

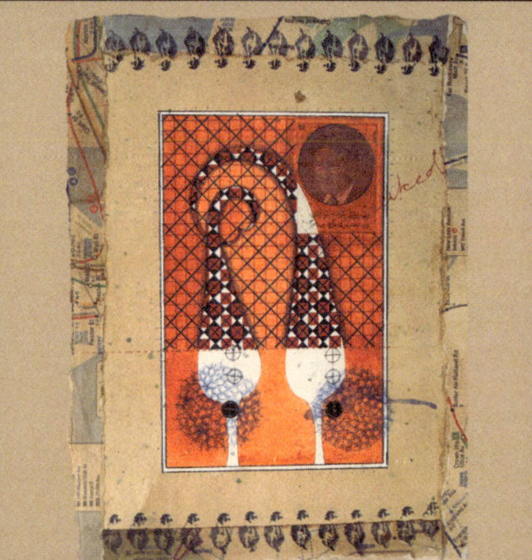

Nusra Latif Qureshi Melbourne

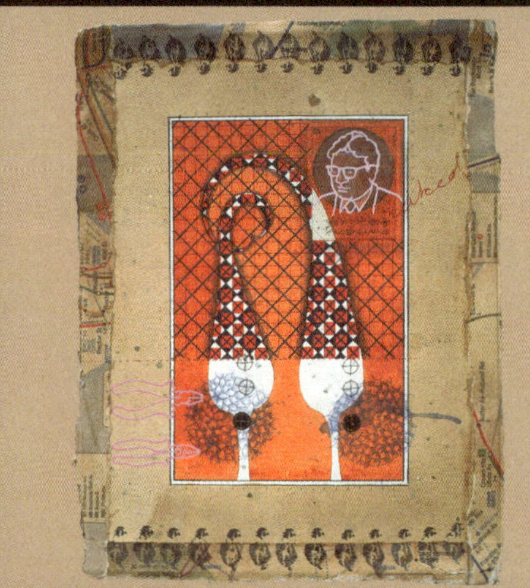

"I wanted to show how these mullahs have hijacked Islam for their own political reasons. While the goat's feet show them to be mostly illiterate, they still wield enormous influence."

Saira Wasim Chicago

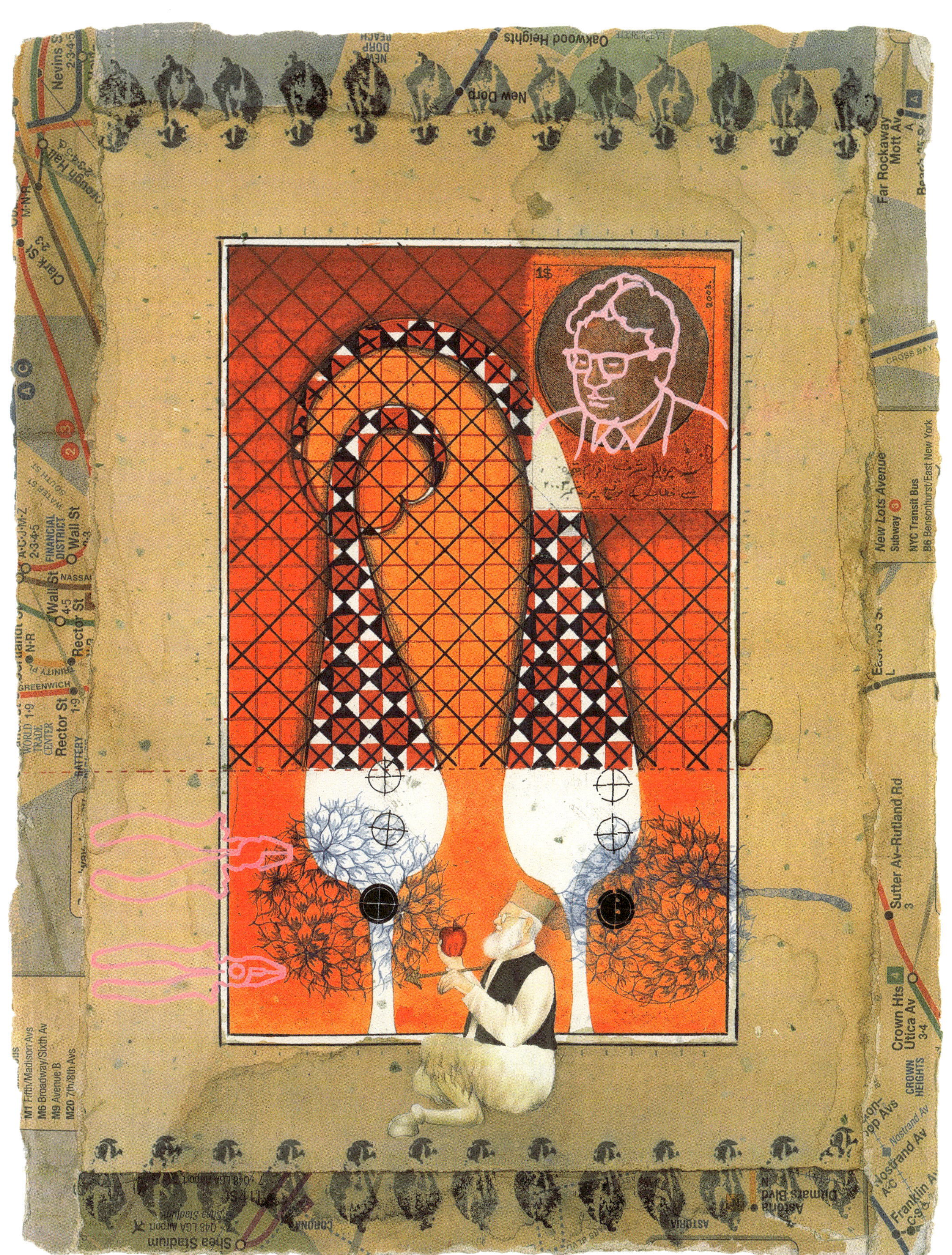

Oakwood Heights
New Dorp
Nevins St
Borough Hall
Clark St
Far Rockaway
Mott Av
1$
2003
New Lots Avenue
Subway
NYC Transit Bus
B6 Bensonhurst/East New York
FINANCIAL DISTRICT
Wall St
NASSAU
Rector St
GREENWICH
WORLD TRADE CENTER
BATTERY
Sutter Av-Rutland Rd
Crown Hts
Utica Av
CROWN HEIGHTS
M1 Fifth/Madison Avs
M6 Broadway/Sixth Av
M9 Avenue B
M20 7th/8th Avs
Nostrand Av
Franklin Av
Astoria
Ditmars Blvd
ASTORIA
CORONA
Shea Stadium

(1) Talha

(2) Imran Qureshi
Sept. 2003

(3) [illegible] oct. 2003

(4) Yasser Khalid oct. 2003

(5) [illegible]

(6)

(1) عمل: طلحه [illegible]

Artists' Biographies

Details of the works reproduced in this section are given on pages 109-110

Aisha Khalid

Born in Faisalabad, Pakistan, 1972. Lives in Lahore

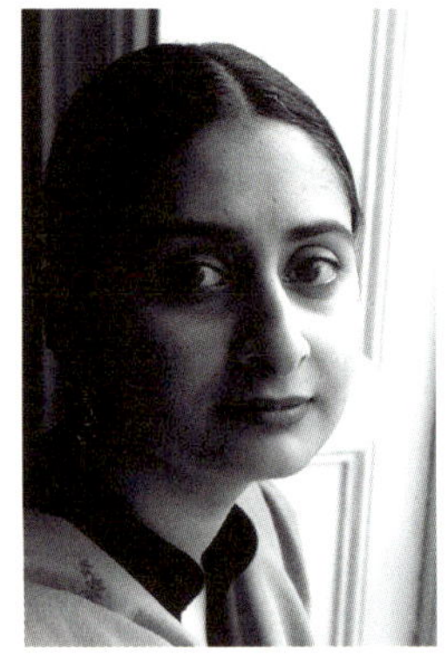

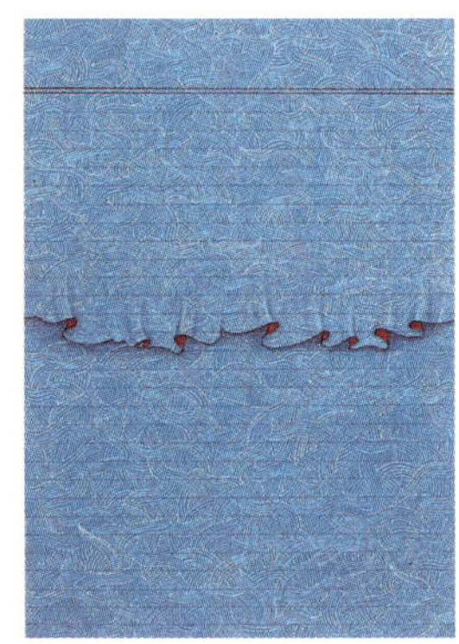

Education

2001-02 Work period at Rijksakademie, Amsterdam, Netherlands

1997 BFA, National College of Arts, Lahore

Solo exhibitions

2004 Corvi-Mora, London

2003 ***Conversation***, Canvas Art Gallery, Karachi, Pakistan

Video installation & other work, Rohtas 2, Lahore

2000 SimSim Gallery, Lahore

Selected group exhibitions

2005 ***Re-inventing Narratives***, Le Galerie Mohamed el Fassi, Rabat, Morocco

Ritu: A Gathering of Seasons, Anant Art Gallery at Triveni Kala Sangam, New Delhi

2004 ***Contemporary Miniature Paintings from Pakistan***, Fukuoka Asian Art Museum, Fukuoka, Japan

Cover Girl, Ise Cultural Foundation, New York

Along the Axis, Apeejay Media Gallery, New Delhi

2003 ***Honey I Rearranged The Collection***, 1a Kempsford Road, London

Karkhana, Touchstones Art Gallery, Rochdale

Contemporary Miniatures from Pakistan, K3—Project Space, Zurich, Switzerland

Negotiating Borders, Siddhartha Art Gallery, Kathmandu, Nepal

2002 ***The Galleries Show: Contemporary Art in London***, The Royal Academy of Arts, London

Threads, Dreams, Desires, Harris Museum & Art Gallery, Preston, UK

Fukuoka Asian Art Triennale, Japan

2001 Corvi-Mora, London

Open Studios, Rijksakademie, Amsterdam

Admit One Gallery, New York

Manoeuvering Miniatures, IIC Gallery, New Delhi; and Sakshi Gallery, Mumbai, India

2000 ***Pakistan: Another Vision—Fifty Years of Painting and Sculpture from Pakistan***, Victoria Art Gallery, Bath, UK; Centre of Contemporary Art, Glasgow, UK; Huddersfield Art Gallery, UK; Brunei Gallery, London

1999 Off Set Gallery, Islamabad, Pakistan

Chawkandi Art Gallery, Karachi

1998 International Commonwealth Exhibition, National Art Gallery, Kuala Lumpur, Malaysia

1997 ***Miniature Paintings***, Lahore Museum

Selected publications

B.N. Goswamy, "Ritu: A Gathering of Seasons," in ***Ritu: A Gathering of Seasons*** (New Delhi, India: Anant Art Gallery, 2005)

Virginia Whiles, "Contemporary Miniature Paintings from Pakistan," in ***Contemporary Miniature Paintings from Pakistan*** (Fukuoka, Japan: Fukuoka Asian Art Museum, 2004)

Craig Burnett, "Aisha Khalid," ***Guardian*** (London), October 2-8, 2004

Marjorie Husain, "Tulips and Camouflage," ***Dawn*** (Pakistan), March, 16, 2003

Virginia Whiles, "News, Lahore," ***Contemporary***, Issue 50 (2003)

Hammad Nasar, "Fine Art Interview," ***Herald*** (Pakistan), March 2003

Edward Lucie-Smith, ***Art Tomorrow*** (Paris: Terrail, 2002)

Salima Hashmi, ***Unveiling the Visible. Lives and Works of Women Artists of Pakistan*** (Islamabad, Pakistan: Actionaid, 2002)

Quddus Mirza, "Threads, Dreams, Desires," ***Flash Art***, October 2002

Quddus Mirza, "Of Missiles and Shrouds," ***Art India***, Vol. V, Issue II (2001)

Virginia Whiles, "In and Out of Pakistan," ***Third Text***, Autumn (2000)

Niilofur Farrukh, "Coming of Age," ***Newsline*** (Pakistan), November 1999

Hasnat Mehmood

Born in Jhelum, Pakistan, 1978. Lives in Jhelum

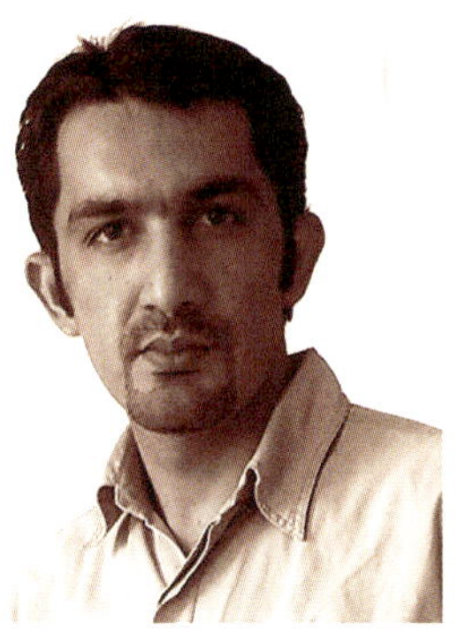

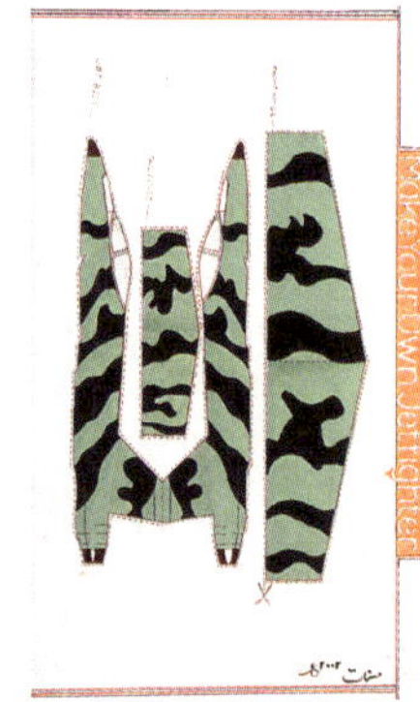

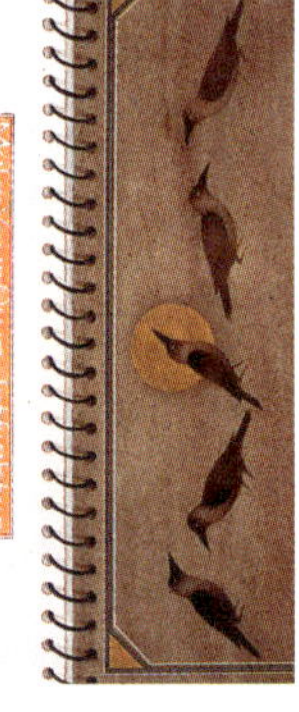

Education

2001 BFA, National College of Arts, Lahore

Selected group exhibitions

2004 ***Contemporary Miniature Paintings from Pakistan,*** Fukuoka Asian Art Museum, Fukuoka, Japan

Transcendent Contemplations, Green Cardamom at Hosains, London

Playing with a Loaded Gun, apexart, New York; and Kunsthalle Fridericianum, Kassel, Germany

2003 ***Contemporary Miniatures from Pakistan***, K3—Project Space, Zurich, Switzerland

Miniatures Pakistanaises, Maison d'Art Contemporain Chaillioux, Fresnes, France

Karkhana, Touchstones Art Gallery, Rochdale, UK

New Voices, Canvas Gallery, Karachi, Pakistan

Around Miniature, Chawkandi Art, Karachi

2002 ***Paintings from Pakistan***, Niavaran Gallery, Tehran, Iran

Ejaz Gallery, Lahore

Translations, Rohtas 2 Gallery, Lahore

Selected publications

Virginia Whiles, "Contemporary Miniature Paintings from Pakistan," in ***Contemporary Miniature Paintings from Pakistan*** (Fukuoka, Japan: Fukuoka Asian Art Museum, 2004)

Laura Smith-Spark "Blair confronts art close to home," ***BBC News Online***, October 2004, http://news.bbc.co.uk/1/hi/entertainment/arts/3708382.stm

Atteqa Ali, "Playing with a Loaded Gun—Contemporary Art in Pakistan," in ***Playing with a Loaded Gun*** (Kassel, Germany: Kunsthalle Fridericianum, 2004)

Hammad Nasar, "Rochdale Remembrance," ***Herald*** (Pakistan), February 2004

Atteqa Ali, ***Impassioned Control: Paintings by Hasnat Mehmood," in Transcendent Contemplations***, eds., Hammad Nasar and Anita Dawood-Nasar (London: Green Cardamom, 2004)

Virginia Whiles, "Miniatures Pakistanaises," in ***Miniatures Pakistanaises: Journal d' Exposition*** (Fresnes, France: Maison d'Art Contemporain Chaillioux, 2003)

Quddus Mirza, "White is Right," ***News*** (Pakistan), June 2002

Saira Dar, "Translations," ***Dawn*** (Pakistan), June 2002

Muhammad Imran Qureshi

Born in Hyderabad, Pakistan, 1972. Lives in Lahore

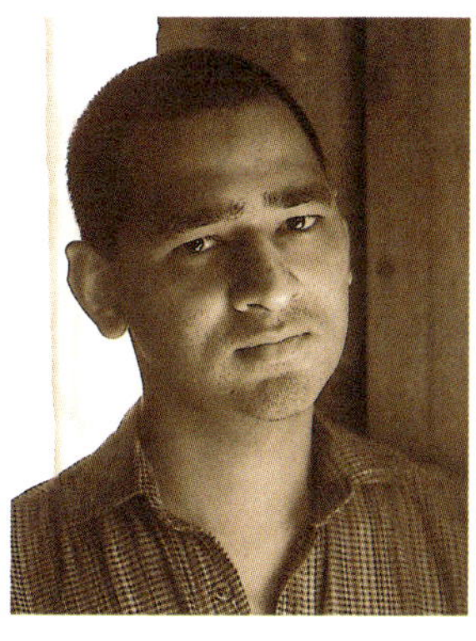

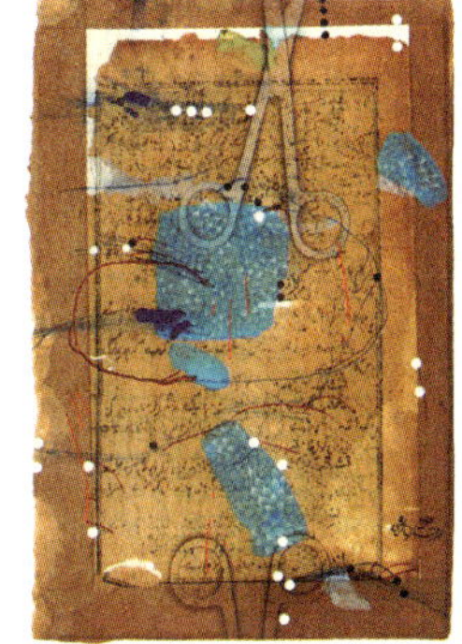

Education

1993 BFA, National College of Arts, Lahore

Solo exhibitions

2004 Corvi-Mora, London

2002 Chawkandi Art Gallery, Karachi, Pakistan

1996 Rohtas Gallery, Islamabad, Pakistan

Selected group exhibitions

2005 ***Re-inventing Narratives***, Le Galerie Mohamed el Fassi, Rabat, Morocco

Beyond Borders: Art of Pakistan, National Gallery of Modern Art, Mumbai, India

Ritu: A Gathering of Seasons, Anant Art Gallery at Triveni Kala Sangam, New Delhi

2004 ***Expander,*** Royal Academy of Arts at Burlington Gardens, London

Contemporary Miniature Paintings from Pakistan, Fukuoka Asian Art Museum, Fukuoka, Japan

Playing with a Loaded Gun, apexart, New York; and Kunsthalle Fridericianum, Kassel, Germany

The Drawn Page, The Aldrich Contemporary Art Museum, Ridgefield, Connecticut

2003 ***The American Effect***, Whitney Museum of American Art, New York

Contemporary Miniatures from Pakistan, K3 – Project Space, Zurich, Switzerland

Karkhana, Touchstones Art Gallery, Rochdale, UK

Negotiating Borders, Siddhartha Art Gallery, Kathmandu, Nepal

2002 ***The Galleries Show: Contemporary Art in London***, The Royal Academy of Arts, London

Threads, Dreams, Desires, Harris Museum & Art Gallery, Preston, UK

2001 Corvi-Mora, London

Ivan Dougherty Gallery, Sydney, Australia

Admit One Gallery, New York

Bluecoat Gallery, Liverpool, UK

Manoeuvering Miniatures, IIC Gallery, New Delhi and Sakshi Gallery, Mumbai

2000 ***Pakistan: Another Vision—Fifty years of painting and sculpture from Pakistan***, Victoria Art Gallery, Bath, UK; Centre of Contemporary Art, Glasgow, UK; Huddersfield Art Gallery, UK; Brunei Gallery, London

1999 ***Asia Pacific Triennial of Contemporary Art***, Brisbane, Australia

1998 ***International Commonwealth Exhibition***, National Art Gallery, Kuala Lumpur, Malaysia

1997 ***Asian Art Biennale***, Shilpakala Academy, Dhaka, Bangladesh

Draped & Shaped, Cartwright Hall, Bradford, UK

Selected publications

Neil Mulholland, "Expander," ***Frieze***, January/February 2005

B.N. Goswamy, "Ritu: A Gathering of Seasons," in ***Ritu: A Gathering of Seasons*** (New Delhi, India: Anant Art Gallery, 2005)

Atteqa Ali, "Playing with a Loaded Gun—Contemporary Art in Pakistan," in ***Playing with a Loaded Gun*** (Kassel, Germany: Kunsthalle Fridericianum, 2004)

Hammad Nasar, "Miniature Makeover," ***Herald*** (Pakistan), April 2004

Lawrence Rinder, "The American Effect," in ***The American Effect***, ed. L. Rinder (New York: Whitney ***Museum of American Art***, 2003)

Holland Cotter, "Playing With a Loaded Gun," ***New York Times***, September 26, 2003

Quddus Mirza, "Imran Qureshi," ***Flash Art***, January-February 2003

Edward Lucie-Smith, ***Art Tomorrow*** (Paris: Terrail, 2002)

Virginia Whiles, "Imran Qureshi," ***Art Asia Pacific***, Issue 33 (2002)

Robert Clark, "Mania, McCarthy and Qureshi," ***Guardian*** (London) June 23-29, 2001

Niilofur Farrukh, "Coming of Age," ***Newsline*** (Pakistan), November 1999

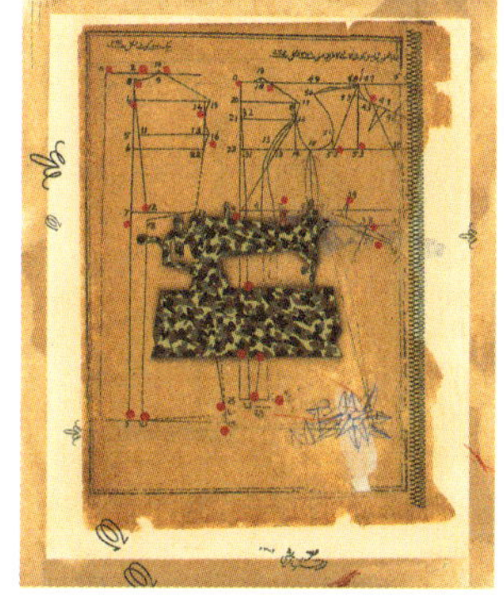

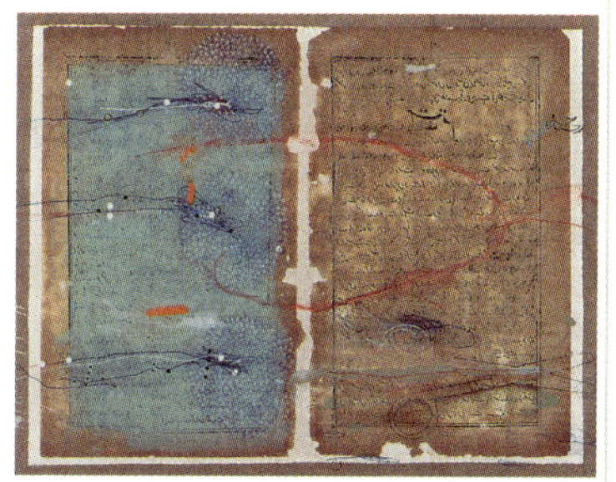

Nusra Latif Qureshi

Born in Lahore, 1973. Lives in Melbourne, Australia

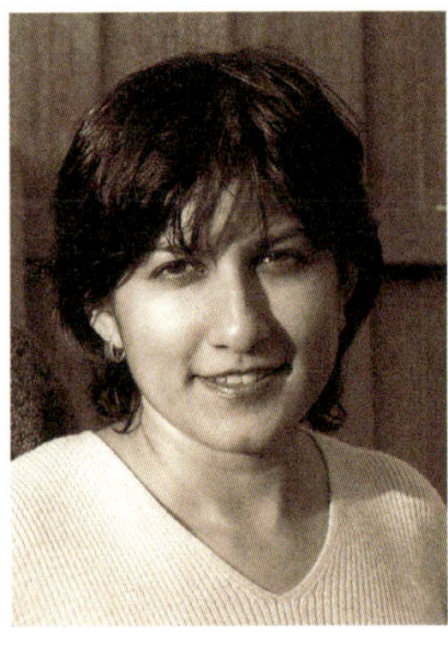

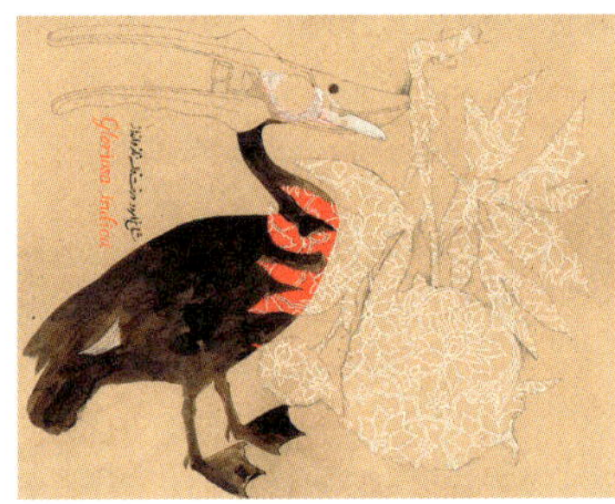

Education

2002 MFA, Victorian College of the Arts, University of Melbourne

1995 BFA, National College of Arts, Lahore

Solo exhibitions

2004 ***Exotic Bodies***, Counihan Gallery in Brunswick, Melbourne

The Way I Remember Them: Paintings by Nusra Latif Qureshi, Smith College Museum of Art, Northampton, Massachusetts

2002 ***Altered Perceptions***, Artholes Gallery, Melbourne

Postcolonial Representations, Joshua McClelland Print Room, Melbourne

1999 Rohtas Gallery, Islamabad, Pakistan

Selected group exhibitions

2005 ***RAPT: Austral-Asia Zero Five***, Sherman Galleries, Sydney, Australia

Ritu: A Gathering of Seasons, Anant Art Gallery at Triveni Kala Sangam, New Delhi

2004 ***Contemporary Miniature Paintings from Pakistan,*** Fukuoka Asian Art Museum, Fukuoka, Japan

Miniatures, Queensland Art Gallery, Brisbane, Australia

2003 The 18th Street Arts Complex, Santa Monica, California

Contemporary Miniatures: India and Pakistan, The Fine Art Resource, Berlin

Karkhana, Touchstones Art Gallery, Rochdale, UK

Contemporary Miniatures from Pakistan, K3—Project Space, Zurich, Switzerland

Negotiating Borders, Siddhartha Art Gallery, Kathmandu, Nepal

2002 Betty Rymer Gallery, Chicago

Canvas Art Gallery, Karachi, Pakistan

Women's Salon, Counihan Gallery in Brunswick, Melbourne

2001 Dickerson Gallery, Melbourne

Manoeuvering Miniatures, IIC Gallery, New Delhi and Sakshi Gallery, Mumbai, India

2000 ***Pakistan: Another Vision—Fifty Years of Painting and Sculpture from Pakistan***, Victoria Art Gallery, Bath, UK; Centre of Contemporary Art, Glasgow, UK; Huddersfield Art Gallery, UK; Brunei Gallery, London

Didrichsen Art Museum, Helsinki, Finland

1999 Rohtas Gallery, Islamabad

1997 ***Contemporary Miniature Painting***, Lahore Museum

Chawkandi Art Gallery, Karachi

1996 ***Fifty Years of Pakistan***, Alhamra Art Galleries, Lahore

Selected publications

B.N. Goswamy, "Ritu: A Gathering of Seasons," in ***Ritu: A Gathering of Seasons*** (New Delhi, India: Anant Art Gallery, 2005)

Virginia Whiles, "Contemporary Miniature Paintings from Pakistan," in ***Contemporary Miniature Paintings from Pakistan*** (Fukuoka, Japan: Fukuoka Asian Art Museum, 2004)

Robert Nelson, "Subverting Love's Sweet Nothings,***" Age*** (Australia), July 7, 2004

Anna Sloan, "The Way I Remember Them: Paintings by Nusra Latif Qureshi," in ***The Way I Remember Them: Paintings by Nusra Latif Qureshi*** (Northampton, Massachusetts: Smith College Museum of Art, 2004)

Hammad Nasar, "Rochdale Remembrance," ***Herald*** (Pakistan), February 2004

Marcella Sirhandi, "Contemporary Indian Miniature Painting," ***Arts of Asia***, May-June 2003

Virginia Whiles, "Manoeuvering Miniatures," ***Manoeuvering Miniatures. Contemporary Art from Pakistan*** (New Delhi, India: Khoj International Arts Centre, 2001)

Quddus Mirza, "The Court Comes to Common," ***News on Sunday*** (Pakistan), May 2, 1999

Talha Rathore

Born in Lahore, 1969. Lives in New York

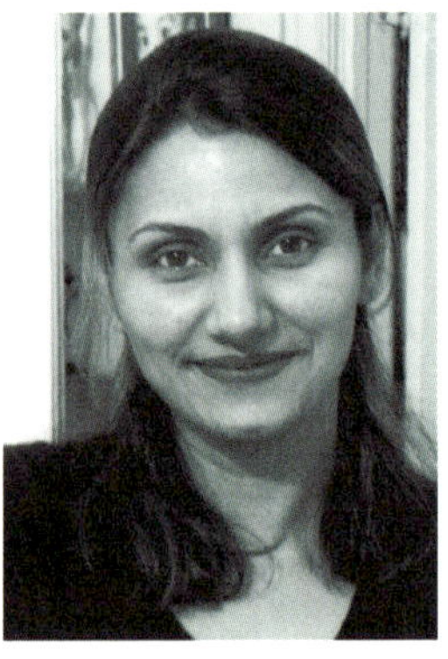

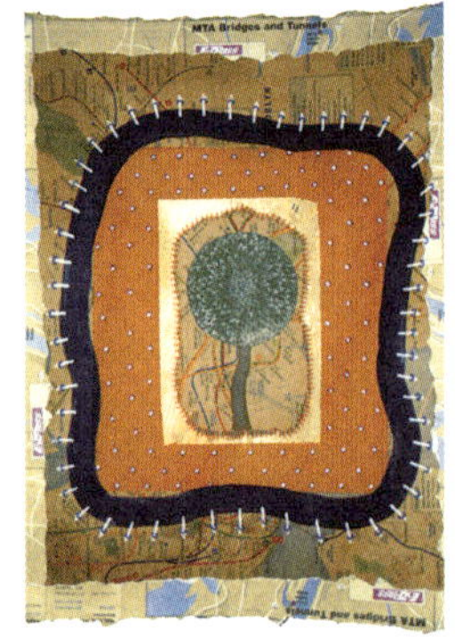

Education

1995 BFA, National College of Arts, Lahore, 1995

Solo exhibitions

2003 ***Between Worlds***, BosePacia, New York

1998 Gallery Espace, New Delhi

Rohtas Gallery, Islamabad, Pakistan

1996 Alliance Française Gallery, Lahore

Selected group exhibitions

2005 ***Re-inventing Narratives***, Le Galerie Mohamed el Fassi, Rabat, Morocco

2004 ***Contemporary Miniature Paintings from Pakistan,*** Fukuoka Asian Art Museum, Fukuoka, Japan

2003 ***Negotiating Borders***, Siddhartha Art Gallery, Kathmandu, Nepal

Karkhana, Touchstones Art Gallery, Rochdale, UK

2002 ***Borderless Terrain***, Visual Arts Gallery, New Delhi

Transforming Tradition: Contemporary Visions from Pakistan, World Bank Art Gallery, Washington DC

2001 ***In an Exuberant and Profuse Manner***, BosePacia Modern, New York

In Conversation, Gallery Espace, New Delhi

2000 ***Pakistan: Another Vision—Fifty Years of Painting and Sculpture from Pakistan***, Victoria Art Gallery, Bath, UK; Centre of Contemporary Art, Glasgow, UK; Huddersfield Art Gallery, UK; Brunei Gallery, London

1998 ***International Commonwealth Exhibition***, National Art Gallery, Kuala Lumpur, Malaysia

Chawkandi Art Gallery, Karachi

Sanskriti Kendra Village, New Delhi

1997 Hong Kong Art Centre Gallery

Hong Kong University of Science and Technology Gallery

Art Connoisseur Gallery, London

1996 Gallery Martini, Hong Kong

Alhamra Art Galleries, Lahore

Selected publications

Virginia Whiles, "Contemporary Miniature Paintings from Pakistan," in ***Contemporary Miniature Paintings from Pakistan*** (Fukuoka, Japan: Fukuoka Asian Art Museum, 2004)

Hammad Nasar, "Rochdale Remembrance," ***Herald*** (Pakistan), February 2004

Holland Cotter, "Art Review; Millenniums of Asia, Packed Into a Week," New York Times, March 28, 2003

Salima Hashmi, "Between Worlds and Other Matters," in ***Talha Rathore: Between Worlds*** (New York: BosePacia Modern, 2003)

Quddus Mirza, "Maps of Mind—the Art of Talha Rathore," in ***Talha Rathore: Between Worlds*** (New York: BosePacia Modern, 2003)

Salima Hashmi, ***Unveiling the Visible. Lives and Works of Women Artists of Pakistan*** (Islamabad, Pakistan: Actionaid, 2002)

Roberta Smith, "Art in Review; In an Exuberant and Profuse Manner," ***New York Times***, July 20, 2001

Salima Hashmi, "Radicalising Tradition", ***Art Link*** (India), Issue 20 No 2 (2000)

Ratnottama Sengupta, "It's Yesterday Once More," ***Sunday Times of India***, April 12, 1998

Amra Ali, "Reaching the Old in New Language," ***News on Sunday*** (Pakistan), December 28, 1997

Saira Wasim

Born in Lahore, 1975. Lives in Chicago

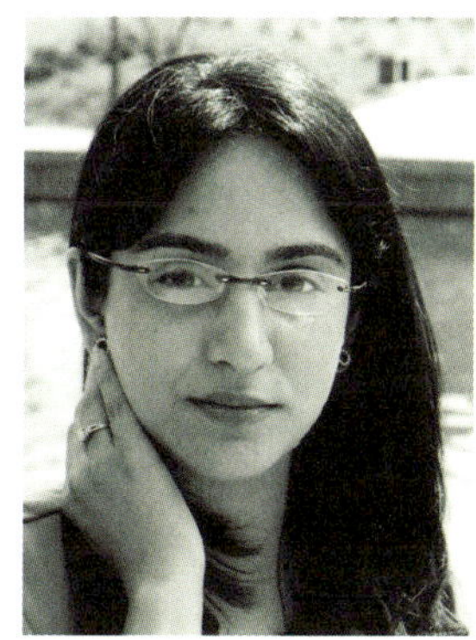

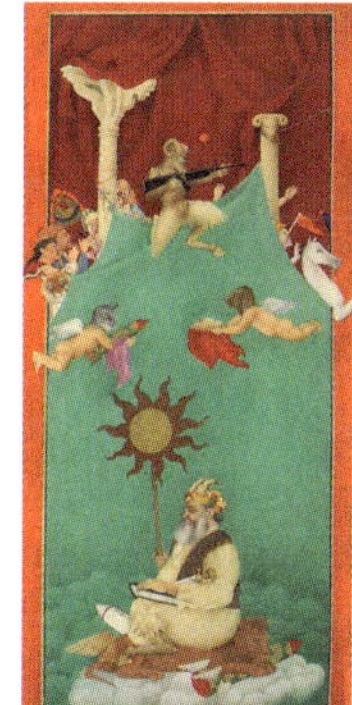

Education

1999 BFA, National College of Arts, Lahore

Solo exhibition

2005 ***Saira Wasim: Political Carousel***, Fine Arts Gallery, Southwestern University, Georgetown, Texas

Selected group exhibitions

2005 ***Ritu: A Gathering of Seasons***, Anant Art Gallery at Triveni Kala Sangam, New Delhi

2004 ***Contemporary Miniature Paintings from Pakistan,*** Fukuoka Asian Art Museum, Fukuoka, Japan

Transcendent Contemplations, Green Cardamom at Hosains, London

Playing with a Loaded Gun, apexart, New York; and Kunsthalle Fridericianum, Kassel, Germany

2003 ***The American Effect***, Whitney Museum of American Art, New York

Contemporary Miniatures from Pakistan, K3—Project Space, Zurich, Switzerland

Karkhana, Touchstones Art Gallery, Rochdale, UK

Negotiating Borders, Siddhartha Art Gallery, Kathmandu, Nepal

2002 ***Exotic Bodies***, Harris Museum & Art Gallery, Preston, UK

Around the Miniature, Canvas Gallery, Karachi, Pakistan

2001 ***Manoeuvering Miniatures***, IIC Gallery, New Delhi; and Sakshi Gallery, Mumbai, India

Six Artists from Pakistan, Jay Grimm Gallery, New York

Rohtas 2 Gallery, Lahore

2000 Didrichsen Art Museum, Helsinki, Finland

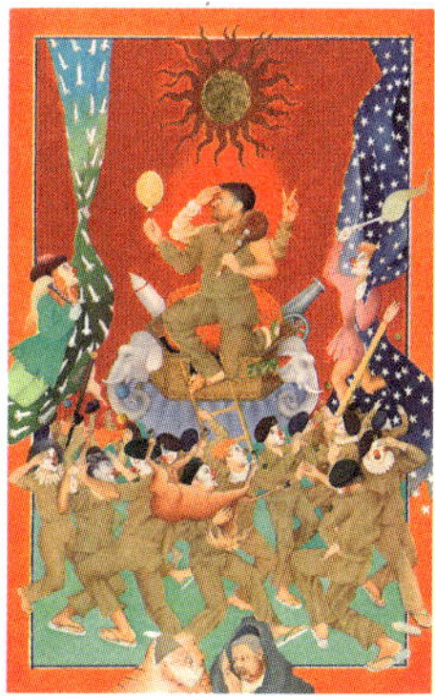

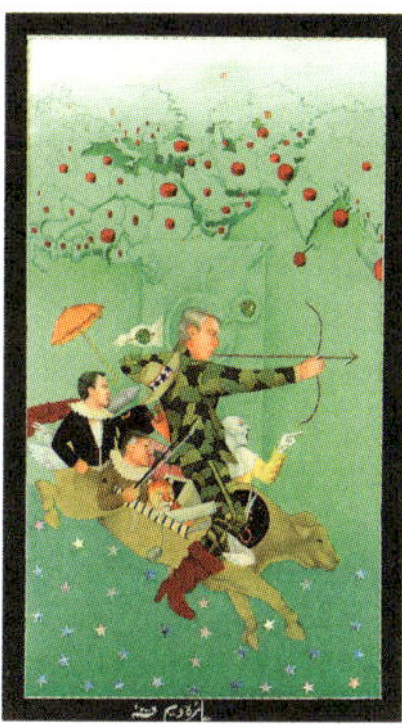

Selected publications

B.N. Goswamy, "Ritu: A Gathering of Seasons," in ***Ritu: A Gathering of Seasons*** (New Delhi, India: Anant Art Gallery, 2005)

Virginia Whiles, "Contemporary Miniature Paintings from Pakistan," in ***Contemporary Miniature Paintings from Pakistan*** (Fukuoka, Japan: Fukuoka Asian Art Museum, 2004)

Anna Sloan, "A Divine Comedy of Errors: Political Paintings by Saira Wasim," in ***Transcendent Contemplations***, eds., Anita Dawood-Nasar and Hammad Nasar (London: Green Cardamom, 2004)

Laura Smith-Spark "Blair confronts art close to home," ***BBC News Online***, October 2004, http://news.bbc.co.uk/1/hi/entertainment/arts/3708382.stm

Atteqa Ali, "Playing with a Loaded Gun—Contemporary Art in Pakistan," in ***Playing with a Loaded Gun*** (Kassel, Germany: Kunsthalle Fridericianum, 2004)

Hammad Nasar, "Rochdale Remembrance," ***Herald*** (Pakistan), February 2004

Lawrence Rinder, "The American Effect," in ***The American Effect***, ed. L. Rinder (New York: Whitney Museum of American Art, 2003)

Ellen Pearlman, "The Art of Saira Wasim," ***The Brooklyn Rail,*** October 2003

Saira Wasim, "How Do We Look?", ***New York Times*** (OpEd essay), June 21, 2003

Virginia Whiles, "Manoeuvering Miniatures," ***Manoeuvering Miniatures: Contemporary Art from Pakistan*** (New Delhi, India: Khoj International Arts Centre, 2001)

Works in the Exhibition

All measurements are height x width. The system in which the work of art was originally measured is presented first. An approximate translation into centimeters (cm) or inches is provided for reference only.

Collaborative works

Muhammad Imran Qureshi, Hasnat Mehmood, Aisha Khalid, Nusra Latif Qureshi, Saira Wasim, Talha Rathore
Untitled (1), 2003 (p.57)
Gouache, mixed media on *wasli*
23.5 x 17.9 cm (9 1/4 x 7 inches)

Muhammad Imran Qureshi, Hasnat Mehmood, Aisha Khalid, Nusra Latif Qureshi, Saira Wasim, Talha Rathore
Untitled (2), 2003 (p.61)
Gouache, mixed media on *wasli*
17.9 x 22.9 cm (7 x 9 inches)

Hasnat Mehmood, Aisha Khalid, Nusra Latif Qureshi, Saira Wasim, Talha Rathore, Muhammad Imran Qureshi
Untitled (3), 2003 (p.65)
Gouache, mixed media on *wasli*
18 x 23 cm (7 x 9 inches)

Hasnat Mehmood, Aisha Khalid, Nusra Latif Qureshi, Saira Wasim, Talha Rathore, Muhammad Imran Qureshi
Untitled (4), 2003 (p.69)
Gouache, mixed media on *wasli*
18.1 x 23.4 cm (7 x 9 inches)

Aisha Khalid, Nusra Latif Qureshi, Saira Wasim, Talha Rathore, Muhammad Imran Qureshi, Hasnat Mehmood
Untitled (5), 2003 (p.73)
Gouache, mixed media on *wasli*
21.1 x 16.3 cm (8 1/3 x 6 1/2 inches)

Aisha Khalid, Nusra Latif Qureshi, Saira Wasim, Talha Rathore, Muhammad Imran Qureshi, Hasnat Mehmood
Untitled (6), 2003 (p.77)
Gouache, mixed media on *wasli*
16.1 x 21.4 cm (6 1/3 x 8 1/3 inches)

Nusra Latif Qureshi, Saira Wasim, Talha Rathore, Muhammad Imran Qureshi, Hasnat Mehmood, Aisha Khalid
Untitled (7), 2003 (p.81)
Gouache, mixed media on *wasli*
22.9 x 17.6 cm (9 x 7 inches)

Nusra Latif Qureshi, Saira Wasim, Talha Rathore, Muhammad Imran Qureshi, Hasnat Mehmood, Aisha Khalid
Untitled (8), 2003 (p.85)
Gouache, mixed media on *wasli*
25 x 18.9 cm (9 7/8 x 7 1/2 inches)

Saira Wasim, Talha Rathore, Muhammad Imran Qureshi, Hasnat Mehmood, Aisha Khalid, Nusra Latif Qureshi
Untitled (9), 2003 (p.89)
Gouache, mixed media on *wasli*
26.5 x 19.3 cm (10 1/3 x 7 1/2 inches)

Saira Wasim, Talha Rathore, Muhammad Imran Qureshi, Hasnat Mehmood, Aisha Khalid, Nusra Latif Qureshi
Untitled (10), 2003 (p.93)
Gouache, mixed media on *wasli*
28.6 x 19.5 cm (11 1/4 x 7 3/4 inches)

Talha Rathore, Muhammad Imran Qureshi, Hasnat Mehmood, Aisha Khalid, Nusra Latif Qureshi, Saira Wasim
Untitled (11), 2003 (p.97)
Gouache, mixed media on *wasli*
23.3 x 18.5 cm (9 x 7 1/4 inches)

Talha Rathore, Muhammad Imran Qureshi, Hasnat Mehmood, Aisha Khalid, Nusra Latif Qureshi, Saira Wasim
Untitled (12), 2003 (p.101)
Gouache, mixed media on *wasli*
23.5 x 18.4 cm (9 1/4 x 7 1/4 inches)

All collaborative works are courtesy of the artists

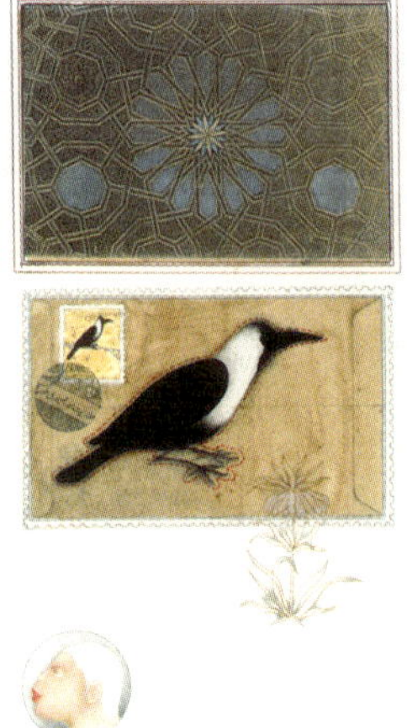

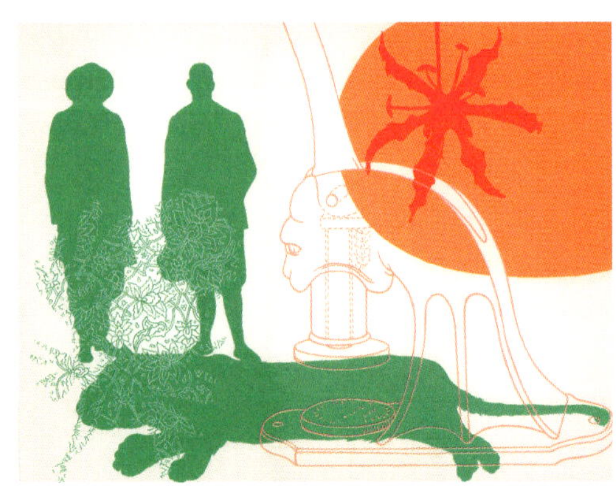

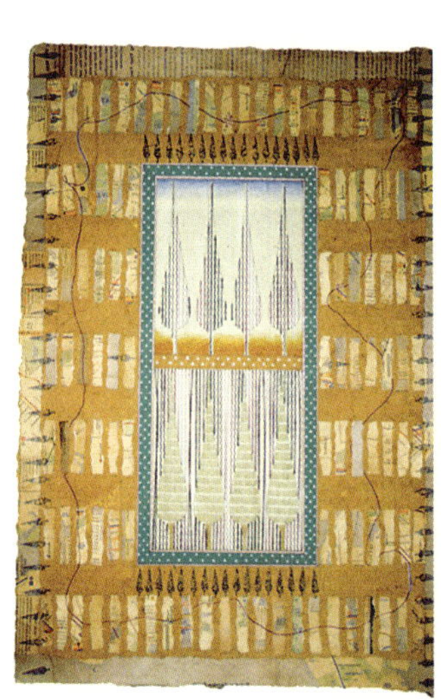

Works by individual artists

Aisha Khalid

Ongoing Conversation II, 2003 (below, left)
Opaque watercolor on *wasli* and paper board; artist's frames
22 x 15.5 cm and 69 x 50.2 cm (8 2/3 x 6 inches and 27 x 19 3/4 inches)
Courtesy Corvi-Mora, London

Ongoing Conversation III, 2003 (p.35)
Opaque watercolor on *wasli* and illustration board; artist's frames
24.5 x 18.2 cm and 69 x 50.2 cm (9 2/3 x 7 2/3 inches and 27 x 19 3/4 inches)
Courtesy Corvi-Mora, London

Veil, 2004
Opaque watercolor on *wasli*
34.2 x 24.2 cm (13 1/2 x 9 1/2 inches)
Private collection
Courtesy Corvi-Mora, London

Veil, 2004
Opaque watercolor on *wasli*
34.2 x 24.2 cm (13 1/2 x 9 1/2 inches)
Courtesy Corvi-Mora, London

Song of Silence, 2004 (p.104)
Opaque watercolor on *wasli*
34.2 x 24.2 cm (13 1/2 x 9 1/2 inches)
Private collection, London
Courtesy Corvi-Mora, London

Hasnat Mehmood

Untitled, 2002
Watercolor, tea stain, graphite on *wasli*
32 x 19 cm (12 1/2 x 7 1/2 inches)
Collection of Aisha Khalid and Muhammad Imran Qureshi, Lahore

Make Your Own Jet Fighter, 2003 (p.104)
Gouache, tea wash on *wasli*
25 x 25 cm (9 7/8 x 9 7/8 inches)
Courtesy of the artist and Green Cardamom, London

To Whom it May Concern, 2003
Gouache on *wasli*
50 x 32 cm (19 2/3 x 12 1/2 inches)
Collection of Aisha Khalid and Muhammad Imran Qureshi, Lahore

Untitled, 2003 (p.108, left)
Gouache, lead, tea wash on *wasli*
11 x 6 3/4 inches (28 x 17 cm)
Collection of Belinda Shattock, London

Conference of Crows, 2004 (below, center)
Gouache, collage, tea wash on *wasli*
33 x 52 cm (12 x 20 1/2 inches)
Courtesy of the artist and Green Cardamom, London

Muhammad Imran Qureshi

God of Small Things, 2002 (p.105, center)
Opaque watercolor, Letraset transfer on *wasli*
27.5 x 23 cm (10 7/8 x 9 inches)
Collection of Aisha Khalid, Lahore

Perfect Harmony, 2003
Opaque watercolor, Letraset transfer on *wasli*
31.2 x 52.7 cm (12 1/4 x 20 3/4 inches)
Courtesy Corvi-Mora, London

Reshape, 2004 (below, right)
Opaque watercolor, Letraset transfer on *wasli*
55 x 59.5 cm (21 2/3 x 23 1/2 inches)
Private collection, London
Courtesy Corvi-Mora, London

U-turns, 2004 (p.105, right)
Opaque watercolor, Letraset transfer on *wasli*
27.5 x 36.2 cm (10 7/8 x 14 1/4 inches)
Courtesy Corvi-Mora, London

Easy Cutting, 2005 (p.105, left)
Opaque watercolor, Letraset transfer on *wasli*
19 x 28 cm (7 1/2 x 11 inches)
Collection of Salima Hashmi, Lahore

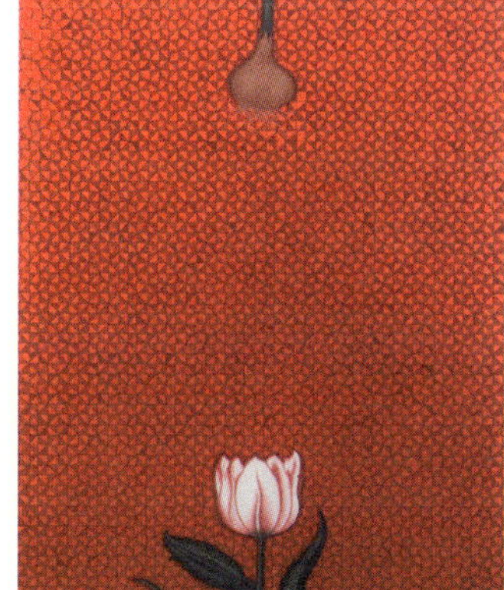

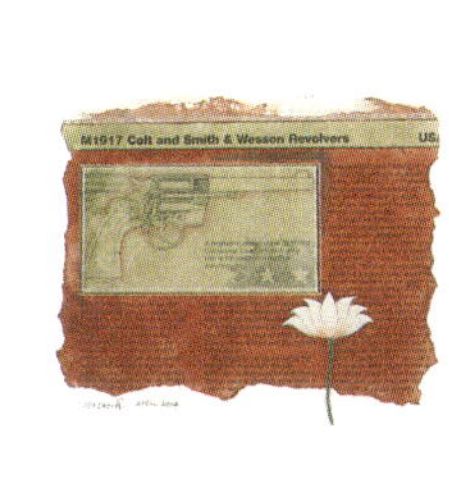

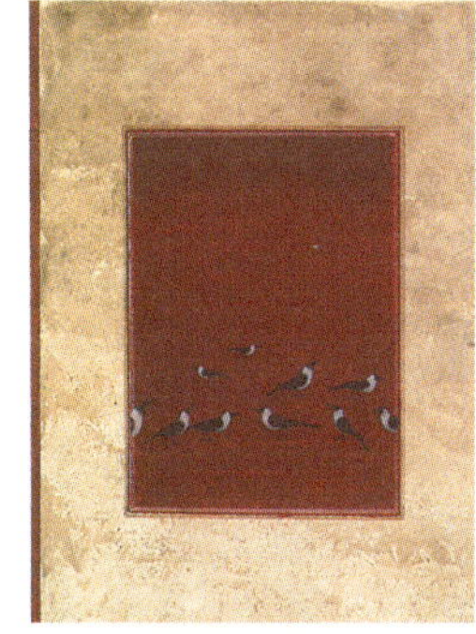

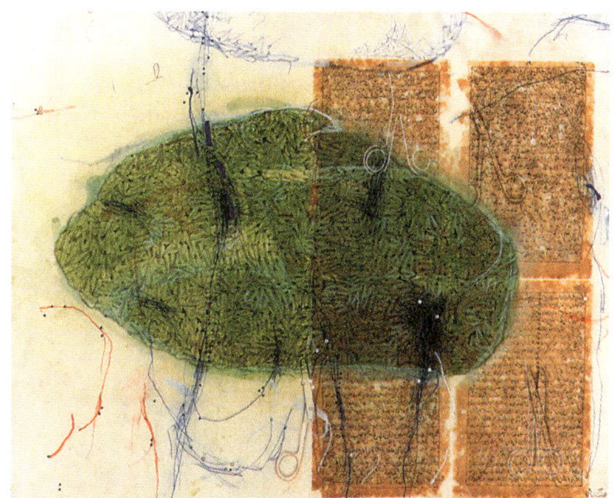

Nusra Latif Qureshi

Specifications of Desire, 2002 (p.106)
Gouache, ink, graphite, watercolor on *wasli*
8 11/16 x 10 5/8 inches (22 x 27 cm)
Collection of Mehrin Masud-Elias and Jamal J. Elias

Specifications of Desire II, 2002 (p.41)
Watercolor, gouache, graphite on *wasli*
11 3/4 x 15 3/4 inches (29.8 x 40 cm)
Courtesy of the artist and Waqas Wajahat LLC, New York

Three Songs of Devotion, 2002
Gouache on *wasli*
9 x 7 7/8 inches (22.9 x 20 cm)
Smith College Museum of Art, Northampton, Massachusetts. Purchased with the Janice Carlson Oresman, class of 1955, Fund, 2004:5

Tropic of Capricorn, 2002 (below, left)
Siyah-qalam (black brush), gouache, liquid gold, and gold leaf on *wasli*
16 3/8 x 10 3/8 inches (41.6 x 26.4 cm)
Smith College Museum of Art, Northampton, Massachusetts. Purchased with the Janice Carlson Oresman, class of 1955, Fund, 2004:4

White Man Still Sitting, 2002
Gouache, collage on *wasli*
15 5/8 x 10 5/8 inches (39.7 x 27 cm)
Collection of Nan Fleming

Manifest Destiny, 2003 (p.108, center)
Gouache on illustration board
14 1/2 x 18 1/16 inches (36.8 x 47 cm)
Collection of Sussan Babaie

Of Birds and Fourteen Year Olds, 2003
Gouache on illustration board
14 1/8 x 17 inches (35.9 x 43.2 cm)
Smith College Museum of Art, Northampton, Massachusetts. Purchased with the Richard and Rebecca Evans (Rebecca Morris, class of 1932) Foundation Fund, 2004:6

Island Dream, 2004
Gouache, acrylic, paper, graphite on illustration board
13 3/4 x 18 1/2 inches (34.9 x 47 cm)
Courtesy of the artist and Waqas Wajahat LLC, New York

Talha Rathore

Their Bodies Turned to Gold, 2002
Gouache, collage, block printing, gold on *wasli*
13 1/2 x 19 inches (34.2 x 48.3 cm)
Courtesy of the artist

Many Matters Remain Unexplained, 2003
Gouache, collage, threads, block-print on *wasli*
40 x 30 inches (101.6 x 76.2 cm)
Courtesy Bose Pacia Gallery, New York

A New Degree of Separation/Togetherness, 2005 (p.108, right)
Gouache, collage, threads, block print on *wasli*
22 x 15 1/2 inches (55.9 x 39.4 cm)
Courtesy of the artist

No Matter What II, 2005 (p.106)
Gouache, collage, acrylic on *wasli*
14 x 11 1/2 inches (35.6 x 29.2 cm)
Courtesy of the artist

The Monsoon Never Came, 2005 (below, center)
Gouache on *wasli*
14 x 11 1/2 inches (35.6 x 29.2 cm)
Collection of Salima Hashmi, Lahore

Saira Wasim

Buzkashi from the series ***Musharraf***, 2003-04 (p.107, center)
Graphite, gouache, gold on *wasli*
11 x 7 inches (27.9 x 17.8 cm)
Smith College Museum of Art, Northampton, Massachusetts. Purchased with the Josephine A. Stein, class of 1927, Fund, in honor of the class of 1927, 2004:25

Mullahs from the ***Terrorism Series***, 2003 (p.107, left)
Gouache on *wasli*
34 x 14 1/2 cm (13 x 5 2/3 inches)
Collection of Steven Rand and Nancy Wender

The Battle for Hearts and Minds, 2004 (p.36)
Gouache, tea wash, lead, gold leaf on illustration board
24 x 16 cm (9 1/2 x 6 1/3 inches)
Collection of Mr. and Mrs. Indar Pasricha, London

Mission Accomplished, 2004 (p.107, right)
Gouache on *wasli*
30 x 16.5 cm (11 3/4 x 6 1/2 inches)
Collection of Mrs. K. Haider, London

War Games, 2005 (below, right)
Gouache, gold leaf on *wasli*
23.5 x 17 cm (9 1/4 x 6 2/3 inches)
Private collection, Washington, D.C.

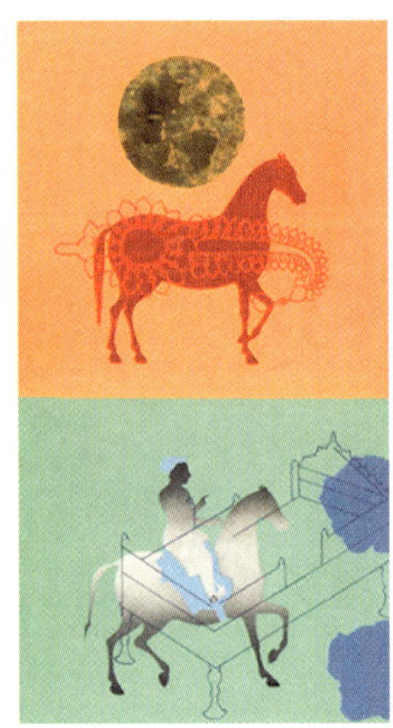

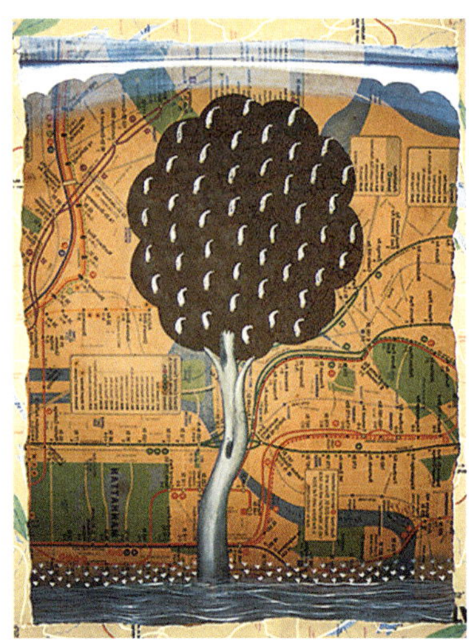

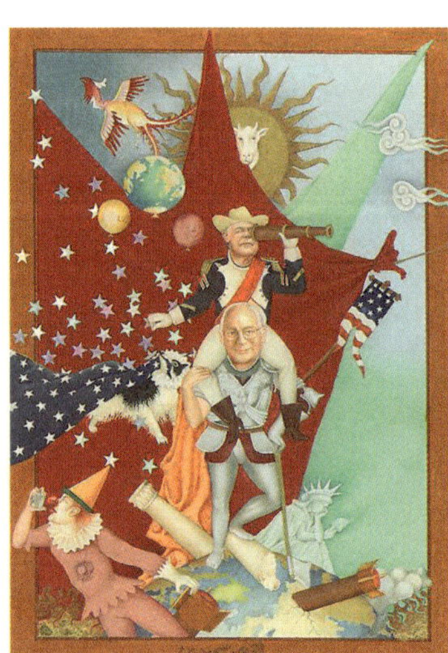

Contributors

Qamar Adamjee, research assistant at The Metropolitan Museum of Art, New York, and PhD candidate in pre-Mughal miniature painting at New York University: Adamjee was part of the Advisory Committee for the exhibition *Fatal Love: South Asian American Art Now* at the Queens Museum of Art, New York, 2005.

Salima Hashmi, head of Visual Arts at the Beaconhouse National University, Lahore, and former principal, National College of Arts, Lahore: Hashmi has been intimately involved in the development of the new miniature movement as Pakistan's pre-eminent art educationalist, writer, and curator.

Jessica Hough, curatorial director at The Aldrich Contemporary Art Museum, Ridgefield, Connecticut: Hough's recent curatorial projects include *Alyson Shotz: Light, Sound, Space; Shahzia Sikander: Nemesis* co-organized with the Tang Teaching Museum and Art Gallery; and *Into My World: Recent British Sculpture*.

Sandhya Jain, conservation specialist with the Department of Scientific Research at The Metropolitan Museum of Art, New York: a Fulbright scholar to India, Jain has worked on conservation issues with leading art museums, including the Los Angeles County Museum of Art and the Philadelphia Museum of Art.

B.N. Goswamy, professor emeritus of Art History at the Punjab University, Chandigarh: a distinguished art historian, Goswamy has written extensively on Indian art and curated numerous exhibitions internationally. He has also taught at the Universities of Heidelberg, Pennsylvania, California (Berkeley and Los Angeles), Zurich, and Texas (at Austin).

Hammad Nasar, independent curator and writer based in London: Nasar is founder of the arts organization Green Cardamom, and programme director, Arts & Humanities, for the Festival of Muslim Cultures, UK, 2006.

John Seyller, professor of Art History at the University of Vermont: a renowned scholar on Islamic art, Seyller was curator for *The Adventures of Hamza* exhibition at the Smithsonian. He has published extensively on Indian painting, and is the author of *Workshop and Patron in Mughal India*.

Anna Sloan, writer, curator, and historian of Islamic and South Asian Art: Sloan has taught at Moore College of Art, Smith College, and is currently at Mount Holyoke College, Massachusetts. She curated Nusra Latif Qureshi's first North American retrospective, *The Way I Remember Them,* at the Smith College Museum of Art, in 2004.

Virginia Whiles, historian, critic, curator, and lecturer at Chelsea College of Art and Design: Whiles has curated exhibitions of contemporary miniatures internationally, including a survey show at the Fukuoka Asian Art Museum, Japan, 2004-05; she is completing her PhD on the birth of the contemporary miniature as an anthropological phenomenon at London University's School of Oriental and African Studies.

Acknowledgments

The genesis of this exhibition lies with Muhammad Imran Qureshi, who brought this group of artists together to collaborate on a suite of paintings, and persuaded Penny Thompson at the Touchstones Art Gallery (Rochdale, UK) to arrange an exhibition in 2003-04 and, equally importantly, to pay the not-inconsiderable courier bill. Hammad saw this exhibition and began a conversation with Imran and Anna about expanding and traveling it, as well as capturing it in book form. A chance conversation between Hammad and Jessica on the public reaction to Imran's contribution to a group show at The Aldrich eventually led to this traveling exhibition being organized by The Aldrich.

At The Aldrich we are indebted to director Harry Philbrick and exhibitions director Richard Klein, who enthusiastically supported the exhibition, and to registrar Mary Kenealy, whose gentle and organized persistence ensured the end result. We would also like to thank Melissa Chiu, director of Asia Society Museum; Bindu Gude and Natasha Reichle, curators at Asian Art Museum (AAM) in San Francisco; and staff members at all three institutions.

This exhibition would not have been possible without the generosity of the galleries and collectors who loaned work to the exhibition: Sussan Babaie; Bose-Pacia Gallery, New York; Corvi-Mora, London; Mehrin Masud-Elias and Jamal J. Elias; Nan Fleming; Green Cardamom, London; Mrs. K. Haider; Salima Hashmi; Mr. and Mrs. Indar Pasricha; Steven Rand and Nancy Wender; Belinda Shattock; and Waqas Wajahat LLC, New York. Smith College Museum of Art loaned four works of art for the exhibition and we thank Aprile Gallant and Louise A. Laplante for their support.

This book contains the work of a group of wonderful writers. Qamar Adamjee, B.N. Goswamy, Salima Hashmi, Sandhya Jain, John Seyller, and Virginia Whiles answered the request for contributions with a range of carefully-considered responses. We are fortunate to have this book, not only to document the exhibition, but also to open up some of the art historical and social issues posed by the work. Its publication would not have been possible without the support of Fayeeza and Arif Naqvi. The Association of Pakistani Professionals and its members: Huma and Asif Alam, Pervaiz Lodhie, Munir and Zeelaf Mashooqullah; Natasha Kazmi and Qaisar Hasan; Shezi and Emily Nackvi; Waqas Wajahat LLC; and our anonymous donors also provided generous support for this publication. Thanks also to David Dibosa, Jean-Paul Martinon and Astrid Schmetterling of Goldsmiths College, London, for acting as sounding boards for many of the ideas in the structure and content of the book. The book looks the way it does because of the creativity, energy, and commitment of Vipul Sangoi. It reads the way it does because of Anita Dawood-Nasar's skillful editing.

Several individuals have supported the exhibition, in particular: Anni and Asad Shamim, who helped in getting the exhibition and the artists to Ridgefield; and, Asim and Isha Abdullah, who acted as midwives in making the exhibition at the AAM happen. Fatima Zahra Hasan was generous with both her advice and her image collection; Asif Alam, Kamran Anwar, Hasnain Aslam, Andleeb Dawood, Mahnaz Fancy, Navina Haider, Nadia and Saquib Hanif, Saneeya Hussain, Umair Khan, Maleeha Lodhi, Adil Najam, Jamil Naqsh, Jaami Shaakir Nasar, Lekha Poddar, Nasreen Rehman, Shahzia Sikander, and Najmi Sura, all acted as great ambassadors for the exhibition and the book, helping in myriad ways.

And lastly, we are grateful to the artists in the exhibition for lending their own work, and the work of their fellow artists, for an extended period of time. Their generosity affords us the opportunity to explore their talents within a coherent body of work. More importantly, it allows audiences on both of America's coasts to partake in the critical dialogue these paintings propose. We are privileged to be associated with these artists and will follow their careers with great interest in the years to come.

Jessica Hough, Hammad Nasar, and Anna Sloan

Photo credits
Fasihullah Ahsan, New York p.106 (right); Andy Keate/Ahlburg Keate Photography, London pp.44-47, 57, 61, 65, 69, 73, 77, 81, 85, 89, 93, 97, 101; Hasnat Mehmood, Jhelum p. 104 (right portrait); R.M. Naeem, Lahore p.105; Thierry Ollivier/Photo RMN, Paris p.15; Muhammad Imran Qureshi, Lahore p.104 (left); Naeem Rana, Melbourne p. 106 (left); Vipul Sangoi/Raindesign, London p.14; Balthazar Serreau, London p.36, 109; Thomas Taylor, London pp.48-51; Haroon Usman, Chicago p.107 (left portrait); Chris Williams, London p.104 (right image), p.107 (center image)

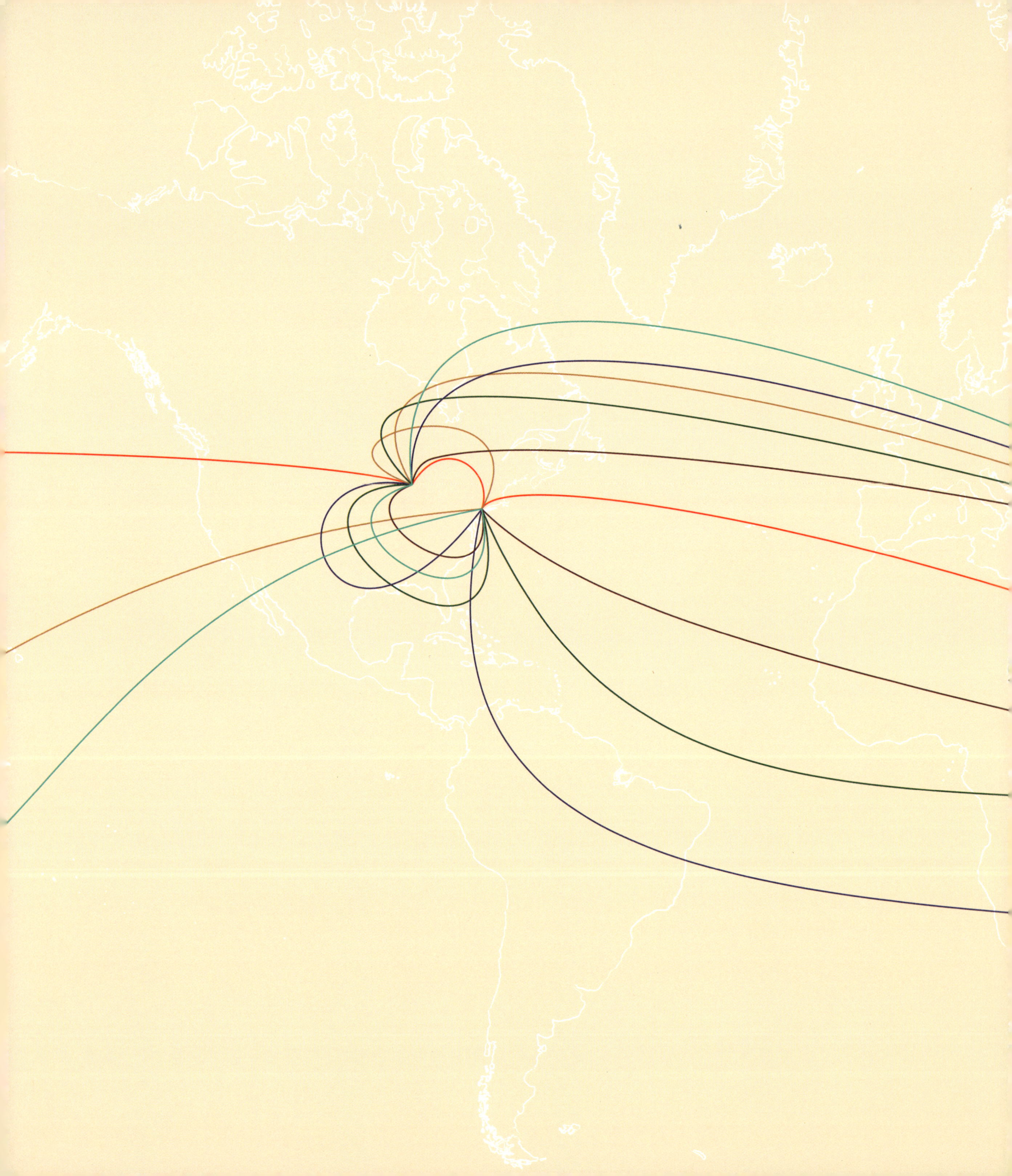